Creating Visual N
Through Photogra

This book provides photographers with the foundation to craft more compelling photos from concept all the way through to creation and distribution, on the path to making a living.

Based on real-life practice and experience, former National Geographic and White House visual editor, Mike Davis, takes readers on a journey starting with addressing the motivation behind an image and how this determines the rest of the creative process. He goes on to articulate best technical practices to create the narrative through photo composition and what to do with your work after the photos are completed. Each section offers exercises for applied learning and a series of appendices cover assignments structures, a compilation of critical words and concepts, a comprehensive resource guide of organizations, competitions, grants, collectives and agencies, book publishers and printers and more.

This is an ideal resource for students and practitioners alike to gain a more informed understanding of photographic expression and learn how to effectively execute these visions.

Mike Davis is a visual consultant, editor, author, photographer and professor emeritus. A visual leader who has worked with hundreds of photographers independently and on multiple staffs, Mike taught visual storytelling courses at Syracuse University and directed The Alexia Grants. He was twice named picture editor of the year, has been on various workshop and review faculty. He has edited more than 40 books.

All photographs in this book were made by the author.

Creating Visual Narratives Through Photography

A Fresh Approach to Making a Living as a Photographer

Mike Davis

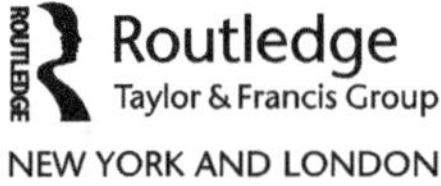

NEW YORK AND LONDON

Cover image: © Mike Davis

First published 2023
by Routledge
605 Third Avenue, New York, NY 10158

and by Routledge
4 Park Square, Milton Park, Abingdon, Oxon, OX14 4RN

Routledge is an imprint of the Taylor & Francis Group, an informa business

ISBN: 9781032262864 (hbk)
ISBN: 9781032262857 (pbk)
ISBN: 9781003287544 (ebk)

DOI: 10.4324/9781003287544

Typeset in Bembo
by codeMantra

For my parents, Jerry and Erma.
They would have been proud.
For my children, Holly and Ben,
for enduring my absence.
For grandsons, Xavier, Jack and Niko,
for helping me see the world anew.
For my wife, Deb, for uplifting me, always.

Contents

Preface

There are more ways to make a living through photography now than ever. The profession continues to evolve from the days of fighting for photography to be considered as an art form, from being perceived as a service department within newspapers and advertising spaces where photographers filled the vision/orders of others. We're moving away from photography being an add-on to photography being the core medium for expression in a more diverse marketplace.

To succeed, practitioners must be visual storytellers who are capable of creating fully realized narratives.

Part of this evolution is recognizing that there is no single standard for what makes photography successful. The profession in all of its iterations is opening to more visual forms and at long last is embracing creators from a greater range of backgrounds and ethnicities. More people in decision-making positions realize that it is the people behind the camera who make photographs engaging and the greater the diversity among the makers, the greater resonance there will be with audiences. We have only begun this essential process that includes greater diversity among decision makers.

With greater voice come greater responsibilities and expectations of visual storytellers. To make a go of it, you have to be thought of as more than someone who takes pictures. You have to be able to fully conceive, pitch and execute work and create a professional and increasingly social presence. Why you create work has to expand as the guiding light for the work.

I wrote this book with students and young to seasoned professionals in mind, to give you a fresh way of thinking about how to approach your visual life, to elevate your why. If you are doing things as you always have, your business is likely sliding and you're finding less joy in the work than you once did.

How to use this book This book presents an additive approach. As you go through the sections, each one builds more understanding about how to elevate your storytelling. Each section brings the previous section's learning forward to build on the application of the next. And each section offers *Try This* exercises to make the learning yours.

The appendixes add value to the body of the book as resources or thoughts that are independent but connected/relevant.

I present my photos in this book because I know the thinking and goals behind their making. Photos will intersect with the point of the book's text. Almost none of the photographs were cropped so you see them as they were created in camera. I cite many visual storytellers and specific work they've produced as further examples of the points being made throughout the book. You can dive further into their work and learn even more from that experience.

A common refrain from the people I've presented this book's methodology to is that they never would have thought of producing or realizing their work this way and that their way of thinking was forever changed for the better. I hope that is the case for you.

Section 1
Why Do We Make Pictures?

Section 1.0 Introduction

What makes a photograph successful? That will vary for each of you, depending on what you're trying to accomplish through your photography. There's no automatic path to creating successful images or a predefined notion of what makes a photograph great. There is a popular postulate that says if your photographs aren't interesting, it's because what's in front of the camera isn't interesting enough. I'd say it's because the person behind the camera isn't doing what it takes to make the photographs engaging. Subject matter is important, but photographs succeed because of what the photographer chooses to do from behind and through the camera.

Another principle, called scopic drive, says it is human nature to see, to look at others or be seen by others. The theory also incorporates how we respond mentally, aesthetically and emotionally to all things visual. Humans inherently respond to the world visually so by extension people will spend more time with photographs that reward their gaze, ones that create a dimensional experience, regardless of what is pictured.

Naomi Rosenblum writes in *A World History of Photography*: "It is a paradox nevertheless that documentary photographs are most memorable when they transcend the specifics of time, place and purpose, when they invest ordinary events and objects with enduring resonance."

Grant Scott, in *New Ways of Seeing* (page 75), says that if photographs have immediacy, emotional impact, engagement and graphic quality, they'll likely be successful.

My iteration of that idea is that photos can last beyond the day if we imbue them with lasting, dimensional qualities and that's more likely to happen when images fall somewhere between being all about what is depicted and all about the photographer who makes the picture.

Victor Lowenfeld, in his 1939 book, *The Nature of Creative Activity*, labels these two ends of a spectrum as either Visual or Haptic, which means they are either literal and descriptive or impressionistic and subjective. Photographs either simply depict what they present or the photographer introduces more through creative craft.

Photographers tend to choose how to make photographs based on the genre of work – or branch of the profession – they're pursuing, whether

DOI: 10.4324/9781003287544-1

it be art, documentary, photojournalism, commercial or advertising. The genre's paradigms dictate much of why photographs are made and subsequently how they are made. Yet, those who rise to the top of their branch of the profession supersede the genre in which they work. Their work goes beyond the parameters and limitations of genre-based photography. If you want to make more "interesting" photographs, advance beyond the boundaries set by genre.

My premise is that why you make photographs determines how you'll create them. Instead of starting from tried-and-true approaches, always start by considering why you're doing anything, in the grandest to the smallest sense, from your career path to saying things about what's in front of you. A parallel notion exists in racing, where the driver looks through the curve to see where they want to go and the car adheres to the eye's destination.

The more clarity and depth you bring to the endeavor, the more often you'll be successful. Photographs will only be what you strive to make them so your path to making successful photos is the process of fully engaging with what you're photographing, forming ideas and understanding from your impressions and using the medium to express your experience.

This way of going about making photographs can take seconds, as a pure response once you're in a setting, or months, as a refined, evolutionary expression to create a body of work.

Equally important is how and where the work will be realized. Creativity in the pursuit of expression is likely to be more successful if you know in what forms the work is best realized.

Genre-based work is how most professional photographers generated income not so long ago. They produced a particular type of work for a set of clients or an employer. People would occasionally cross between branches, but it was the exception. Now, most photographers have income streams from a variety of entities and sources. Self-initiated work is now regularly the germination of all work. Your unique way of saying things through your imagery is what will propel your career.

Another way of saying this is that specialization is now the driving force of visual professions. The idea of being a specialist is not new. Historically that meant you were known because you photograph sports, still lifes, products, portraits, architecture … Or, you were known for your technical prowess, such as being able to light anything. And in those days the expectation was to produce single photos or a handful of options from which people could choose. These ways of making a living still exist, but there are fewer practitioners in these singly focused realms.

What has grown the most are specialties that derive from unique ways of creating narratives and this is happening in several ways:

- On topics in which the creator is completely invested when the specialty is an extension of self: Joshua Rashaad McFadden is known for his portraiture, but his specialty embraces themes related to identity, masculinity, history, race and sexuality.
- Those who become experts in specific areas and can produce bodies of work on that topic in a way that only they could: Cristina Mittermeier has dedicated her life to protecting oceans as a marine biologist, conservationist, photographer and co-founder of Sea Legacy.
- Those whose work is unified by their idiosyncratic way of engaging with the world through their camera to create narratives: Aileen Son is a photographer "whose work centers around still life, portraiture, beauty and austerity."

People such as Jimmy Chin encompass all of these: He knows the mountain climbing world, is an accomplished climber, creates powerful narratives using moving and still images in extreme conditions anywhere in the world.

You're not a world-class mountain climber? What is your passion? What compels you? What can drive your why?

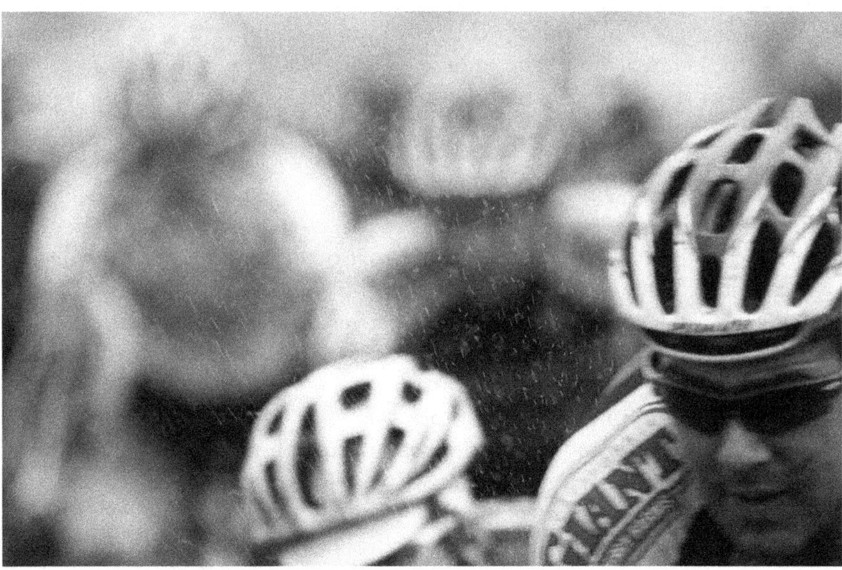

Photo 1.01 One of my passions was to photograph the bicycling communities in Portland, Oregon, here one of the hundreds of cyclocross races that a group of us made pictures of. The why for this photo was to convey the feeling of racing in the rain.

Section 1.1 The Spectrum of Why

Some of you make photographs for a living, some as a hobby, others to capture the flow of your lives as they pass, to memorialize birthdays and important life events. Each of these reasons as to why you make pictures likely guides how you're making them because each reason comes with a standard approach and both a type and depth of why that determines what kinds of photos result.

This way of thinking about The Why is letting the functionality of photographs guide the making of them. We may want to preserve the memory of happenings through photographs so create the standard family portrait – everybody say cheese. Or the goal is to show people doing something and sure enough, there they are doing it. The why, or intention, is straightforward.

Regardless of what box or genre is your current starting point, you can rise above its paradigms by thinking about why you're making photographs in a different way, by striving to say more.

The most precise way I can say it is with another spectrum, the endpoints of which are: You either make photographs to present information or to convey something about what you put in front of your camera. David Bate, in *Photography, The Key Concepts* (page 214) distinguishes the two ends of this spectrum as either denotation or connotation – what is pictured being most important versus what can be derived from the picture based on the combination of what is shown and what the photographer brought to the creation of the photo.

In real-world context, amateur or family or simplistic photojournalistic photography sits on the left side of the spectrum. More compelling communicative photography sits in the middle grounds and artistic work anchors the right.

Photos at one end of this spectrum are made to show things happening, describe or explain settings, or present what objects look like. Information is what they strive to show and the decisions made in the creation of the photo are based primarily on showing what is happening – the verb – or showing physical aspects of the settings – the nouns. Informational-leaning photographs will be interesting to the viewer to the extent that they are interested in the information.

In the middle grounds of this spectrum are photographs made to express the photographer's impressions, to help people visually experience what is portrayed, to convey unique qualities, ideas or concepts. These are the adverbs and adjectives of the setting. In theory and in practice, this approach is more likely to engage a viewer regardless of whether they are interested in what's pictured.

Informational aspects are often what put you into a setting, such as a foot race that is being held in a desert. But the goal driving the making of the photos is to convey the uniqueness of the race – where your approach

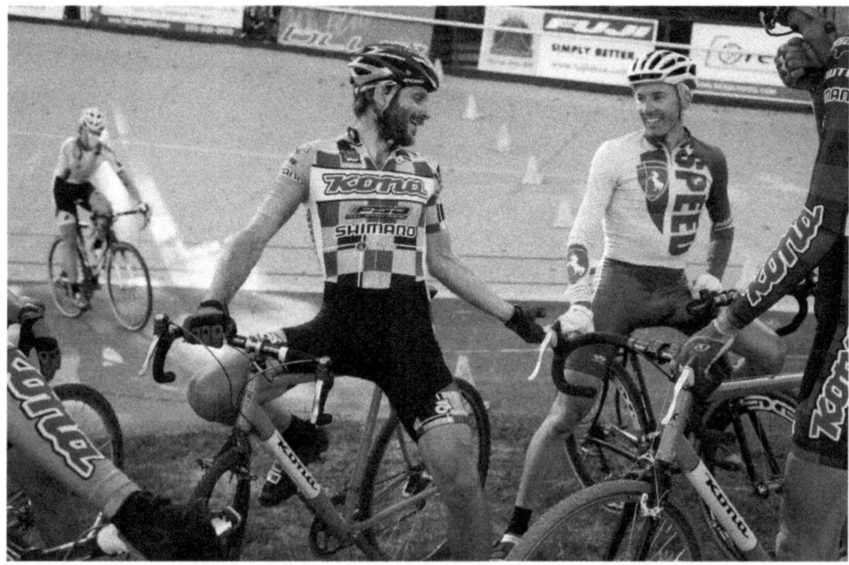

Photo 1.02 The goal here was to convey the sense of community among cyclo-cross racers.

to making photographs can express the qualities of remoteness, of exhaustion and heat, etc. You can still present the informational aspects in descriptions of the photos but what fully realized photos convey more than the verb to run, they introduce adjectives and adverbs.

At the right extension on this notion is creating images nearly independently of what is happening. Purely conceptual photography grows from this starting point. It is all about the photographer's expression or presentation of concepts and ideas.

It follows that the more dynamic the visual vocabulary you build into the creation of your photos, the more people will respond to them, regardless of where you are on this spectrum. You are giving them an experience, not just information.

Making photographs involves a series of decisions, a set of puzzle pieces that you discern and put together to create images. You can let the process determine your puzzle pieces or you can be the one creating the puzzle.

(Uninformed vs. informed Diagram)

Purely informational photographs are like verbs and nouns, a drab usage of the visual language, that depend on what's in front of the camera to be interesting. If you make informational photos, you're probably compromising most of photography's potential, too. Because, to show information, how you make photographs won't vary much from setting to setting, because the why doesn't change and therefore neither does the how.

To only show something happening you must stand at a certain angle to and distance from the happening – probably parallel to and far enough to include everything happening. You've just conceded quality of light, color, composition and distance as means of expression.

You can tell whether you make informational photos by describing your pictures with words and then asking whether the images elicit anything that the words didn't adequately describe, if not they are informational pictures. If how you place elements in photos, the composition, doesn't change much regardless of what you photograph, if light is rarely a critical quality, if the color doesn't contribute a lot: informational pictures.

As John Berger says in *Understanding a Photograph*, "You cannot take photographs with a dictionary."

This is not to say that informational photographs have no value or that photographs are either informational or not. The informational aspects of even a purely emotive or lyrical or aesthetically driven photograph are still there, sitting in the shadows of the photo.

Back to the opposite end of this spectrum, which is to convey our impressions through photographs, with the intention of producing photographs that elicit emotive responses, beyond the informational. These images utilize adjectives, adverbs, the entirety of a visual language. Words can never describe the whole of what lyrically crafted images convey. You'll achieve the highest state of your photography when you strive to create images that only you could make because they reflect your impressions, ideas, thoughts, experiences, your unique visual language. This

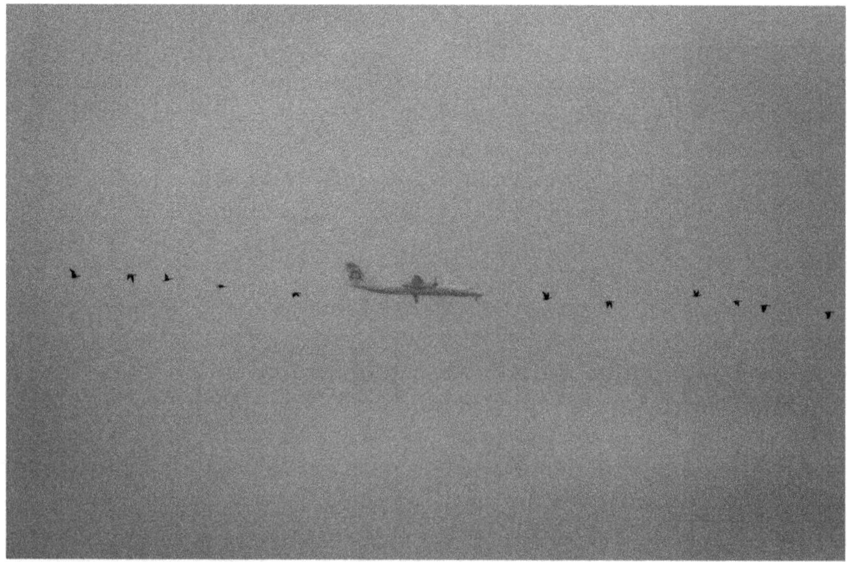

Photo 1.03 Photographs can exist just because they present juxtapositions.

expressive ability is what matters, now more than ever, if your goal is to rise above the masses.

Anyone can make informational photographs, let's start down a path that defines how you can make photos that say things in a way that only you can say them and move your work toward the other end of the spectrum.

Photography throughout its history has arm-wrestled this dynamic of whether the medium should present informational, truthful, objective images or be recognized as art where the photographer's voice is what matters. There never was such a thing as objectivity. And there are many truths. The photographer's voice produces engaging and lasting images only if there is great depth and meaning in why the creator produces work.

This more compelling realization starts by passionately determining what will be in front of your camera, fully engaging with whatever that is and then dimensionally expressing what matters most about what you've engaged with. That's when truly magical photographs result. You can achieve more dimensional photos no matter the genre in which you work or your current why.

What can you say with your pictures or what kinds of experiences can you create for the viewer? The most direct way is through a pure response. If you listen to the voice in the back of your head as you photograph, you might hear it saying this guy is a jerk, is really nice, quiet, a pontificator, slovenly or whatever; or this is a beautiful or catastrophic or harmonious or jubilant setting. Making decisions about how to make pictures that convey the range of your impressions is the goal.

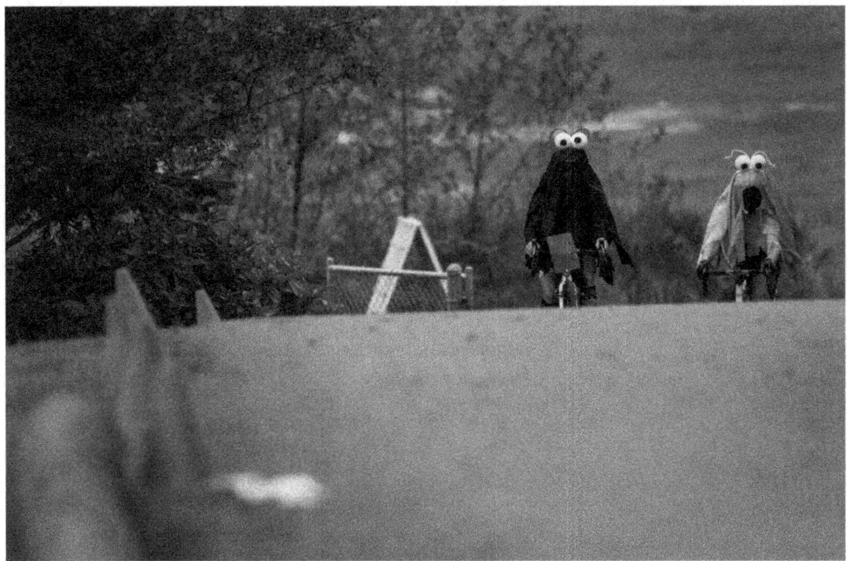

Photo 1.04 The voice in my head was saying, this is hilarious.

Another way is to present an idea or explore a concept or address social issues through your photography. For example, I've been struck by the combination of the choices people make for the two things most of us spend the most money on: where we live and what we drive. My visual solution to that has been to respond to that combination by making pictures when cars are parked in front of houses. I use the same composition, lens, aperture, focal length and distance and make the pictures when light contributes to the quality.

Photojournalists in the crowd might say that's not your job, that you're there to represent what happened without offering your impression. In fact, the best photojournalistic images are impressions rooted in understanding and the desire to say what it was like to be there.

This is not a new idea.

"The purely descriptive or informative is almost as great a threat to the art in photography as the purely formal or abstract. The photograph has to tell a story if it is to work." Clement Greenberg said that in a book titled *From Context and Narrative in Photography*, in 1964.

Determining where you and your work land on this spectrum of information vs abstraction is the goal; knowing that there is a choice is the critical thing.

Here's what Larry Fink, in "*on composition and improvisation*," offers on this notion: "For me, there is the underlying force of perception and perspective, and certainly, judgment can be a part of that, but it should not be the dominant force."

Latoya Ruby Frazier addressed inequality and many other aspects of her family's life in a body of work titled *The Notion of Family* and a 5-year project about Flint's water crisis titled *Flint Is Family in Three Acts*; Chien Chi Chang addressed mental health care in his work *The Chain*; Darcy Padilla in *Family Love* photographed one person's life for nearly 20 years and dealt with poverty, AIDs and other social issues.

What you take on doesn't have to be socially driven. It can be that you like the color red because of its energy or think that hats are silly or wonder why so many people drive pickups and SUVs or just love a certain kind of fashion ....

These are ideas that create bodies of work but the notion of them can also apply to smaller efforts or individual photos. That voice in your head generates them all the time, if you listen and have a camera with you to capture the rapture.

We do not have to photograph big events or have massive intent to create lasting, meaningful experiences with our photographs.

As John Simmons was quoted in a July 14, 2017, New York Times article:

> Every time the shutter is released I feel like we bring our entire life to that. The interesting thing is to be open to the most common,

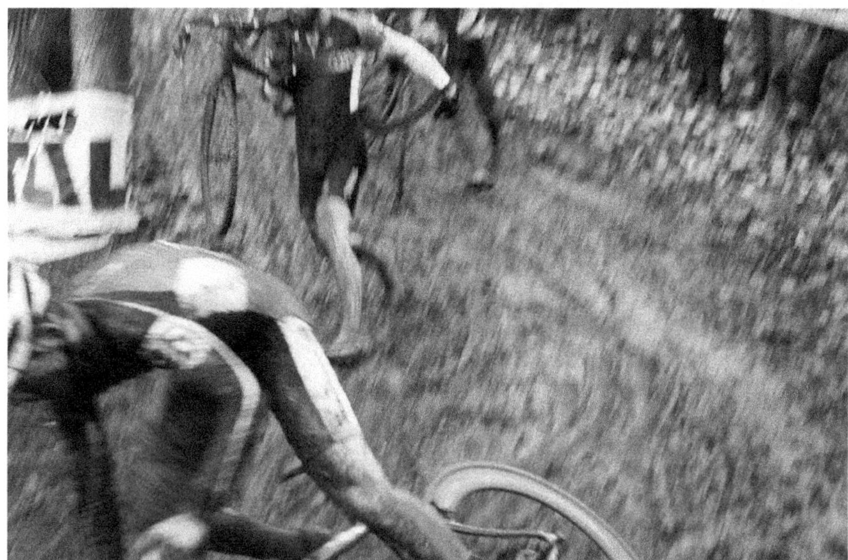

Photo 1.05 Here the point was to convey the sense of tight rope that riders walk when mud and slopes challenge them.

> seemingly insignificant moment and preserve it. Then it takes on a life of its own.

Pew Fellow and Penn State Professor Lonnie Graham says in a TEDx talk that art is best when the artist connects with a community. He quotes a student who responds to his question of why a set of photographs exists: "These pictures for all the people that live here with me." Micaiah Carter's *American Black Beauty* exhibition is an example of how representing your community can create a deeper revelation.

This notion of why determining everything else doesn't just apply to photography. I realized recently that if we recognize stress points in our lives and enact ways to reduce that stress, our lives would be better. For instance, I do whatever I can to avoid the feeling of pressure that can come from deadlines, the down-to-the-wire "Did I do everything I was supposed to?" To prevent that pressure from happening, to the extent possible, I devise systems and processes to back out from the deadlines to ensure that things get done. A bonus is that things get done better. It's good if this seems simple. This *why* connects to a larger one of being as efficient as possible with every effort and devoting the right amount of time to whatever needs to get done. *Why* doesn't have to be complex. Derivations of the why can range from clarifying a goal to correcting a tendency, to defining what matters to you.

If you start by asking yourself why you're doing something and then strive for a balance of expression, effort and realization as you pursue dynamic intention, then everything you do will have greater merit.

Section 1.2 How Do We Experience Photographs?

If the goal in producing images is to elicit a response from the viewer, then it's important to understand how people respond to photographs you make. There are as many ways of addressing this notion as there are people explaining it.

Scholars who study images tend to nullify the viewer's experience by breaking visuals into their component parts, for instance, through "compositional interpretation," a term that Gillian Rose says she invented, in her book *Visual Methodologies*. Rose cites content, color, spatial organization – including geometrical perspective, the logic of figuration, vocalizers and more – and light and expressive content. These are good things to be aware of but fall short, as Rose says, because they don't consider medium or the context of what is depicted. I would add the lack of consideration of the uniqueness of the moment depicted as a shortcoming. (Content in this context usually means what is pictured informationally.)

John Berger, in *Understanding a Photograph* (page 26) addresses the moment: "A photograph is effective when the chosen moment which it records contains a quantum of truth which is generally applicable, which is as revealing about what is absent from the photograph as about what is present in it … Nor can this truth ever be independent of the spectator."

Which I read to say: We capture a moment within the continuum of a setting in a way that expresses the sum of our experience within that setting. How people respond to our representations is unique to each person and is based on their collective life experience.

By extension, the more expression and meaning that you can introduce to photographs during their making, the more people are likely able to "hear" at least some of what you're saying.

This played out for me one day at The White House. There's a tradition of placing "jumbo" prints on the walls of the West and East Wings. (President Nixon coined the phrase jumbo to say that he wanted bigger prints than the 8 × 10s that were then produced to give out.) Callie Shell, vice president Gore's photographer, started to put framed jumbo prints on the walls of a hallway in the lower level of the West Wing and the tradition has grown in each administration since – now they're 20×30-inch prints.

We used groupings of prints in various areas to speak to different aspects of the life of the president. Among the groupings is one of ten jumbos hanging down the hall from the cabinet room. I'd build sub-narratives into that grouping and because that set hung over a staircase, we had to have GSA (Government Services Administration) guys with ladders hang

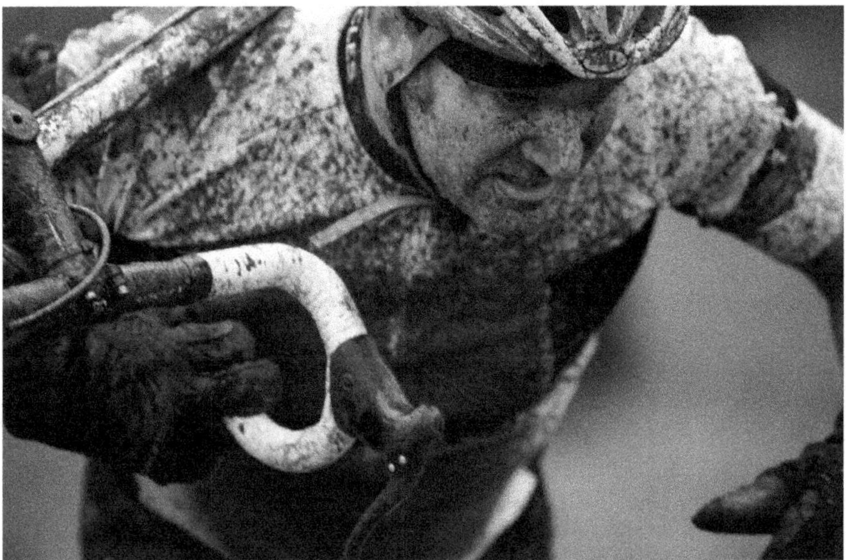

Photo 1.06 Expressing individual intensity was the goal of this photograph.

them. We finished hanging one set that had a subtle layer and one of the guys says, "I like what you did with this set." What do you mean I asked? "The thing with the hands," he said. There was the interplay of hands from one photo to the next, but it was a subtle aspect of the selection and sequencing. People do get it when we introduce dynamics into photographs.

Ask what you can do during the making of photographs to increase the depth and range of what people can respond to when looking at our photos. Here's a way to think about that: People respond to photographs in three ways: with their minds, their eyes and their hearts. Another way of describing the three things is: What does the photograph make us think about; how rich is the experience of looking at it; what do we feel because of the photograph?

Everyone's mind processes the structural aspects, the visual forms, of images through visual processing centers as they deal with lines, circles, squares, colors, spatial relationships and the like. The more organized and dimensional this aspect is the more the mind is engaged but more generically. What engages our minds uniquely is when we challenge the mind's higher processing centers that respond to experience – conflict, joy, exasperation, sadness, intensity … – and ideas, concepts and impressions, which are limited only by the photographer's perception and ability to express them.

Our mind starts to do its thing within milliseconds and the more dynamic there is within the image, the longer our mind's stay engaged. The mind also introduces other senses to the experience of seeing. The mind's eye translates texture in photographs to the sense of touch, it hears objects that make noise in photographs, it smells and hears and even tastes what is pictured. Extend that notion and your mind also responds to the sense of space and motion in still photographs. Again, not everyone will respond alike but the less you introduce to photographs, the less there will be for people to respond to.

Expanding on this experiential aspect, we also hear the things that are pictured in photographs, what Wilson Hicks called sound symbols in his seminal 1952 book, *Words and Pictures*. Combinations of sounds that emanate from pictures can create musicality and when put together in sequence, the effect can be like creating a song, or a symphony, with the inherent possibilities of introducing and utilizing cadence, discordance, unison, atonality/bitonality within individual photographs and in sequencing or grouping sets of photographs. Even volume can be a critical aspect of how we hear photographs.

Images can also trigger smells that are associated with what's pictured.

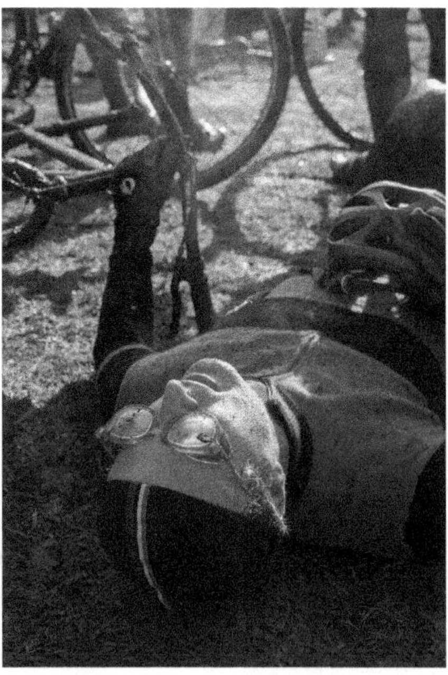

Photo 1.07 I hope you hear the exhaustion in this setting.

The eye receives images both as the pathway to and interpreter for the mind. There's a dichotomous relationship for sure. My reference here is the eye as the guide for the mind, meaning that photographs must fully iterate things visually for the eye to have a meaningful experience. That means having a clear structural hierarchy in the image, so the eye knows how to travel through it. The eye's journey should be spatially geometric and rewarded by the experience of color and light.

The heart feels the emotive aspect of photographs if the maker has introduced qualities to which the heart can respond. That happens not only because of what is pictured. A photograph can show someone crying but we may not have an emotive response to the photo. How the photographer expresses the light, color and distance from the person crying and how the person is placed within the frame are what will elicit a response, as much as the crying.

Engagement of the mind, eye and heart only happens if the photographer introduces what the eye, mind and heart can potentially respond to. Every viewer brings themselves, and their collective experiences, to your pictures so the more dynamically you create photos, the more you strive to say, the greater the chances are that people will respond to your photographs.

Maligning a quote attributed to President Lincoln, "You can make photos that some of the people like some of the time but not photos that all of the people like all of the time."

Section 1.3 The Milking Stool, or Three More Things

Three-legged milking stools work best for the purpose at hand. It's tough to milk a cow while sitting on a one- or two-legged stool – I learned this because my uncle had a busted stool on which I learned to milk cows grouping up in rural Nebraska. Similarly, photographs that sit on binary considerations tend to be less fully realized. Dimensional photographs are more compelling when they sit on these three legs:

Leg 1. A compelling *Why*
Leg 2. A fully realized aesthetic expression
Leg 3. An astute technical application

Photographs tend to wobble without a dimensional *why*. You can make technically astute photos that are boring; you can make aesthetically engaging photos that are otherwise humdrum. You can make technically, and aesthetically accomplished photos and they'll still fall flat compared to what they'd be with a more dynamic *why*.

Dawoud Bey, in *Photo Work: 40 Photographers on Process and Practice*, says "I think the main thing is that each individual photograph has to function in a way that compels a viewer to want to engage with. Making photographs, for me, is always about how one uses the visual poetics of picture-making and then weds that notion to a meaningful intention and subject."

Bey's intention and subject are my *why*. Poetics comprise the other two legs of the milking stool, the technical and aesthetic choices we make.

The technical leg means the choice of camera and decisions related to the photographic process, including aperture, shutter speed and ISO, choice of lens, etc.

Aesthetic uses are how we see and express color and light, how far away the camera is from what is being photographed and how we compose these in the photographic frame. Color, light, distance and composition combine to achieve what I call moment value, a derivation of Henri Cartier Bresson's Decisive Moment. Both words – value and decisive – are terms that describe the coming together of many decisions to create a photograph that is unique in the experience that it offers.

Or as Bresson says in *The Mind's Eye*, "To me, photography is the simultaneous recognition, in a fraction of a second, of the significance of an event as well as of a precise organization of forms which give that event its proper expression."

Keywords in the sentence are recognition, significance, organization, expression and more importantly their modifiers.

Section 2 goes into detail with each of these three legs.

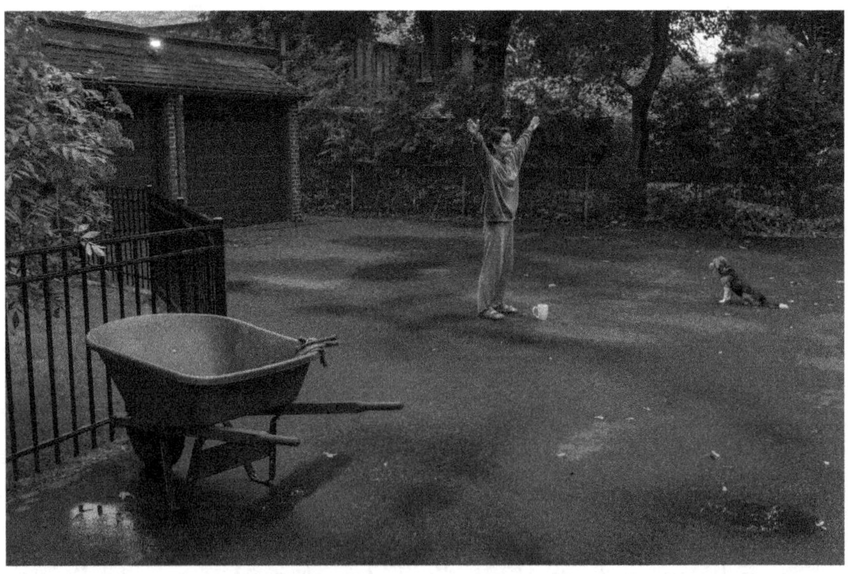

Photo 1.08 Bring all three legs of the milking stool together and even the mundane events of life can have a greater sense.

Section 1.4 Complex Simplicity; Simple Complexity; Perfectly Imperfect

Simple complexity. Complex simplicity.

We can strive to say so much in our photographs that the message is lost in the complexity of the making and the resulting photos lack clarity and are nothing but chaos. That would be complex complexity, as opposed to either of the terms above.

Or the opposite is striving to say so little and being so simple in the making that the resulting photos are simplistic and don't merit more than a passing glance. Being simplistic is the crime here, for me. Simple can be compelling; simplistic is usually boring.

In either case, the missing component is clarity of realizing how best to approach a given scene or topic – if the goal is to go beyond showing the informational aspects of what you put in front of your camera.

A starting point is to look for the opposite of what might seem obvious. If what you're trying to address is incredibly complex, try to find a representative aspect of it that you can embrace to represent a revealing aspect of the whole. Melissa Lyttle sought to address racism in a significant way but what a complex topic. She narrowed her focus through a project called *Where They Stood*, showing what happened to U.S. Civil War-era statues in communities that chose to remove them.

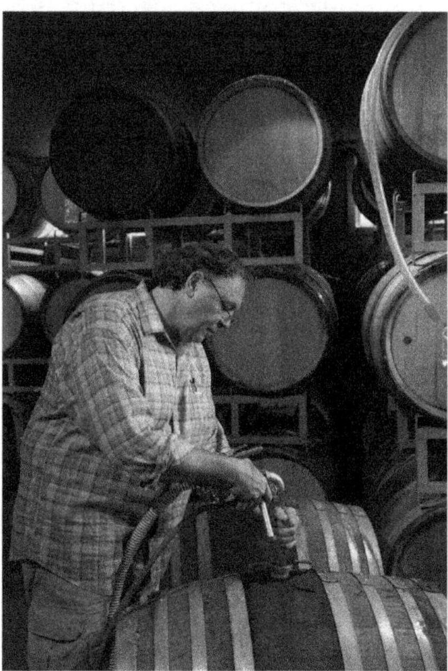

Photo 1.09 This photo oversimplifies the setting – Doug Tunnel during the wine-making process at Brickhouse Vineyard.

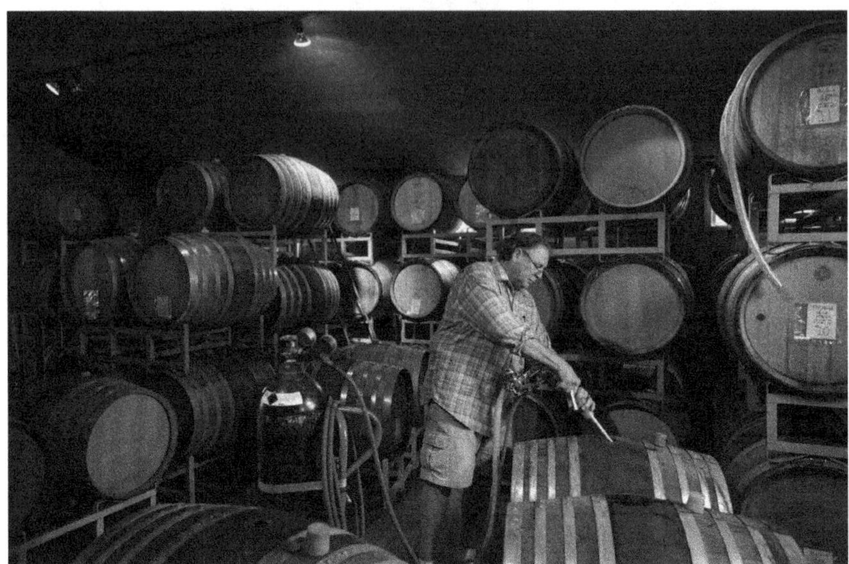

Photo 1.10 While this photograph offers much more.

On the opposite end of this simple/complex spectrum is being aware that what might seem simple has complexity, or what you perceive to be singular might be dimensional. The richer result of engaging with a complex topic might come from connecting with the complexity in an accessible form. A lot of essays result from this starting point. (Essays are groups of photographs on a shared aspect, as opposed to a picture story that follows one person or setting over time. W. Eugene Smith was among early groundbreaking storytellers who employed both story forms. His 1951 story about Nurse Midwife Maude Callen is a picture story while *Spanish Village* and *Pittsburgh* were essays.)

Béatrice De Géa's essay *Church for Everyone* is a series of portraits. "I hope to show what it feels and looks like to be on a lifelong search for a higher spirituality," she says, in a Washington Post Magazine article. What a complex topic and approach. Essays typically have to embrace enough of their topic to convey it wholly if not completely.

Joel Parés' *Judging America* is another essay that uses portraiture pairings to address prejudice.

Another notion is that of making perfectly imperfect or imperfectly perfect photographs. This is borrowed from the traditional Japanese way of thinking and acting called Wabi Sabi. Introducing imbalance, discord, asymmetry in ways that are still balanced is the goal.

Robyn Griggs Lawrence says of Wabi Sabi: "It takes a mind quiet enough to appreciate muted beauty, courage not to fear bareness, willingness to accept things as they are without ornamentation … to slow down, shift the balance from doing to being, appreciating rather than perfecting."

Wabi Sabi is a guiding principle in some interior design and architecture and can play out even in how we treat objects. For instance, Kintsugi is the practice of repairing damaged pottery, beautifully, instead of throwing it away.

In a way, this is borrowing from the design principle that substance precedes form, or how something is designed should be based on what it's supposed to do.

Translating Wabi Sabi to photography: Connect, let the essence of what you're photographing drive the resulting expression of it as opposed to applying a pre-determined set of rules or approaches. Photographers who exemplify this approach include Tanuma Takeyoshi, Izima Kaoru, Daido Moriyama, Yoneda Tomoko, Yumna Al-Arashi, Fabiola Ferrero, Meyrem Bulacek, Delphine Diallo, Nicole Tung, Hajime Kimura, Kita Cahana, Fethi Sahraoui, Aida Muluneh, Baudouin Mouanda, Cristina de Middel.

Section 1.5 This Is Not About Style

Do an online search for photography and style and you could read the search results for the rest of your life and come away, just before your last breath, thinking that style is the most or least important thing to achieve in your photography. Style is either superficial or essential, it evolves or gets newly applied.

One end of this spectrum says that style is you, it's your visual statement, your unique reason for and approach to creating photographs. On the other end, style is a superficial layer of accouterments or timely gimmicks that you apply to photographs in the hope that the *style* makes them engaging. It's the difference between an approach to image making that you craft uniquely and a pull-down menu solution that changes like software upgrades.

In the former definition, your style evolves gradually over time as you are able to elevate what it is you strive to say and how you achieve that expression through your photography; your current and past work will visually and substantively connect. In the latter definition, you'll change your style regularly to make your photography "fresh" and your style's past will progressively look outdated, though the same superficiality will connect your past and present work. If your *style* doesn't change time will leave you in the dust.

Style gets appropriated in a variety of ways, through the latest gizmo or the latest technical capability of software. Get a drone, switch to 360 or VR, snag that massive wide angle, adopt HDR. Or by applying a look to your photos through this or that filter pack during post-processing.

Think of substantive style more accurately as your visual language. It is your intentional selection of a visual vocabulary to sonorously reveal what you've chosen to engage with. Yes, photography shares qualities with sound and music. We can hear the best photographs. Some photos are single notes, others chords and when conceived and realized as a group they can be choruses and songs, movements and symphonies.

How do you achieve your unique visual vocabulary? By putting challenges in front of yourself and working through the solutions to those challenges through your camera. Building your language can be as simple as going into a space and only seeing light and how it affects the pictures you'll make in that space, to starting from ideas or concepts and striving to express them through your photographs, as heady as the injustice of how some people treat others or as experiential as what it feels like to be out on the first warm day of spring.

If you successively elevate and expand these challenges, your ability to make photos will continue to evolve because you continually try to express more. The goal is really the pursuit of growing your self-understanding and it happens by creating increasingly strong connections between receptors – your intention with a set of actions on the path to achievement.

Look at Nadav Kander's work through the years to see an evolution of seeing that goes beyond the application of style.

On your evolutionary path, you may know where you've been but not know where you're going. The not knowing is the fun part as each step

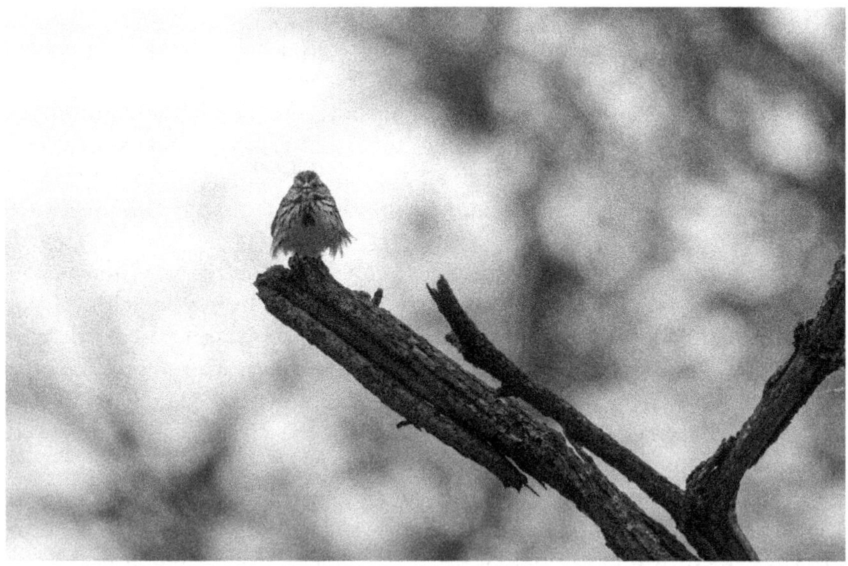

Photo 1.11 In approaching a new topical area – wildlife – I had to make many decisions, all of which stemmed from defining the why of the making of pictures. It was simply to say things about what it's like to be a bird, in this case a song sparrow after a rain.

forward informs and guides the next. But do look back and figure out what has worked well and not so well in the past and how to make the good better and stop doing the not so good.

As Star Trek Captain Michael Burnham says: "You will make the path by traveling it."

Section 1.6 So Many Ways to Express the Why

One observation of the past is that photography creation and delivery systems were so complex and expensive that they required a massive profession for the making and presenting of images. Knowing how to operate cameras and having the money to pay for them was the biggest price of entry for a large swath of how people made money with a camera. And only entities that could pay for printing processes could present the work.

This historically tended to produce a narrow mindset of what made a photograph successful; it only allowed certain types of people into the profession; and predefined how work was presented.

You gained access to these hallowed halls largely only if you became connected to someone who already was, it was a pipeline fed from the same wells. And most everyone looked like you, if you were white, European and male.

Fast forward to nowadays. Anyone can make a picture, anytime, anywhere, with anything that records an image. Minimal technical knowledge is required, no Visa, passport, expense account, company car. Anyone can publish anything digitally at minimal cost and with limited expertise. Social media outlets further amplify whatever you want to put out there – which can be positive, or not.

Instead of being able to own and operate a camera as the primary entry criteria, the far greater burden today is on being able to make photographs that say things people are willing and able to engage with. That's what gets you hired.

Within this new context, a much greater range of media is being used to approach and communicate what we address and how we present it. We're no longer limited to the sequenced still image, whatever story forms best convey what we're speaking to are the best choices. See how uniquely Diàna Markosian approaches narrative as one example. This evolution in visual communication falls somewhere between the genres of art and traditional work produced for clients, whether they are editorial, commercial or advertising.

It was wonderful to see World Press Photo recognize this trend by creating a new category or its global competition, called *Open Format.* Isadora Romero was the first recipient of her project *_blood is a seed.* Reference Louie Palu's *Front toward Enemy* presentation to see another example of multiple mediums coalescing around a theme: conflict.

It would be easy to decry the multi-discipline evolution, and many do. I celebrate it. Among the things that have changed is the openness to a greater range of types of images. We collectively have redefined what successful is. Instead of following rules that are genre specific and limiting, the best settings have no rules, "publishers" respond to images that speak uniquely to them.

Also, seemingly suddenly, who is behind the image-making machines is gradually changing; they are decreasingly predominantly white men. That is a massively good thing.

If photographs are the expressions of the people who make them – they are who we are – then it goes to follow that as a greater range of people are creating images, then more can be said in more ways. Any one person might be the right choice to photograph a given setting but not all settings. We need the full spectrum of humanity behind the camera to reflect upon and create the ever-increasing type of imagery that people respond to and value.

All of this current remolding of the profession stands on the shoulders of those few who were trying to make these, and many other changes happen for decades but were again and again thrown against the wall and shouted down. Efforts such as Yunghi Kim's *Trailblazers of Light* and *Kamoinge, The Continuing Legacy of an African American Photographic Collective*, bring the past forward. And many more recently formed groups bring more people to the viewfinder. Among them are Diversify Photo, Women Photograph, Natives Photograph, MFON, The Authority Collective, Foto Féminas. Furthermore, photographic collectives have emerged throughout the world to make the business of photography more efficient and provide shared community.

Now the challenge is to find your unique way of operating the machines and expand beyond traditional approaches and business models to say things about the world and get paid for doing it. If you are feeling left behind by this evolution or hear yourself blaming others or the system that left you behind, the need to update your way of producing work and finding a new market for it is clear.

Try This: Change Your Why

- Make a list that shows what motivates you to make pictures.

Ask yourself, as you're in a specific situation, what is your process of making photos and why is it the way it is? Slow down and really watch yourself make pictures from the time you enter a space until you leave. Make a list of what you do and say why you chose to do it that way.

Look at what you've produced and assess whether the reasons you made the photos as you did resulted in successful pictures, as you perceive success now. Then ask if they could have been better, what else could you have spoken to? In other words, how could you have changed *The Why* to make better photos?

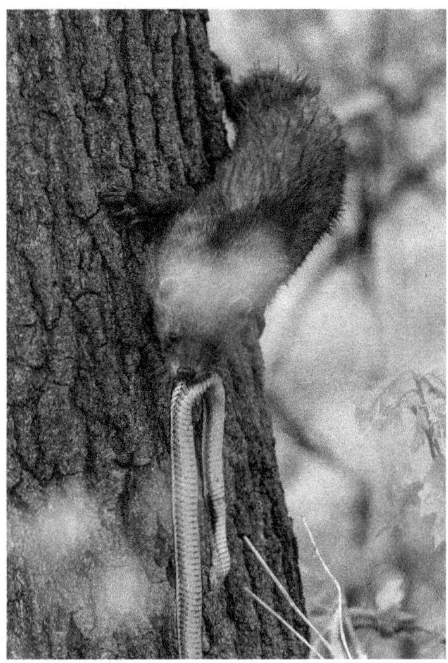

Photo 1.12 This fisher, a member of the Marten family, scared the heck out of me. Maybe you feel that from this photo.

Then put yourself in front of something or someone you've never photographed. Something new to you will likely inspire new approaches.

Then reconsider why you're going to make pictures. What qualities are you responding to, what ideas can you speak to, how can you approach the making differently from the past? Set a goal of making pictures that say something you've never said about what's in front of your camera. What could you say beyond showing it happening or using tried and true approaches?

Get to know the person and setting until you hear the words in the back of your head, the adjectives. Then strive to make pictures that convey the adjectives. What can your pictures make us feel?

If you think you've got the range of what can be said, keep pushing and exploring until you've really exhausted the possibilities. You'll know you're done when you've run out of things to say.

Section 2

Photography's Means of Expression

Section 2.0 Introduction

Your means of expression as a photographer are how you see and express light and color or tonalities in black and white, determine distance and compose settings within the frame. I express the fruition of these four means as the moment value of a photograph. The more dimensional and precise the seeing of each means, the greater the moment value – or the more unique and engaging the photograph will be.

Responding to settings and then translating how your eye sees to how the camera sees can seem overwhelming. But like wading into a cold, deep pool of water it's best to gradually ease in until the water no longer feels cold or fearfully deep. The experience becomes more intuitive as you continually challenge yourself.

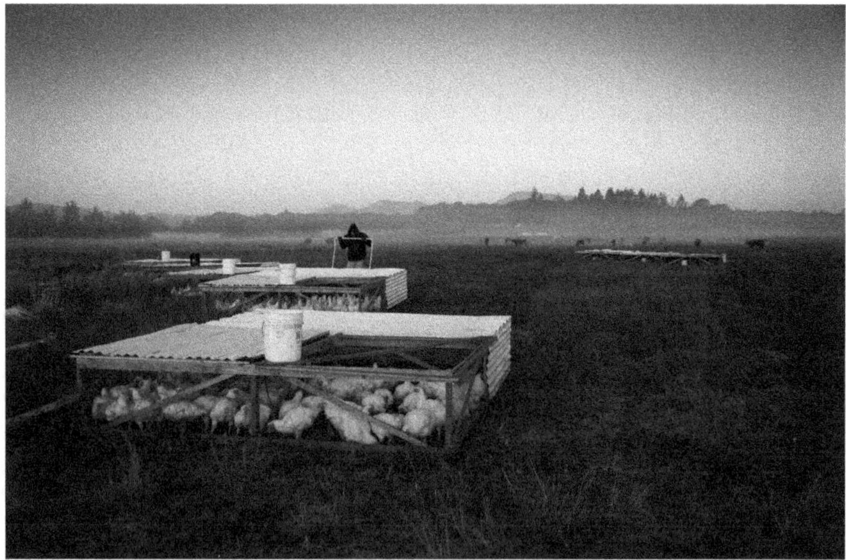

Photo 2.01 High-moment value photos engage the viewer through the number of occurrences that had to come together.

DOI: 10.4324/9781003287544-2

Photographers become known for their heightened realizations of one or more of them, such as Sarah Moon's seeing of color, Ming Smith's bond with light, Akira Kurosawa's compositions (in films), Andreas Mühe for distance in *Pathos of Distance*, and moment value is off the charts for all of them, each uniquely.

You too will convey the nature of what you photograph by realizing these different tools in a way that only you can.

Section 2.1 Achieving High Moment Value

Moment value is a way of speaking to how dimensional a given photograph is. Dimensionality comes from fully realizing photography's means of expression in tandem with the coming together of elements within a setting and all that it took for this to happen. To say a photograph has high moment value is to say that it is a rich and unique experience.

What comes together for photographs to have high moment value? There's the uniqueness of an individual moment, the coming together of multiple moments in a way that only happened once and the full expression of color, light, distance and composition – those are photography's means of expression.

Bringing together color, light, distance and composition to create photos that stop time uniquely in the service of saying things about what you photograph is what you have the most control over. Your choices reflect your uniqueness and create images that only you would make, as opposed to following a predetermined process.

If photographs are music, the goal is to create images that are more chord-like than single note. That means fully achieving all the means of expression in the service of saying things about what you're photographing. As opposed to relying on what is happening to make photos interesting or producing images that only one works well in one or two of the means.

Photographs that you can experience anew every time you see them have high moment value and are the most magical. Conversely, the more didactic or simplistic your photos are, the less engaging they're likely to be – seeing them once will be plenty.

How do you increase moment value in your photographs? Early on we're taught that we must "get" the picture, that we "shoot" photos, as if you raise the camera like a rifle and hit whatever you're shooting at.

In fact, high moment value photos result from a more considered, less reactive approach. Here too, why determines how. Here's a set of steps to use when photographing to increase moment value:

- Define *The Why:* Form an impression: what are you responding to in a situation, what is important to convey, what can be said, what do you want people to understand. (This is different from offering your opinion through your photography, which would be about you and not what you're photographing.)

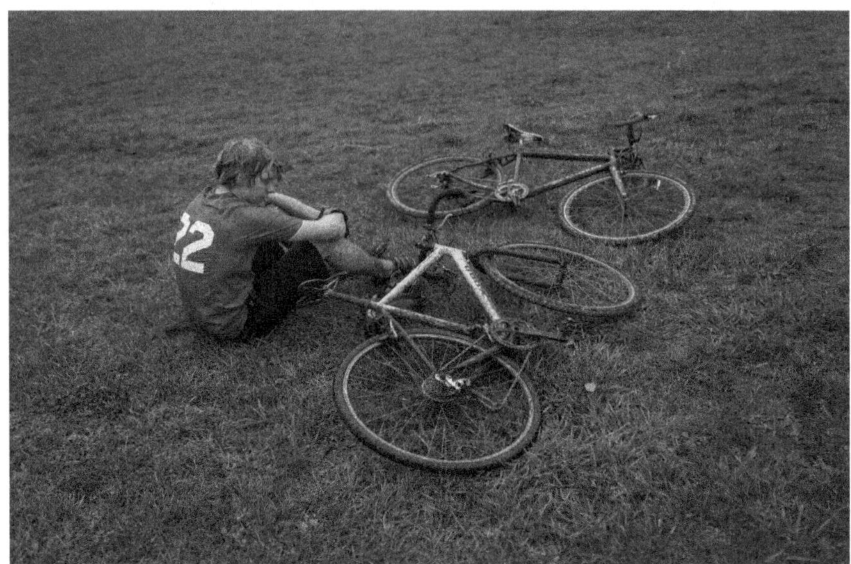

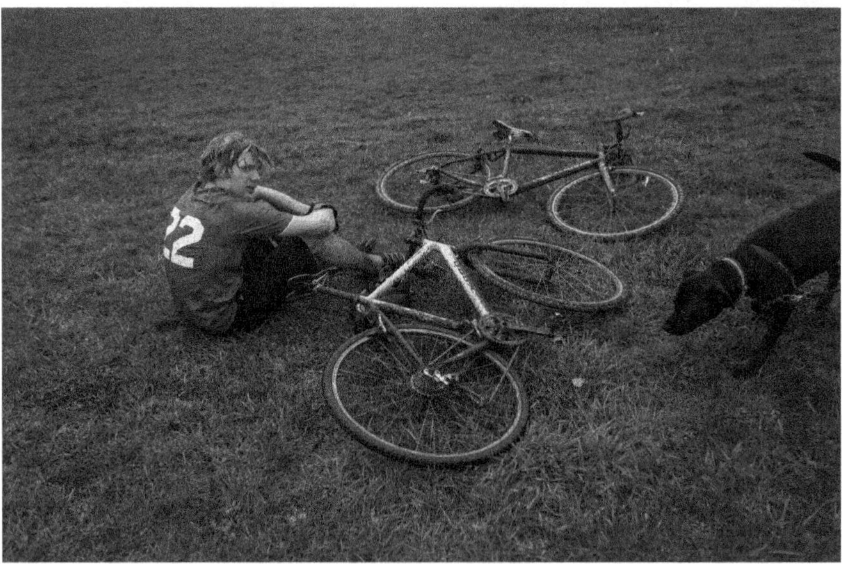

Photos 2.02 and 2.03 Just waiting for more elements to come to fruition in the frame can create higher moment value.

- Read the color. Where in the setting does the color of objects help or hinder what you're trying to say; are there different colors of light that you can use to elevate an expression or should avoid them because they distract? If you're making black and white photos, tonality or the scale of black to white is your means of expression.

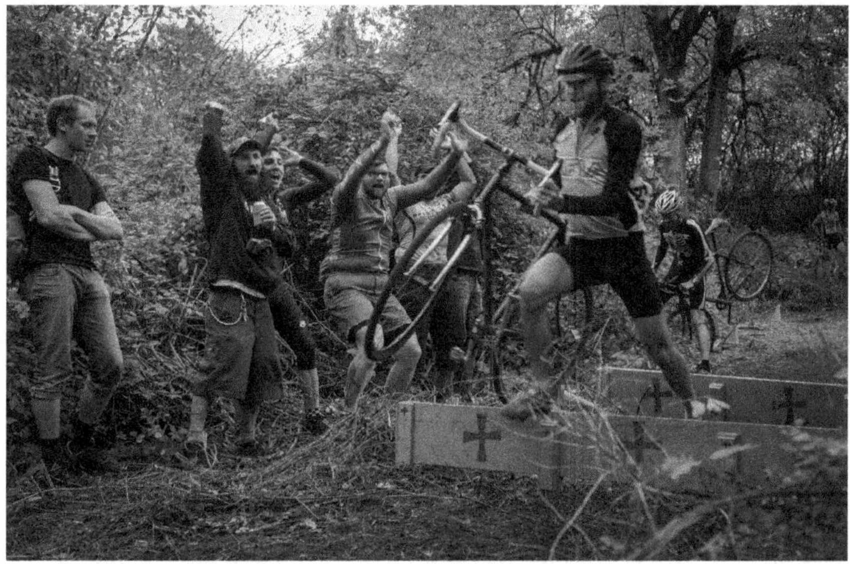

Photo 2.04 It's not just about how many things are going on. Careful placement of elements in different planes within the photograph, including the deepest point, is one way to make high-moment value photos.

- Map the light and determine where the quality of light best reflects what you're trying to say. How many different qualities of light are there, and which should you strive to photograph within?
- Choose the distance, how far away from the setting you need to be to convey what you're wanting to say and then compose and wait for the moments to come to fruition.
- Then change the distance and your seeing of all the other tools to say something else. Repeat until you've exhausted your seeing.

Oh, my god, that'll take forever, you might be saying. Maybe so, at first, because this is a different way of thinking about how to make photographs. But as you train your mind's eye anew, you'll find that you can do all of this in short order, once you understand what's important in a given setting and then respond using this relearned approach. This does become intuitive.

Other variables of moment value include the fact that every active situation has a rhythm, they begin, rise and conclude. You'll learn how to interpret the setting, anticipate and compose for the action and flow from beginning to end with it.

You can say many different things about every setting you're in and each will have a different quality of moment value, a unique application of seeing, based on each why as each fits into the narrative you're creating.

An additional challenge is to strive to make photographs that you can't fully see when making them.

Section 2.2 The Technical: Beyond Knobs, Dials and Sliders

Cameras and lenses are complex machines. They have so many knobs and dials and settings and sliders. In the same way that it's important to know how a piano works if you want to play it well, it's important to understand the technical aspects of photography in the service of making musical photographs with your camera. More compelling photographs result when you knowingly translate the way your eye and mind see through the camera's way of seeing.

What's the difference between your eye's way of seeing and the camera's? Here are a few:

Centered Sight

Your eye can only see an oval field of view and it can only focus on one, centered point. The further from the middle objects are, the less your eye can discern them. Your eye auto exposes, and most people can see greater volumes of light than cameras. Each of us sees light and color differently. The camera, in contrast, sees everything in the viewfinder equally, left to right, front to back, corner to corner. It can vary how much is in focus and render color and light uniquely.

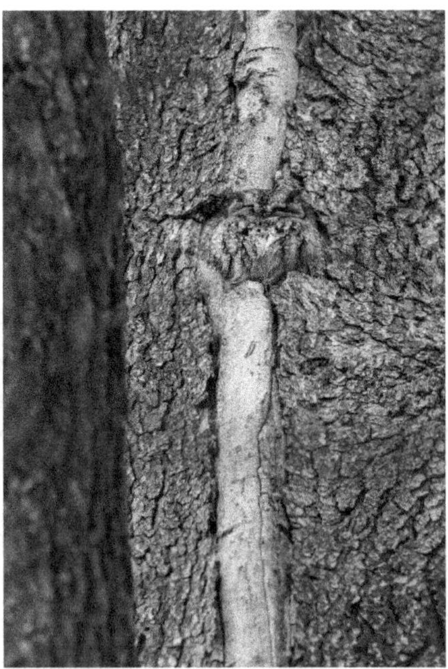

Photo 2.05 All of the means of expression come to play in this photo in the service of conveying how camouflaged this eastern screech owl is. Lens choice and quality of light are the primary means.

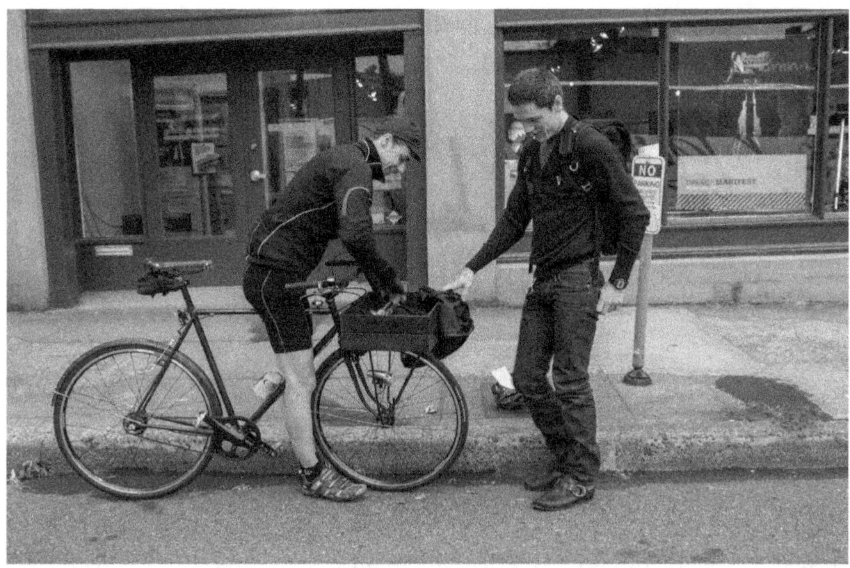

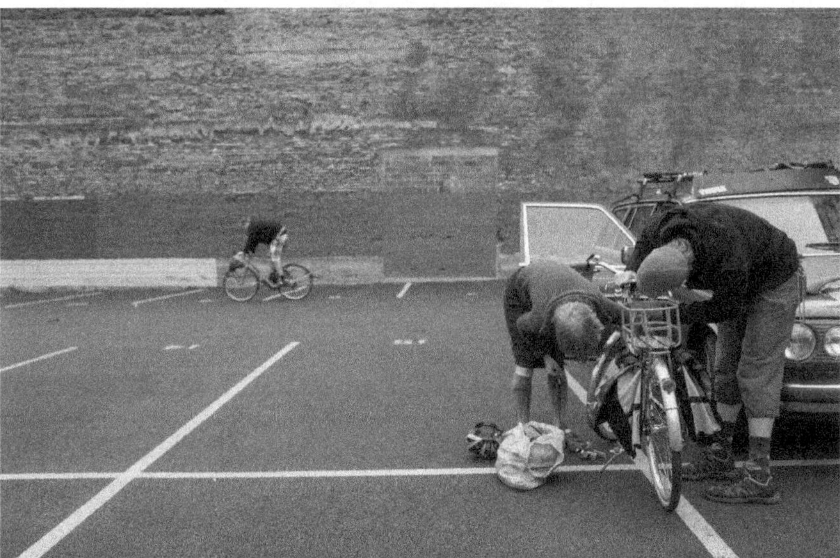

Photos 2.06 and 2.07 The first photo is how your eye sees – centered and unconcerned with foreground and background. The second photo translates the eye's view to how the camera sees, a more complete iteration of the frame.

Two Eyes versus Cyclops

Your eyes see in stereo. What you see has depth/dimension/roundness because of that. Objects are separated from their backgrounds and appear rounded. They have shape because your eyes can see from two points simultaneously. The camera is a one-eyed creature. It relies on how light falls on objects and careful placement through composition to create a sense of depth that your stereo eyes can see automatically.

There's only one setting on your eyes' way of adjusting how it sees: P for Program, compared to many choices on the camera.

Exposure Triangle

Among those choices is which combination of aperture, shutter speed and ISO produces the result you're looking for. There are plenty of articles that proclaim there are good or bad, right or wrong combinations, or rules to follow in choosing the "right" combination of these three. Instead, think of each of them as creative choices. Aperture offers choices of the depth of field and what the out-of-focus parts of the frame will look like. Shutter speed will determine whether all of parts of the photo are "sharp." The choice of ISO affects sharpness in a different way by introducing "grain" and affecting the dynamic range of the sensor or film. The combination of the three, if chosen to convey qualities of what you're photographing, can be magical.

Depth of Field

Your eyes can't vary the depth of field, except somewhat by their distance from an object. Depth of field isn't a complex concept. It's simply how much of a scene is in focus the further objects are from the camera. Depth of field is one of the camera's most powerful tools. Use depth of field as a creative expression. Tell your camera how much of a scene that you want to be in focus by choosing the aperture that conveys the quality that you want the photo to convey, and how much you want to be in focus front to back. Choose a larger aperture opening, such as f/2 and less of what's in front of the camera will be in focus relative to its distance from the camera. Shallow depth tends to isolate objects within a scene and, depending on the scene and what you want to say, can create a sense of loneliness or intensity, a closed space, separateness from a setting or invite the viewer into the setting. Shallow depth can also create a hierarchy of what's most important in a scene by blurring less important elements.

Distance from what you're photographing varies the depth of field. The further objects you've focused on are from the camera, the greater the depth of field and vice versa.

A smaller aperture opening will create greater depth of field, yet the smaller the opening the larger the f/stop number, which used to confuse me. Having more in focus gives the viewer more to respond to, and more to look at. But that puts greater responsibility on the photographer for deciding what to include and how to structure the photograph with a clear hierarchy – start looking here, then go there, then there, etc. Greater depth of field can create a sense of chaos if objects are jammed together and connected in different geometric planes within the scene. You can more easily make qualitative and physical connections with scenes with greater depth of field. Or you can isolate lone objects within an expanse that's completely in focus to create a sense of isolation that will be different from the sense given by shallow depth.

Dynamic Range and Exposure

People's sight generally has greater dynamic range than any camera, which means they ascertain more range of highlight to shadow than cameras.

It's important that you understand how much of a scene your camera will be able to record. Most can "see" in the 14-stop range. You determine exposure in part by placing the exposure within the range of what the camera will record with details. Whether you expose so more of the shadows have detail or expose so highlights are rendered with detail is a creative choice. Exposing for highlights can create shadows without detail, which can convey a somber quality, among others, while blown-out highlights and greater shadow detail can introduce vibrance.

Not everyone has the same sensitivity to light. Just ask my wife. I generally don't turn lights on in a darkened room that I walk through while she generally needs to keep from running into objects.

Cameras, on the other hand, have a whole system in place to ensure that all of them see volumes of light equally, based on their ISO, basically the sensitivity to light of the camera's sensor or film. How the camera reads the volume of light through its light meter is also said to be consistent. Camera meters are becoming more sophisticated in interpreting the light in scenes and there are multiple metering choices. In-camera meters display the median point of the volume of reflected light seen through the viewfinder. (Incident meters measure light falling on the meter's sensor dome.) If a scene has a lot of dark areas relative to light ones, the light meter will tell the camera to let more light onto the sensor, which would overexpose the highlights. So, it's up to you to understand why the camera is telling you what the exposure should be and knowing when you have to override its way of seeing to make an exposure that is specific to what you want to convey through that choice.

It's also worth noting that the higher the ISO the less dynamic range there is.

Shutter Speed

Use how long the shutter remains open as a creative control by deciding whether you want everything to be sharp, moving things to be blurred or sharp, or nothing to be sharp. Each choice creates a feel. Decide which ones work best for what you're saying about what you're photographing.

ISO

Film accomplishes higher ISO ratings by using larger bits of light-sensitive material, which we see as grain. Digital has the equivalent feel the higher the ISO you choose. Introducing grain can be a creative decision.

White Balance and Color Temperature

White balance is another camera setting that might seem simple. Pick one of the camera's offerings – cloudy, sunny, fluorescent, incandescent – to render the color temperature of a scene and you're done. Or just go with AUTO and don't even think about it. But what is white balance and what creative choices can you achieve through setting the white balance?

Typically, the choice of white balance is meant to render a white object as white, regardless of the "color" of the light in each setting, and by extension, all other colors fall into place. You might have seen broadcasters holding up a white piece of paper in front of their video cameras to set a neutral, or balanced, white. Color of light as your camera understands it is expressed on a Kelvin color temperature scale, going from warmer to cooler, while your eye tends to auto-shift the temperature of light in scenes to being more neutral than is actual.

Incandescent light bulbs, flames and warm sunsets are in the 1700k–3000k range; early morning and dusk after sunset are in the 3000k–4500k range; bright overcast and direct sun are in the 4600k–6500k range and above.

If you choose to match the kelvin on your camera to the kelvin in each setting or go with Auto White Balance, you will render the setting's color temperature quality more the way eyes see. Photojournalists and people who want to render scenes as they appeared to tend to go this route.

If you choose to contrast the kelvin setting or choose to represent one of the color temperatures in a mixed-temperature setting, you are making a choice that affects the rendering of the scene. Movie makers are among those who use this approach. For instance, if there is both a warm and cool light source in a setting and your set for the cool kelvin, the warmth of the light in the scene will feel all the warmer, whereas AUTO would split the difference in the same way the light meter would land the exposure in the middle.

Choosing opposing kelvin settings can turn scenes warmer or cooler to affect the feel of the photographs.

Lens Choice

Deciding which focal length of lens to use in each setting can be an extension of the creative process, as opposed to choosing a lens based on it being wide enough to include everything you want in the frame or being long enough to compensate for your inability to move closer. You can choose to use zoom lenses with the same considerations. Choose the focal length

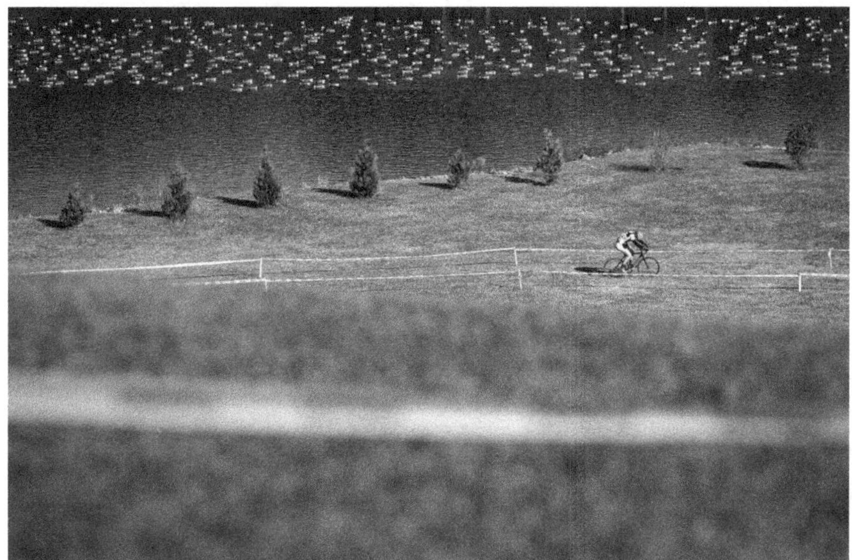

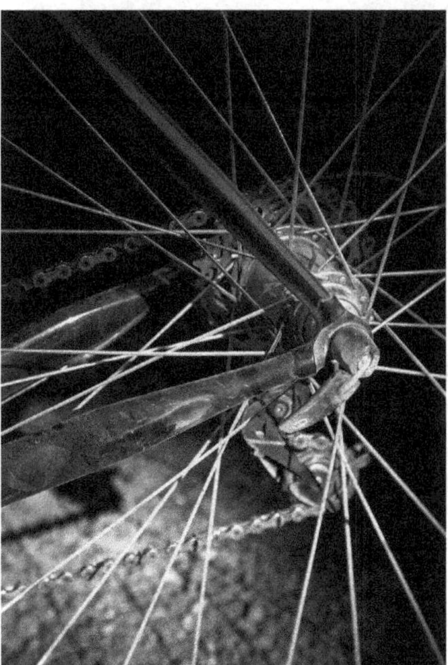

Photos 2.08 and 2.09 You can use lenses against their inherent qualities. Telephotos are usually used to minimize and bring the distant closer and wide angles are chosen to include more of scenes. Lens usage in these two photos does the opposite.

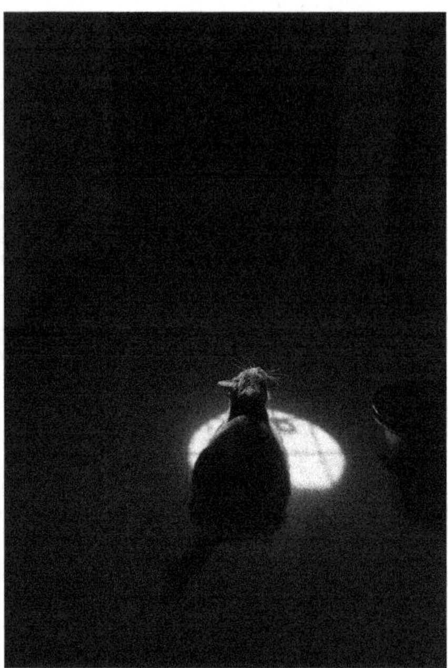

Photo 2.10 Be like a cat. Always know where the light is.

on the zoom that best conveys the qualities that you want to express and then move to the distance to best realize that lenses expression, as opposed to staying put and ratcheting the focal length to include what you want in the picture.

Nathaniel Brunt recommends starting out by using only a fixed focal length lens – 35 or 50 mm – to ground your seeing in how that lens sees, which in turn develops your spatial sensibility. You can then choose other lenses and adopt what is different from each.

This is not an all-encompassing technical description. I hope there is enough to awaken your awareness of the relationship between technical, aesthetic and *The Why*.

Section 2.3 Seeing and Expressing with Light

Photography is nothing without light. The judicious seeing of light can elevate the ordinary to the extraordinary. Light can bring warmth or a chill, it can repel or embrace, it can introduce a sense of conflict or resolution, happiness or sadness, elevate you or send you crashing.

I've heard the excuse: "The light sucked so I couldn't make a decent picture." Such a notion often happens when trying to craft a picture at noon outdoors or in a florescent-lit space or when it was "too dark" or off-color.

Yet each of these situations could result in telling photographs that reflect the exact qualities of light you might have found bad.

Thinking of light as being either good or bad, as with most binary measures, is counterproductive. A better way to think of this is that the light was wrong for what you were hoping to say. Every setting has the quality of light but if you hear yourself saying the light sucks it might be that you're working against the light.

You're likely compromising the light by deciding the photograph must be made from a specific angle and in a specific part of the scene where the quality of light isn't telling. That usually happens because you think the photograph has to directly show what is happening, an informational or verb approach. If your starting point were trying to convey qualities of what is happening, you'd determine where the light in a setting imbued those qualities and make seeing the light a primary determinant of how to craft photos.

Another common misperception is that "good light" is something specific, that it happens only in some settings and certain times of the day. You could do a content analysis that tracks what time of day photographs that appear in National Geographic magazine were made through the decades. Chances are that as the years passed you would see photographs being made during a greater range of times during the day and night. When I worked there it was still the time of believing that photos should be made in the golden hours, soon after sunrise or before sunset or better yet, just after a rain when the sun comes out from the clouds. Now, photographs

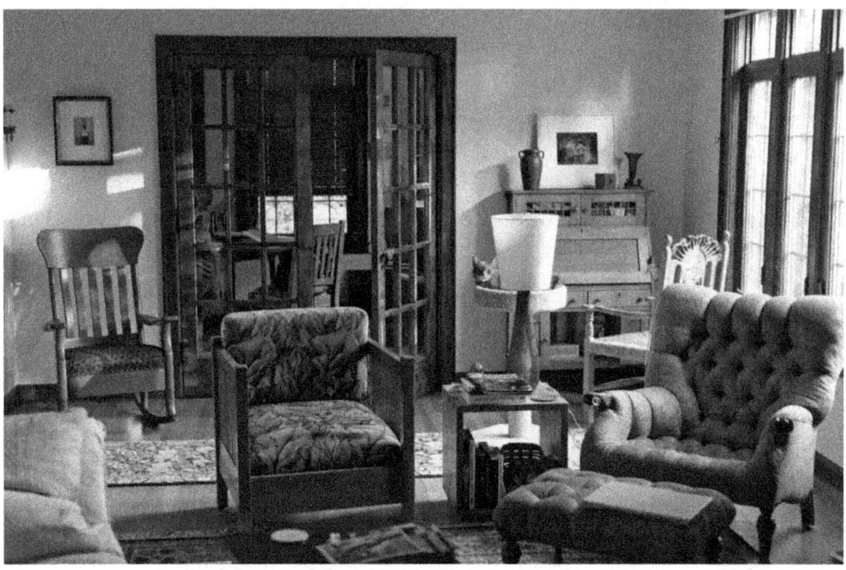

Photo 2.11 Most settings will have a range of qualities of light. This one has many. Decide where to make a picture based on what quality you want to convey with the light.

the magazine runs are made during more times of the day and night and they present a far greater range of qualities of light.

Know that starting from a point of lightness is a western cultural concept. Some Asian cultures "celebrate the complexities of darkness not just as the mere absence of light but as the place from which poetry and possibility originate," quoting Dr. Zun Lee. Zun cites Junichiro Tanizaki's 1933 essay *In Praise of Shadows*, in which the author contrasts The West as searching for light and clarity, compared to The East's appreciation and exploration of shadow and subtlety.

We all experience and therefore express light differently, both as a matter of our physical uniqueness and as an extension of our personalities. Scott Thode said that Stanley Greene spoke of the photographic journey as each person finding their light within. This was during a tribute to Stanley on the anniversary of his death, and his birthday, February 14. What if, from this day forward, you create photographs that express your light with clarity and dimension?

Map the Light

Mapping the light in settings is my way of saying that you look at the number and types of light sources in a setting and see how the light they produce falls on what you want to photograph, from different angles. Read their angularity. That will tell you better and lesser places within the setting from which to make photographs.

Start mapping by noting how many light sources there are. A light source can be anything that illuminates a setting: Light bulbs, windows, reflections, doorways, smartphones, computer screens. If you are outdoors, light sources include the sun and objects it bounces off or is absorbed by. Then scope out how many directions the sources come from. Determine the relative volume of each in a given part of a scene and how does that change as you move to different parts of the scene? Are there non-qualitative settings or dead zones – if so, avoid those? If you are in a space where you know you'll make photographs over time, note how the light changes throughout the day and as seasons change.

Then make note of what kinds of qualities the cumulative light conveys in the different spots within a setting. Look at how the light falls on objects or people and move completely around the people or things to see how the light changes from different angles in different parts of a setting. Choose to photograph from where the qualities of light permeate your photos. If you're lucky, the people you're photographing will be like actors and find the light in scenes.

Range of Quality

The size of a light source relative to its distance determines whether light falling on what you're photographing will appear soft or hard, diffused

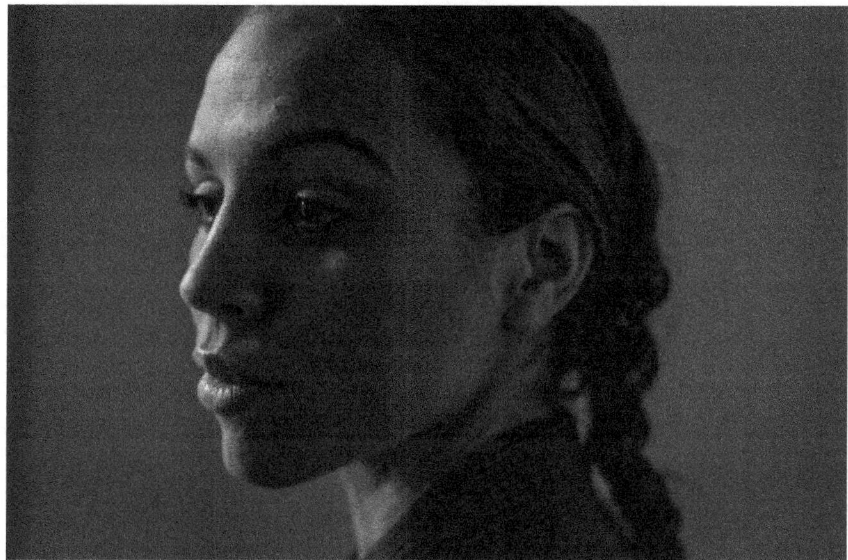

Photo 2.12 There was only one angle from which the two primary light sources landed on and reflected off of Aneshea's face, including the critical catch light in her eye.

or specular. Larger light sources produce softer light while, smaller light sources produce harder light; matte vs reflective sources determine diffused or secular qualities.

Sunlight bouncing off of a large matte surface produces softer, diffused light and if off of a highly reflective surface the light will be hard or specular. And sunlight softens when passing through clouds.

Be sensitive to light sources' size, type of materials light bounces off in settings and distance from the source to what you're photographing.

Incidence = Reflection

Light's angle of incidence equals its angle of reflection, which means that there's a sweet spot at which light goes from its source, lands on a surface and reflects, or bounces, into your lens. Water without reflection will look flat, and eyes that don't have a catch light will look dead. Find the sweet spot of reflected light by moving at an angle to light sources to see which angle produces the best result as the light falls on and bounces off of what you're photographing.

Directionality of Light and Viewer's Brain

The brain's experience of looking at photographs gets richer when photographs present angularity. Our brains engage with the directionality of

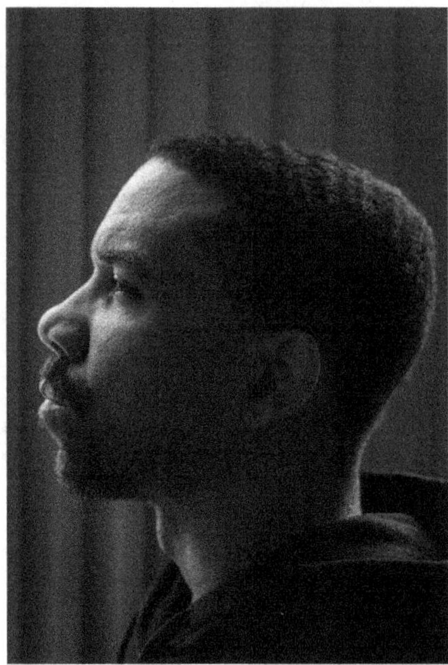

Photo 2.13 The light source to the left is closer to Leonard's face than the one on the right, so is brighter, an example of the inverse square law at play.

light in a photograph relative to the viewer by imagining the light source, as if your brains traced the path that light took to reach our eyes. Light sources from behind the viewer are less engaging and generally produce less dimensional photographs. Light sources at angles from the viewer create widely varied visual experiences, just because of their angle of incidence. The more light sources there are and the greater their variability, the richer the experience for the brain.

Light Falls Off

Also remember that light falls off exponentially, meaning that as the distance from a light source doubles, its volume, or brightness, halves. (In physics, this is known as the inverse square law.) To put this in photographic terms, the exposure must increase by one stop as you double the distance from a light source. Contrast ratio – the difference in the volume of light between highlight and shadow – diminishes as you move away from a source. Considering these two dynamics helps you more completely realize the potential of expression based on the light in every setting.

Lighter the Further from the Camera

Another way to express light is inherent in landscape photography, where the image gets lighter the further the scene goes from the camera. Our mind's eye expects closer objects to be darker, further objects to be lighter. Changing that relationship, by placing lighter elements in the foreground and darker in the background can create a contradictory feeling.

There can be a dozen different expressions of light in a single space so choosing the spots where the quality of light matches what you think is important to convey about what's in front of you is critical.

Color Temperature Considerations

Be sensitive to the different temperatures of light in a setting because using the contrast between warm and cool or maintaining a consistent overall temperature can be a powerful consideration in conveying qualities. (More on this in the next section about color.)

Follow this process whether you have 10 minutes, days or years to make a picture in a given environment. It might seem like a lot to try to accomplish but this becomes second nature the more you do it and the more success you have in the doing.

Once you have a good sense of how light expresses where you're photographing you can use that as a building block for a set of pictures. You can

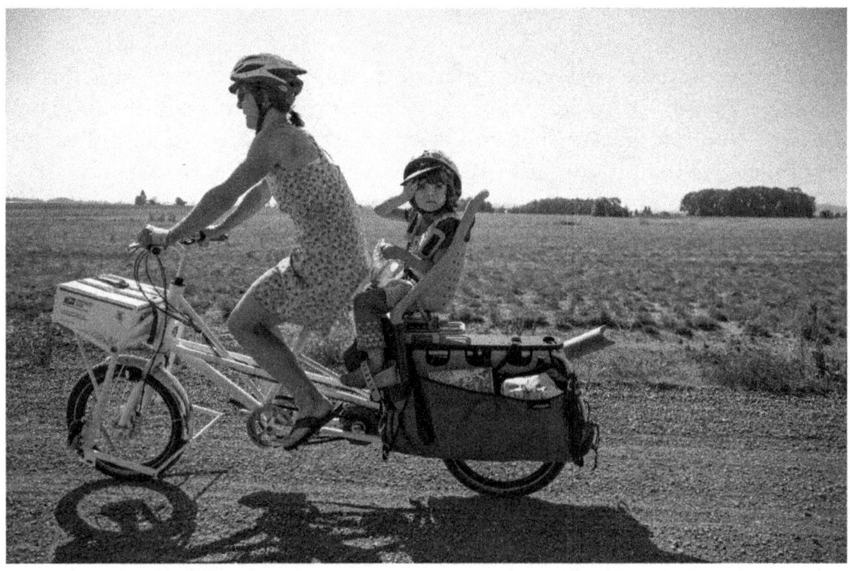

Photo 2.14 Sunlight in the middle of the day is usually considered to be *bad*. But if what you want to convey is the heat and exhaustion of a setting, then that's the right time to make photos.

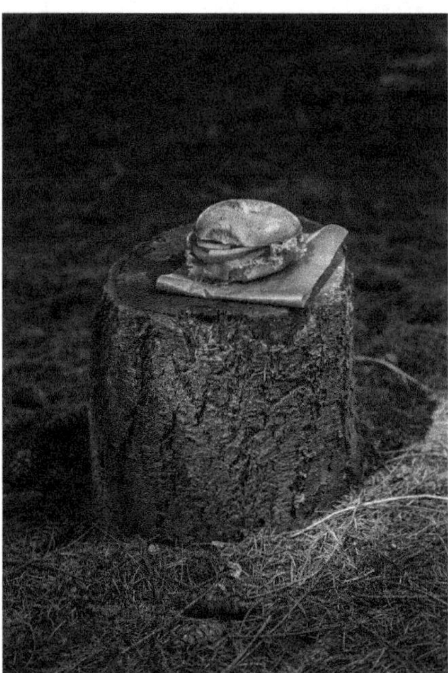

Photo 2.15 Introducing light can be a primary or additive source to bring out what is most important in a setting, if as in this case the existing light is not working but the setting was good.

reinterpret a setting by seeing different qualities of light within it. Strive to make a range of photographs that convey different qualities in every setting you photograph. That will offer greater potential when building a set of pictures than if you just make one type of picture in a setting.

Light's qualities can then either hold a set of photographs together as a group or create distinctive subsets. You can create visual narratives in limitless ways that build on contrasting or similar qualities of light, in combination with all the other tools and aspects that this book addresses. Quality of light *is* the foundational, essential element.

When to Introduce Light

If the light as it is won't convey what you want to say in a given setting, or if it is non-qualitative in every part of where you have to make photographs, should you introduce light to the setting? Increasingly people are answering that question, yes. And with reason. With the advent of smartphones, almost anyone can make a picture that is fine but lacks the quality of light that elevates photos to a higher state. Among the things that distinguish an uninformed smartphone user from successful professionals is how much more completely the latter expresses light purposefully.

Some photographers choose to introduce light into every setting they photograph.

Your choices in introducing light are some combination of a reflective, moveable surface, a constant light source, such as an LED or incandescent, and strobes with modifiers. Use the combination that's right for what you want to say.

Among the attributes and abilities that introduced light brings to your photographs is controlling light ratios, which can be a powerful creative choice, either raising or lowering the ratio to exclude or include more details within scenes.

There are many books that speak about creating light. Among the strongest is Gregory Heisler's *50 Portraits: Stories and Techniques from a Photographer's Photographer*, because Greg talks about the whole of making portraits, including lighting choices.

Section 2.3 Color – See, Feel, Interpret

Once you've mapped the light in a setting, begin to understand how you could say things through the expression of color, or tonality in black and white, in that setting. Color and tonality affect our perception of photographs in three ways: By directing the eye, by creating spatial relationships and by conveying mood.

If color/tonality is perceptibly seen, it can direct the eye through the photograph. A brighter color or tone in a scene is where the eye generally falls first.

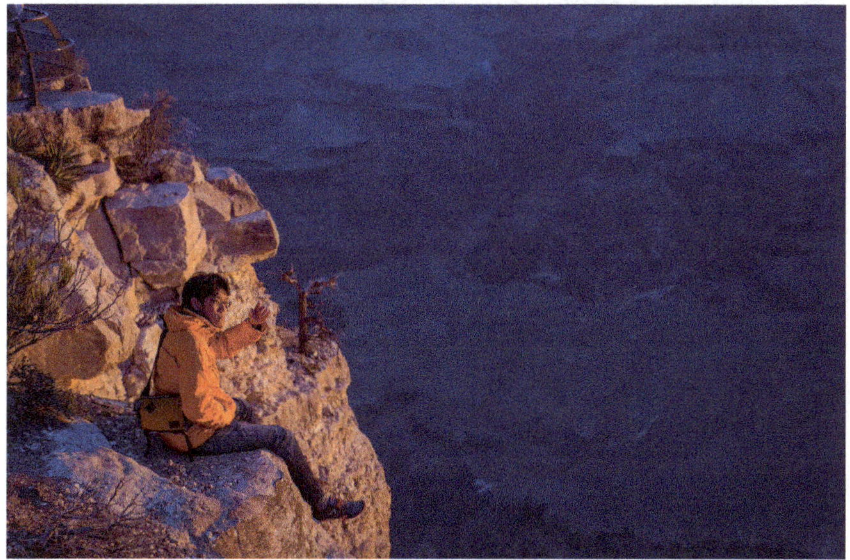

Photo 2.16 Warm foreground color separates from the cool background color.

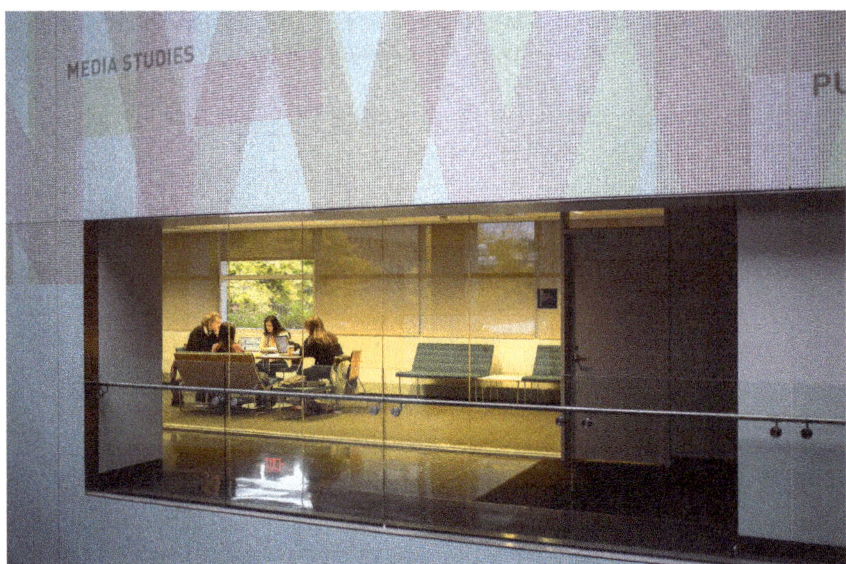

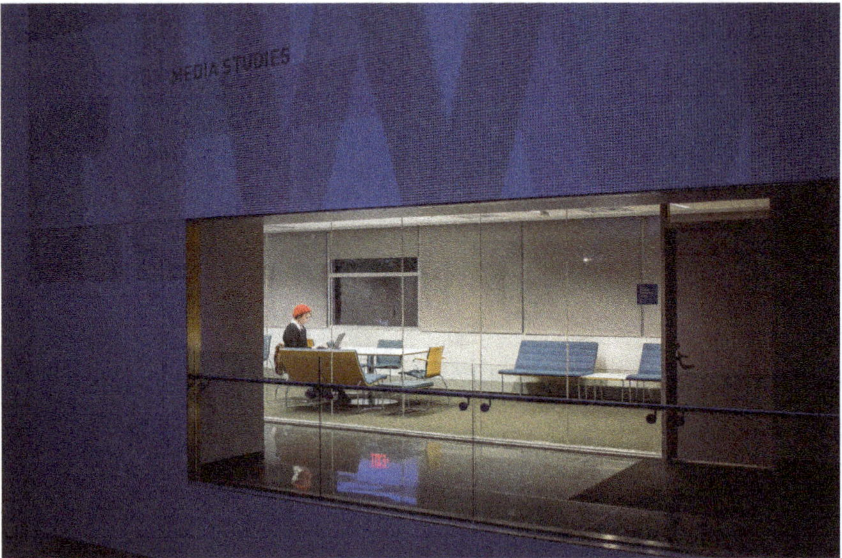

Photos 2.17 and 2.18 Different times of day produce different color temperatures and colors of objects within a setting.

Color can create spatial relationships between planes and objects in the scene. A warm object in the foreground will come out to the viewer even more if there is a cool aspect to the background of the setting. A range of carefully seen black to white tones creates similar spatial dynamics.

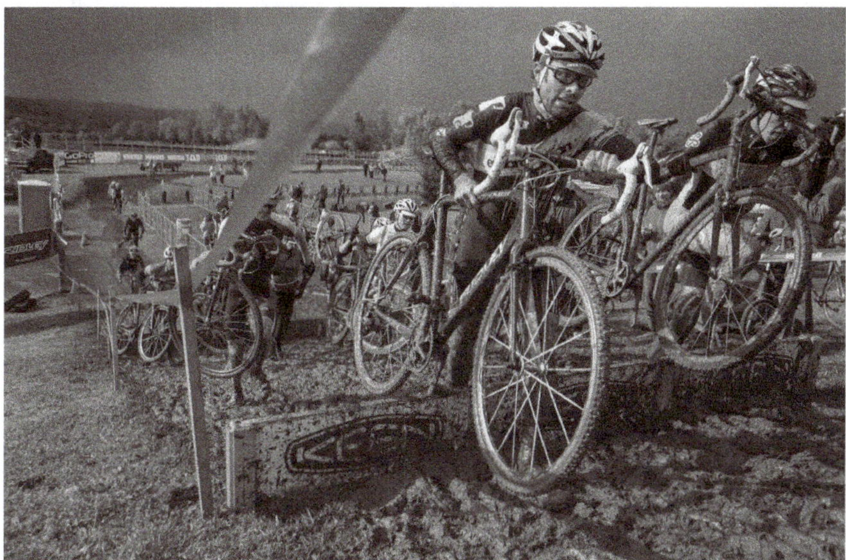

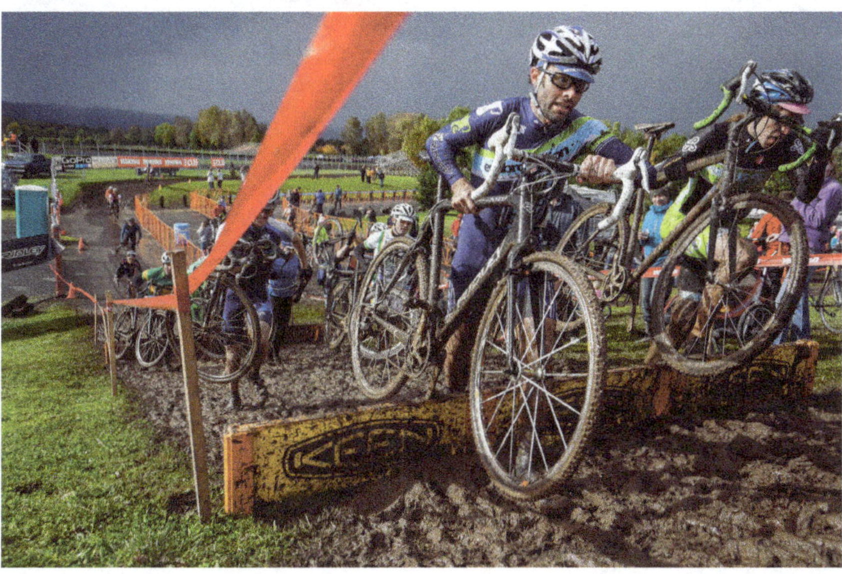

Photos 2.19 and 2.20 Map the color in a setting by seeing if specific colors take the viewer astray from where you want them to look. In these two, where does your eye start in the color photo compared to the black and white? The photo was seen in black and white.

Mood from color: Warm colors can convey comfort or happiness or be uplifting or ... Cool colors can convey crisis or discord or sadness. Different colors have different associations in different societies, so this aspect is not globally universal.

Making color a critical component of your photographs is an active process. You can't just say, this is what's here, so I'm stuck with it. In the same sense that you should map light in a setting, you have to be sensitive to how the color lives within a setting.

Types of Color

There are two types of color as they apply to making photographs: The color of objects and the color of light, as described in the light subsection. The color of objects is what most people think of in the context of making pictures. Light emits waves on a color spectrum from cool to warm, its temperature. You can consider the two separately but together is better because the color of light and the color of objects together affect the color of objects – a warm light makes warm objects all the warmer and it could warm the quality of cool objects. If there are contrasting light waves and object colors you can use that dynamic creatively.

This assumes that the starting point for any of these decisions is what you're striving to say about what's in front of you.

A color wheel is one way to see object color relationships, with wedges of yellow through orange, red to purple, shades of blue and shades of green, as if each color handed off some of itself to its neighbor and picked up a bit from the coming shade.

Color of light has a similar representation, on a spectrum from darker blue at one end to deep orange at the other. Wavelengths of light also affect how much range of detail your camera will record, with sunlight at the fullest and sources such as mercury vapor at the lower end.

On the wheel and light color spectrum, colors opposite of each other in settings create tension, separation, opposite moods, conflicting notions, the variance of depth within the frame and more. I call them frienemies. Similar colors create the opposite effect: cohesion and connection and whatever sentiment that shade elicits.

Mapping Color

Start seeing color in a setting by noting if specific parts of the scene you're photographing have stronger color representations. Warmer colors might dominate one part of a scene, another might have contrasting color (opposites on the color wheel). Or maybe the color in some parts of a given space conflicts with what you're striving to convey in that setting – everyone is wearing purplish red and yellowish green but the mood is one of cohesiveness. The color of light might be consistent throughout or there may be varying temperatures of light in a scene.

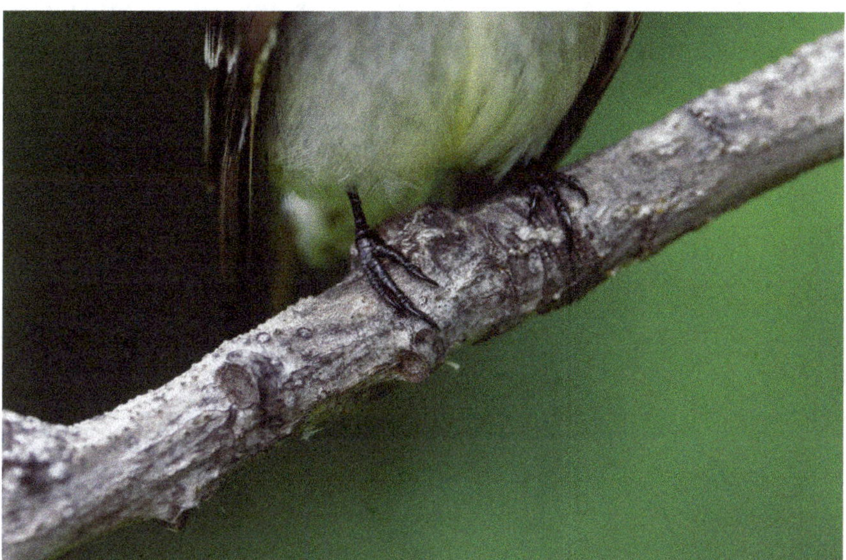

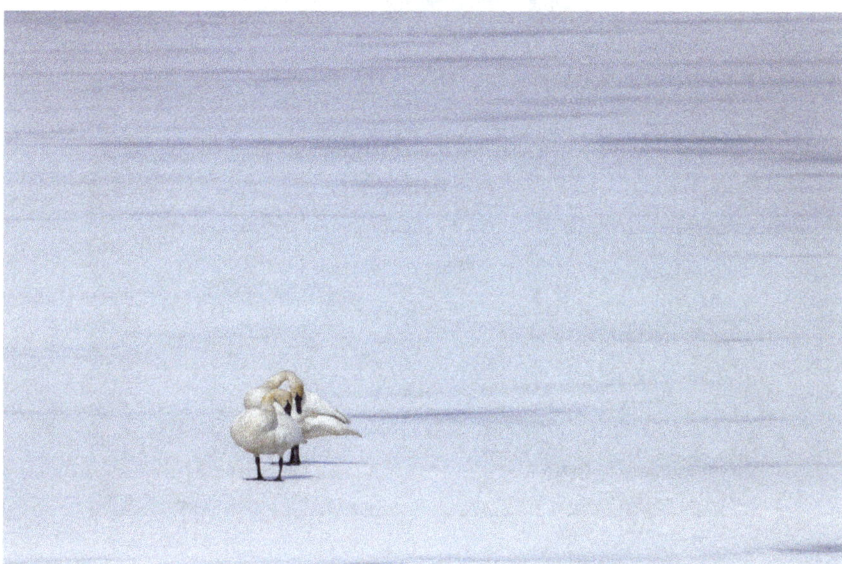

Photos 2.21 and 2.22 How far the camera is from what's being photographed is as important a decision as any other. Proximity to an eastern wood-pewee offers a unique experience while putting trumpeter swans in the context of place creates a very different sense. Both were made with long telephoto lenses.

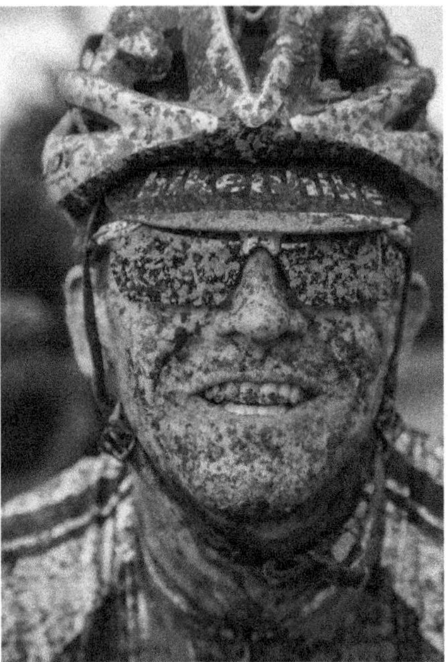

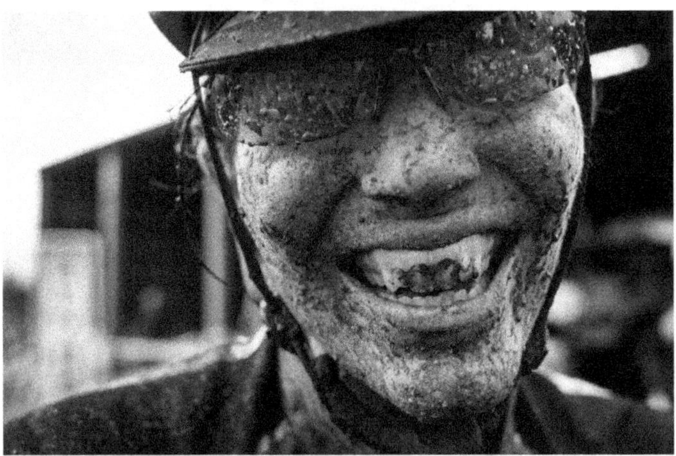

Photos 2.23 and 2.24 Similar conditions, what changes is focal length and distance. The first is an 85 mm lens, the second a 35 mm, both at minimal focusing distance.

Once you've read, or mapped, the scene, think about what to include or exclude to enhance color's voice in the photograph. Include colors that add to the experience of the photograph; exclude those that distract.

Think about where to place color relationships within a scene. For instance, red in a scene will almost always be the first thing people look at in a photograph so if you want to pull people into a scene and therefore the photograph, place an important red object deep within the setting. Red and green or blue and orange in a photograph will create a sense of conflict or contrast so you're in charge of carefully managing where you place those frienemies in relation to each other within the photo.

It's as simple as determining in which parts of the setting colors would contribute to or detract from what it is you want to say; avoid the bad spots, work within the good.

Section 2.5 Distance as Voice

This is the least considered, yet potentially most impactful decision in making a photograph that conveys qualities. How far the camera should be from what's being photographed is usually an automatic function: It needs to be this far to be able to *show* what I'm photographing. Which means that most photos made through this default are made from similar distances, regardless of what's in front of the camera. Detail photos are a subset of default distance choices, by showing some singular aspect of a setting.

This method is akin to how films are photographed. Films often introduce us to a scene from the widest view necessary to give it context, show us the characters interacting within the setting and then enmesh us deep within the scene, not necessarily in that order. A film made from one distance would put you to sleep, as do most sets of photographs made from one distance.

Intentional distance choices create varying vantage points, from which you can say different things about what's out there, from the very close to middle distance to the furthest distance from which you can make a telling photograph. The furthest distance can range from a sweeping landscape to the whole of a room, depending on the scope of the setting in which you're photographing. This distance can give all other photos of the same setting context and are often the most important to create – but too few people step back to make them.

Wide perspectives are the most difficult to dynamically compose because they don't have the inherent main character or action layer that closer proximity includes. Composing the wide scene has the same burden as closer distances, it's just that the elements are further away, meaning that you still must place elements within the setting on a hierarchy, three dimensionally within the space. Light and color are even more important, and challenging, because they will be critical to guiding people into and through the scene while conveying qualities of the setting.

The middle view is observational. It's the default distance of most photographs because you can include the actions completely. It's easy to make verb photos that do nothing more than show what's happening from the middle distance and as I explained earlier, showing usually compromises most of photography's toolbelt.

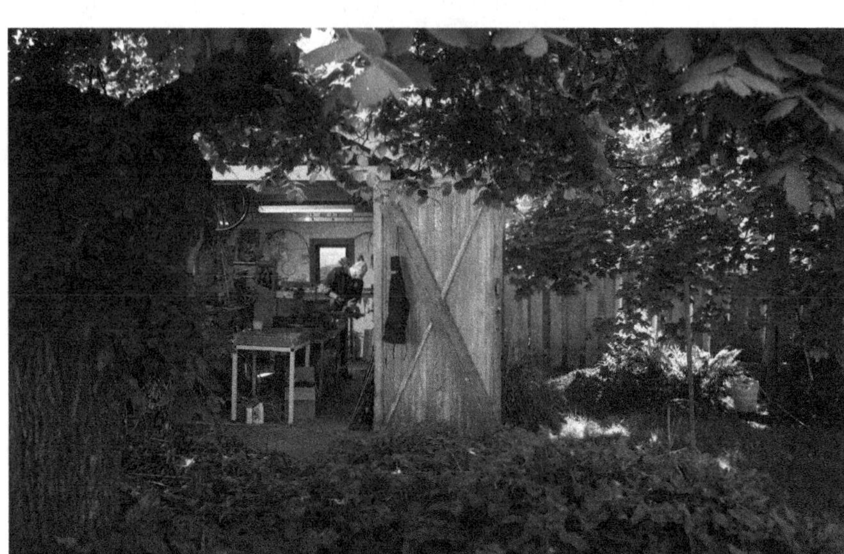

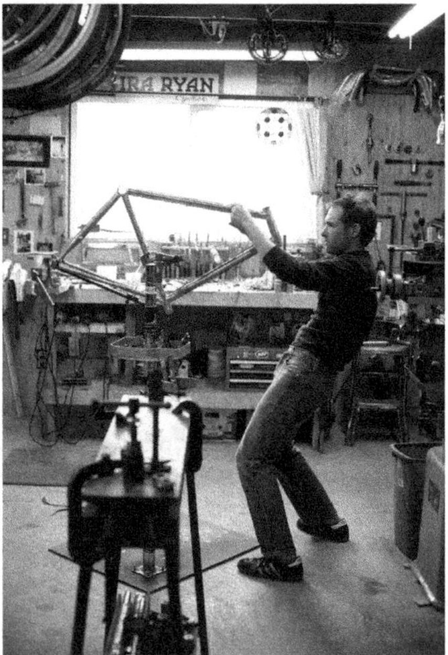

Photos 2.25, 2.26 and 2.27 Say different things from different distances and use that variability as an important narrative tool. I photographed 20 people who build bikes by hand and would always show the wider work setting, a middle-distance view of them working and a tighter view, of their tool wall.

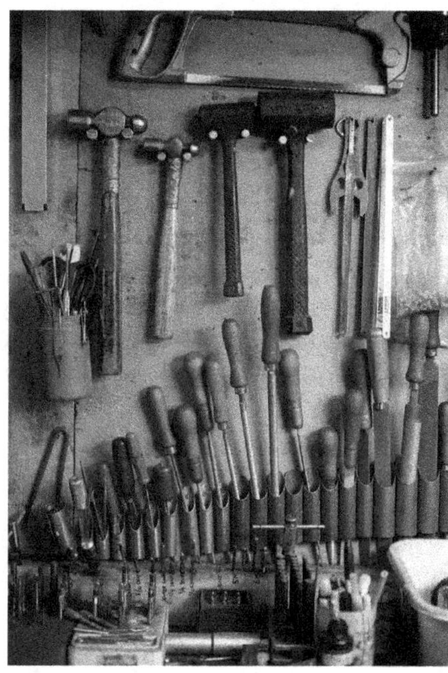

Photos 2.25, 2.26 and 2.27 (Continued).

Determine what you can speak to from a middle distance and then consider the whole of the space that's in your viewfinder, not just the "layer" where the action or most important thing is. Create the frame from infinity forward, is how Sam Abell once described it to me. That means, decide where you want the deepest point in a scene to be and build the rest of the frame from that point forward to the camera. More on this in the next section on composition.

Getting close enmeshes you, and subsequently viewers, in the scene. They will feel like they are part of what happened not just an observer.

You can say different things about a setting from each of the three distances. From each distance, you'll have to see the color and light and compose and make technical decisions differently from the others. Explore every setting you photograph from variations of each of the three distances and you'll be creating the chords of your song about that setting.

Determine whether you're using distance intentionally now by how much the sizes of people's heads in your photographs vary. If they don't change much, or heads only change because you put on a longer or shorter lens, but the camera hasn't moved, then you aren't using distance effectively.

I suggest three distances because the dynamics of three elements has been essential to the creation of visual media throughout history. I even strive to have three reasons for doing anything of substance before committing the time to make the effort.

Section 2.6 Composition – Order from Chaos

Composition brings qualities to images; it can elicit emotional responses. You can create chaos and friction, you can be aggressive or passive, offer complex simplicity or simple complexity, you can frustrate or bring joy to the viewer, all through compositional choices. Choose how you build the frame based on what you want to say, compose the setting to convey those qualities and make people feel what it was like to be there. Go beyond just showing what was in front of you.

Think of the photographic frame as a three-dimensional space, into which you intentionally place what is in front of your camera with a hierarchy and spatially geometric structure. That is composition.

I say that successful compositions are whole frames. Every part of the photograph contributes to the whole, from left to right, front to back and every corner; your mind's eye can walk into the space you've created through the viewfinder.

Some people think of the photo created in the camera as a starting point that they can revise later by cropping it. I think a higher state is to create a fully realized composition in the camera. That doesn't preclude knowing in the creation that some part of the frame is the whole frame – see the un-cropped versions of Arnold Newman's photo of Stravinsky or Elliott Erwitt's Chihuahua dog standing by a woman's feet. Intentionality is the key. Sometimes you

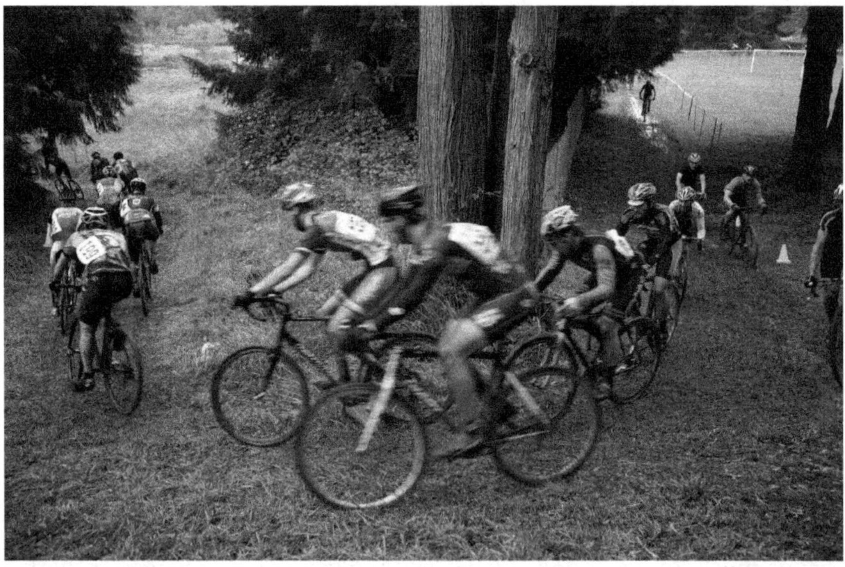

Photo 2.28 Photographs are ideally three-dimensional experiences where your eye travels to every part of the frame. Start by determining the deepest point of a setting that you will include and ensuring that there is value in that part, then move forward. In this case, riders in the far right side of the frame were critical.

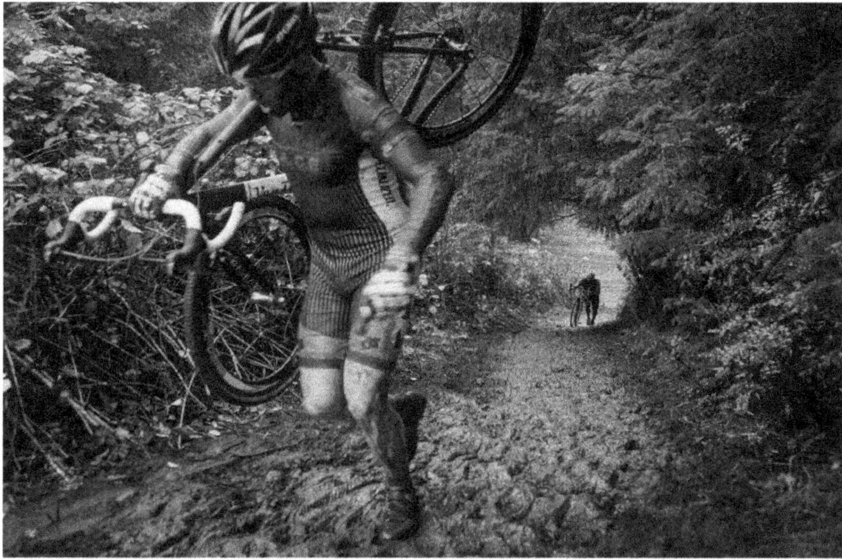

Photo 2.29 Decide where you want people to start in a frame based on what quality that realizes. Here, having people start deep within in the frame at the bottom of the hill enhanced the sense of how hard the hill is to climb.

may see the scene as a square or a panoramic or you don't have the lens that allows a composition you want so have to crop after the fact to realize a full frame. So, you make the picture knowing it will be cropped.

Creating a hierarchy in the frame means deciding where you'd like people to look first, second third, etc. You are the tour guide through the photograph. You can have people start their journey deep in the frame – the furthest point from the camera – or at the closest, the left side, the right side or the middle. And then take people on a tour through the rest of the photograph. Color and light have equally important voices on this tour.

Spatially geometric structure means that you visually connect elements within the frame: This one at the top left foreground talks to that one in the bottom right background, which then talks to that one in the mid-bottom right. Triangulating elements at different depths of the frame and on different planes, adds to the sense of depth. Collectively, this is what makes the photograph feel three dimensional.

For inspiration to create photographs that are more geometric, look at the paintings of Martin Lewis, who is said to have inspired Edward Hopper. Lewis often connects three elements on an angular plane and then makes them speak to a singular element elsewhere in the painting.

You create an experience for the viewer through your compositional decisions, which are additive to the expressions of light, color and distance.

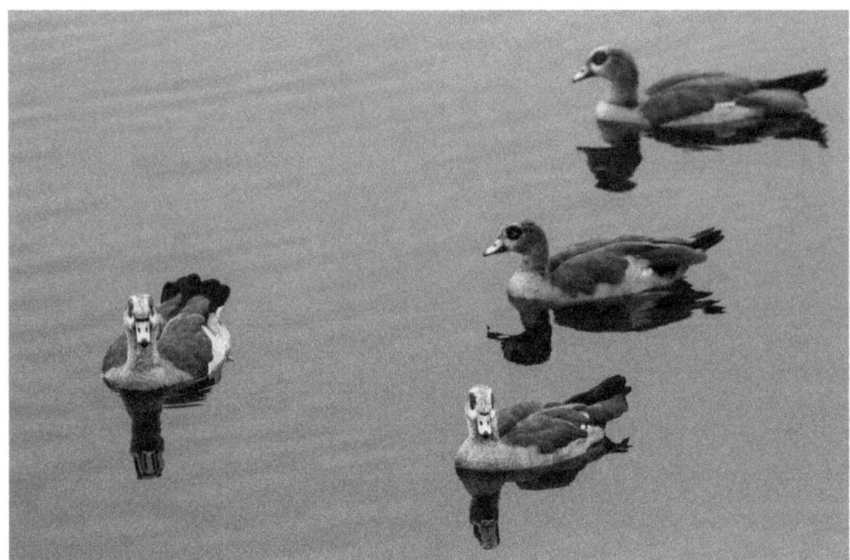

Photo 2.30 Odd numbers of elements are generally better but juxtaposing three against one can be successful. Martin Lewis often did this in his paintings. Here, Egyptian geese swim on an Austin, Texas, lake.

A bonus compositional notion is a principle I learned in an undergraduate psychology course: The more elements between you and an object you're looking at, the closer that furthest element will appear to your mind's eye and you will be pulled into that setting. That's why placing out-of-focus objects in the foreground makes you feel like you are more enmeshed in the scene.

Default Compositional Approaches

In my experience, many people compose by default in ways that aren't good. These defaults fall into categories: almost always putting elements in the middle; splitting the frame horizontally and/or vertically; aligning elements parallel to the camera; not seeing the full frame top to bottom or left to right, foreground to background; constructing the frame from middle outward or starting from the left, right, bottom or top; putting the main element in the plane closest to the camera. (Most of these default approaches to composition are exactly how our eyes see, as compared to how the camera sees.)

Which of these is your default?

Centeredness

Ever give your camera to a passing stranger to make a picture of you and your friends? Inevitably your faces in that photo will be dead center in the frame. Putting the main element in the middle is generally not intentional composition but it is how your eye sees. Try to focus on the edge of a setting with your eye, the edge becomes the middle. So, if you tend to put things in the middle in your photographs you are making them as your eye sees.

Do this test, to see if your default is the middle. Put your finger in the middle of your screen as you scroll through a bunch of your photos. This can be every photo you made in a day or your best photos. As you scroll through the photos, see how often the main element in the photos moves away from your finger. Are you surprised? (This test also works to determine if you're using other default approaches: Watch where your eye first lands in your photographs and ask if that's where you wanted people to look first; note whether you tend to put the main aspects at a specific depth within the frame or in the same plane; is there foreground middle ground background.)

Centeredness also comes from thinking that you have to watch the active part of the setting to be sure and get it. A more productive approach that leads to more full-frame photographs is for you to pay more attention to mindfully placing secondary, tertiary and other elements in the frame as the action unfolds. Let the camera capture the action by pushing the shutter as you consider how the action fits into the rest of the frame. The thinking is that only you can control all of the other elements, but the camera can get the action if you push the shutter button enough times.

Centeredness usually produces oval compositions, meaning the main element is in the middle of the frame with decreasingly critical elements the further they are from the middle – like centered above. Oval compositions also typically have nothing important in front of the main element and the background is not fully considered. If you can draw an oval on many of your pictures and nothing important is outside the oval, or in front of or behind it, then you're seeing as your eye sees and making compositions accordingly.

Splitting the Frame

Pull up a selection of what you think are your strongest pictures and put a ruler in the middle of your screen. Then scroll through your pictures and see how often a line-up of elements within the frame falls on or near the ruler – splitting the frame with a horizon line is one example. Then hold the ruler vertically in the middle of the screen and scroll again. If elements in your pictures align with the ruler often, then you're splitting the frame. If you do both, vertically and horizontally, that's really bad. I'm not sure why people do this, though I see it happen regularly. It could be that the rush of making a picture produces this default solution in some people. Where you place your auto-focusing point could also make this – and centeredness – more likely to happen, if you don't recompose after focusing.

You can usually overcome this by moving your auto-focus point higher or off center. Compositions that split the frame diagonally are generally not good because they reflect a lack of intention in placing elements actively. There are times when splitting the frame does work.

Parallelograms

Aligning elements parallel to the camera's focal plane tends to produce less dimensional compositions. We experience only one layer of the space photographed, when the goal is generally to create photos that feel three dimensional. Some people say wow, that photo has a lot of layers, referring to photographs that feel dimensional – and those usually just have a lot of things going on in the photo. Plywood has a lot of layers but it's flat. A better way to describe photos that connect elements at different depths, that do appear three dimensional, is to say that the photo is spatially geometric. Increase spatial geometry by placing yourself at an angle to what you're photographing, unless being parallel is the best choice for what you're striving to convey. Then structure the frame to connect parts of the scene that are at different depths, which creates planes at angles to, as opposed to being parallel to, the camera.

Not Seeing Whole Frame

This default has to do with not fully seeing the frame fully through the camera. People often leave a quarter of one side of the frame unrealized. It's just sitting over there saying: "Hey, what about me?" If you can consistently crop a certain part of the frame and the photos get better, then you are not fully seeing the space. The unseen part can be at any edge, or many incompletely seen photos get better when cropped to squares. This happens because you're building the frame from the bottom up or from one of the edges but your eye didn't make it all the way to the other side of the frame. See if your photos are better if consistently cropped, then going forward push your seeing into the areas you cropped.

Main Element Closest to Camera

If, when you look at your photos, the starting point, or main element, is nearly always the closest to the camera, then you're likely composing informationally. People who do this tend to put the main subject in the middle of the frame, too. It should be a choice as to where you place the most important aspect of the scene and that can be at any location or depth within the scene. Another way to think about this is asking where you want people to start looking within the photograph you're creating.

Where you place the starting point will affect how people experience each photo and become a critical variable when sequencing photos. You can create rich sequential experiences if in one photo people are pulled deep into a setting as a starting point and then in the next photograph the starting point leaps out at them and then the following has a neutral perspective. If in each case the starting point also moves left or right, up or down, wow, that's rich.

Imagine going to a movie and every scene is presented exactly like the previous scene. How long before you'd leave the theater? This is what happens when you only use your default approaches to composition.

More on Plywood Compositions

Another approach to avoid is plywood photos. That's where the only important elements are in one "layer" of the photograph. You've not considered what's behind that layer and there usually isn't anything in front of it. This is the opposite of infinity-forward compositions.

This and That

An extension of plywood compositions is the this-and-that composition, which connects two parts of a scene because they relate to each other. One might be the action and one the recipient, for instance. Connecting elements visually is important but only connecting two aspects is two-dimensional, or binary. Connect a third element to form triangulation and do this more than once in the composition and you'll create a three-dimensional feeling.

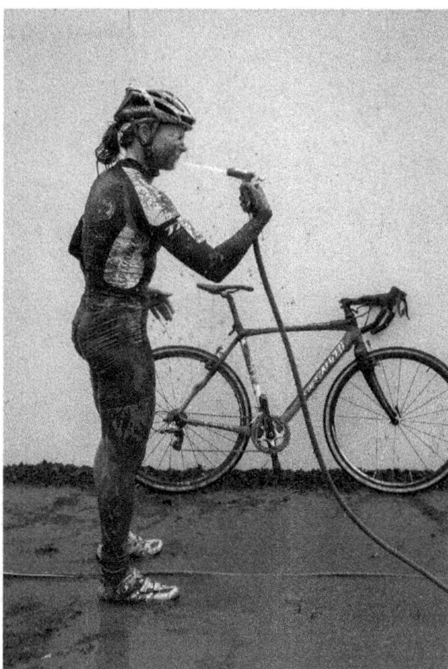

Photo 2.31 How much room you give the main element in a frame is both a compositional and distance choice.

Too Snug to the Edge

A generally bad approach is one I call the copy editor composition, because back when copy editors laid out inside pages of newspapers they would cut stories and photos to fit the space available. For photos that

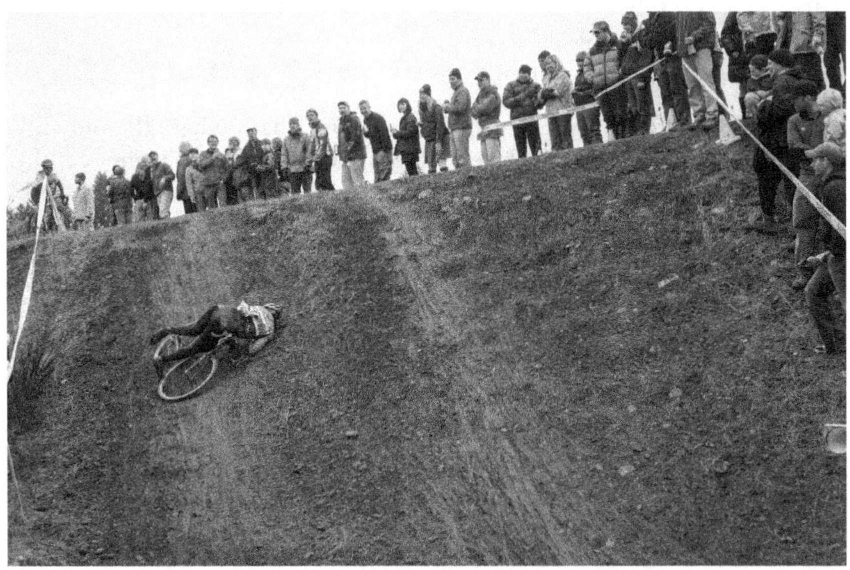

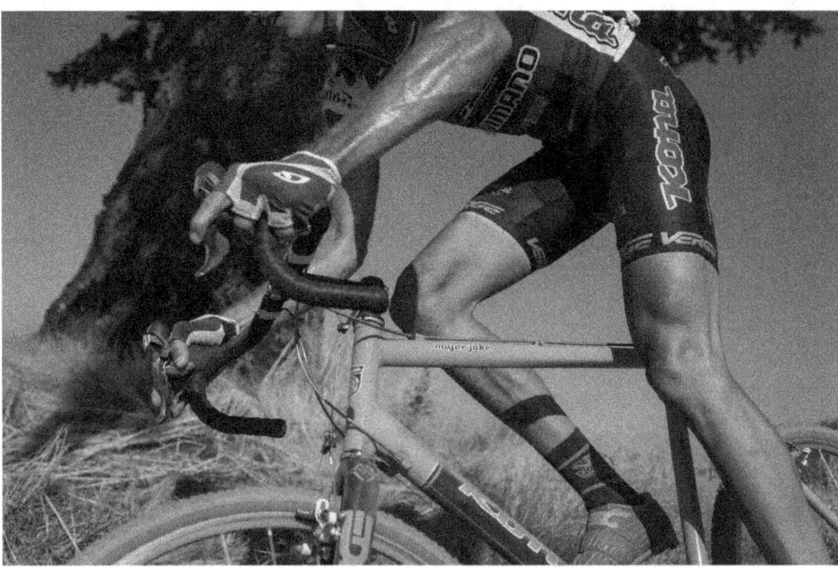

Photos 2.32 and 2.33 How much room you give the main element in a frame is both a compositional and distance choice. Let happenings within photos breathe to varying degrees or have them break the frame, depending on the feeling that you're striving to convey.

meant bringing the edge of the frame into what mattered in the photo at the same distance on all sides, no matter what was in the photo. Generally, avoid nudging elements close to the edge of the frame. It diminishes the spatial experience, it's just saying, simplistically, here it is. Placing elements too close to the edge of the frame can also cause pinch points, where it's hard for the eye to travel around those points, clogging or interrupting the flow of the composition.

Approaches to Powerful Compositions

Moving on from default derelictions, your decisions about how to create hierarchy and spatial geometry should include full realizations of the seeing of light, color and determining distance. You must discern and bring forward the other tools to the composition to achieve high moment value.

Every setting you photograph deserves its own composition. You should approach the placement of elements uniquely every time you start to build a frame, in the same way that you see color and light uniquely every time and determine the distance to express the scene specifically. Don't be a developer who only builds one kind of house for eyes to live in.

Imagine that the frames you're creating are dioramas where every element is carefully placed and meaningful and worth spending time with, again and again. Or, think of what you're photographing as first creating the stage and waiting for the actors to act within the completely seen stage. As the scenes change, you recompose the stage and wait for the actors.

Emotional Aspects

Compositional decisions also affect how we feel by either creating the sense that the subject is jumping out at us, that we are allowed to safely observe these unique circumstances being pictured or are being pulled into the setting. Composition affects which experience the photo creates through the placement of elements within the frame. Deciding which experience you want the viewer to have can help guide compositional decisions. You can create dramatically different photos in the same setting just by deciding on how you want the photos to engage people.

Break the Frame

A critical compositional decision is whether you include all of the active aspects of a setting completely within the frame or let some of the important elements continue outside the confines of the frame. When important aspects of a scene continue outside the frame, the mind will complete those elements, so the experience of the photo is more active, for the viewer's brain. Breaking the frame creates tension and brings us into the settings as well. It's as if the actors have come into the audience space, like breaking the fourth wall of the theater.

Successful Centeredness

It is possible to place the main element in the middle of the frame and have a successful photograph, as long as the rest of the frame is fully realized – it's not an oval composition. Paolo Pellegrin's compositions mostly place the main element in the middle, but they are generally complete frames nonetheless. Might some of them be better if the starting point changed from the middle? I think so.

Centered photos do win competitions, a lot – I've been tracking this for several years. Editor extraordinaire Sue Morrow just mailed the most recent version of NPPA's *The Best of Photojournalism* magazine, which presents BOP's awards. Of the 203 photos presented in this magazine, 95 are centered compositions. That's a lower ratio than in previous years, owing to Dudley Brooks deciding who the judges would be and chairing the competition. Of the 95, about half were full frames, as I define the term. The other half could have been cropped to be better, they were incomplete compositionally. The more amateur, or lower level of professional, a competition is the higher the ratio of incomplete-centered compositions, which speaks to both the level of the entrants and the sophistication of the judges' response to photos. Communication Arts and World Press Photo competitions tend to have fewer, Sony World Photography Awards more and Pictures of the Year somewhere in the middle of the pack.

Negative and Positive Space

The opposite of breaking the frame is letting the active aspect of a scene occupy a small part of the frame. Back to the actor analogy, think of the actors in the frame as either occupying negative or positive space within the stage, or frame, or as above, breaking the frame, or stage. Positive space is usually where the action aspect is, the *most important* component. Negative space is the rest of the stage that you've created or included in your composition. The decision of how to craft the negative space is as important as focusing your efforts on the positive, or active, aspect of a scene. How much negative space there is in your frame and the shape of that space dramatically affects the feel of the photograph. Consider carefully how much of the composition the active part of the scene will occupy, how much breathing room is there for the actor. A lot of space conveys one feeling; breaking the frame, where the actor isn't contained within the frame, creates a different quality. This is both a compositional and distance consideration.

Equally important is deciding how far to let people's eye travel in each setting. Do you contain to a tight spatial representation a few feet from the camera or do you include the farthest part of a scene, to infinity? One creates a confined feel, the other gives relief or escape. This factor is extremely important when producing a group of photos on a topic. Varying or being consistent in how you treat the depth within frames offers the opportunity to create yet more musical chords in your photographic song.

Being aware of whether you should overlap or separate elements within the scene is another critical decision. When elements in the foreground, middle ground and background touch each other, the sense of depth decreases because the elements are visually connected in the photos, even though they were separate in their original space. When separate elements, don't let them overlap, depth increases because your eye can travel around them and your mind puts them in space relatively.

Collectively, these compositional considerations build foregrounds, middle grounds and backgrounds into every photograph and triangulate elements within the space and let objects breathe in the frame or break the frame.

Your job is not done once you've built the frame and actors begin to act. Aspects of the scene will evolve so you'll have to continually make micro-adjustments to the composition, adjusting for overlapping elements, finding the sweet spot between foreground, middle ground and background elements, moving slightly left or right or closer or further to maintain a full frame and let things come to fruition within the photo to achieve high moment value.

This is not a one-size-fits-all approach. Back to the idea of the spectrum: Compositions can either be quick reads or take some time to absorb. In hierarchical terms, that means you can clearly tell people where to start and where to go thereafter (the tour guide approach with varying lengths of tours) or you can create chaotic compositions that encourage the viewer to explore the frame at will, with no ingrained hierarchy – the *Where's Waldo* approach. The latter is more challenging to do successfully but should be in your toolbelt.

How a Composition Can Develop

Bringing the previous subsections of Section 2 forward, here's a way to think about achieving a fully realized composition that is specific to the scene in front of you. Read and map the light and the color in a setting, then determine where within the setting those happen best, pick a starting distance from which to make pictures based on what you intend to convey from that distance, then compose the elements in the setting to a fully realized, three-dimensional iteration of the frame. To create a more complete representation of what transpires in front of you, move to other settings within the scene, at different distances and repeat the above steps and repeat until you've created every chord possible.

Section 2.7 Ditch Rules, Rise above Clichés

Another spectrum within the photographic realm has to do with people at one end who want to follow the *rules* of photography and those at the other end who find rules to be limiting or not particularly helpful. If you prefer to make informational photographs, then you likely prefer to follow

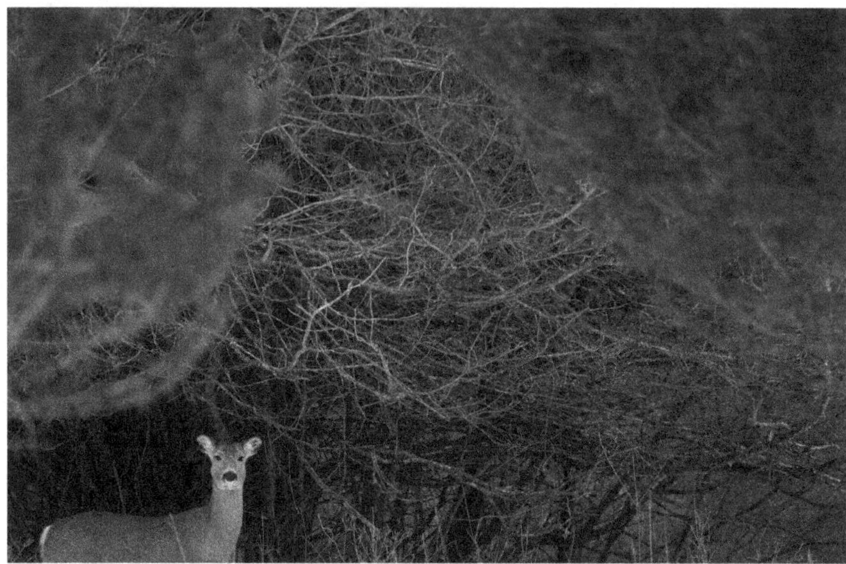

Photo 2.34 Place elements based on what you're saying as opposed to following rules. Isolating the deer in the frame spoke to the barrenness of winter. The point wasn't to *show* the deer.

the rules; if you would rather strive for impressionistic photographs then you probably find rules of little use.

What are the rules? There are so many.

Many have to do with composition. On the more formal side are rule of thirds, golden ratio and leading lines. Less formal include: Don't cut people off when placing them in the frame, especially not at a joint; moving objects should move into the frame not out of it; simplify compositions to make them easier to read; always have a straight horizon line (a crooked horizon, or tilted framing is called Dutch angle); clean up the edges of the frame, don't have partial elements on the outskirts; follow the rule of odds, meaning that odd numbers of elements are more engaging; don't merge foreground and background elements; vary the height from which you make photographs; put the dominant eye of the person you're photographing in the middle of the frame (this one I've never understood); crop your photos at will into whatever shape you want; make motion go from left to right; repeating patterns make photos more interesting; balance elements in the photo, and on and on.

The challenge, for me, is that there are more situations where more compelling photographs would result if you didn't apply the standard set of rules than if you did, especially in the pursuit of conveying qualities and impressions of what you're photographing. I recognize that this book in a way presents a set of *rules* to follow but I hope this approach is expansive as opposed to restrictive for you.

Those Pesky Cliches

Oh, and what about clichés, which are generally produced by people who follow photography's rules.

What are photographic clichés? A shorter list might include what are not. In teaching, I'd use a fictitious list when a cliche would pop up in student's work, such as Cliche #26 = tight portrait of craggy-faced homeless person; Cliche #12 = child playing in sprinkler; Cliche #2 = anything silhouetted. That list was hundreds long.

Why do cliched photographs come across as being successful? Because chances are that at some point someone made a photograph in that setting that was held up as being a good photo. Popular culture began to repeat that image until it became a rubber-stamp-like process of thinking that if you make a similar photo of the same thing, then it too would be good.

Know the Antecedents

How do you rise above clichés? It's important that you know the work that precedes you, your antecedents. Build a photographic library in your memory that continually grows and that will inform your work now. The more photos your memory holds, the less likely you are to repeat what has been done, if your goal is to make unique photos.

Before you go into a setting to make photos, spend time critically looking at photos made in similar settings that were judged to be successful. Ask yourself why they are strong. Use the five photo tools to gauge the strength of images. And then challenge yourself to make photos that are different from those that have already been made.

Find photos in a range of settings: museums, bookstores, libraries, competition websites. Build a library of websites and join newsletters that point good work your way.

One thing I did as both an undergrad and while a graduate student was to go to the campus library, identify the photo book section and then I'd spend time every week methodically looking at every book. Now, to continue building my internal photographic library, I get a bunch of newsletters from organizations and competitions and publishers and workshops that present me with an ever-expanding approach to visual storytelling. Thanks to the pandemic I've been able to join scores of interactive sessions and attend workshops remotely.

Once you're in a setting the challenge is to make photographs that go beyond the clichéd and what has been done before. Apply what you've read so far in this book and you're more likely to do make fresh photos. Continue reading to learn how to leave clichés in your dust.

Try This: With Camera in Hand

See the self-assignment appendix for more ideas to try.

Light: Look at your past work and assess how you have seen light. Was your intention clear; were you striving to say something about the scene? Did you compromise light by positioning yourself to better show what's happening? Could you have made a stronger photo by making the quality of light a higher priority in deciding how to make the picture? Were you in a setting at the wrong time for the light to be evocative?

Distance: Assess your previous photographs for how much you varied the distance from what you were photographing. If you did, why did you change how far away you were? Could you have made stronger images or photos that said different things by getting closer or moving back?

Composition:

1 **Test your centeredness, structure:** Pull up a wide selection of your photographs on screen and put your finger in the middle of the screen. Now scroll through the photos and see how often and how far the most important element moves away from your finger. If not often,

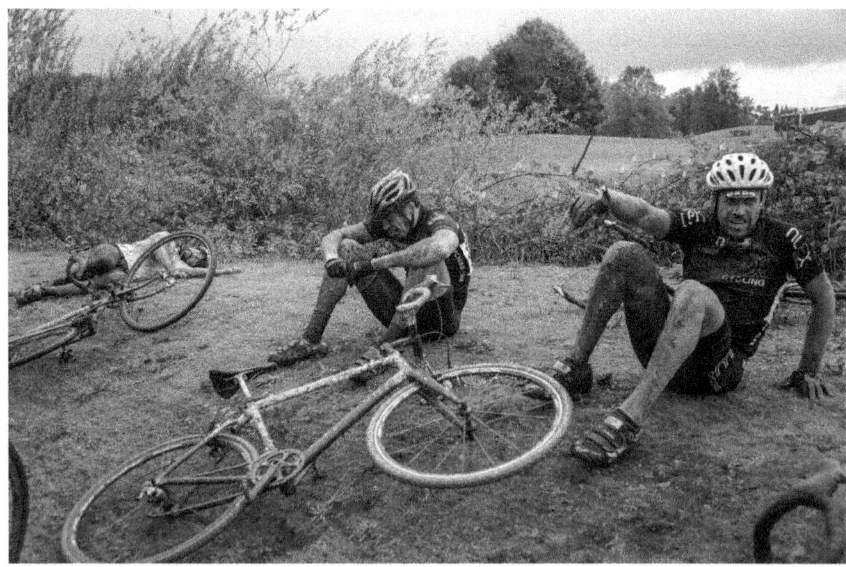

Photo 2.35 When I started to photograph cycling I looked at as much work on the topic as possible, both current and historical. I chose to make pictures that felt current but often had a historical nod, mostly through composition and the choice of black and white. Photographing more than the action, putting riders in a wider context also adds to the longevity of images.

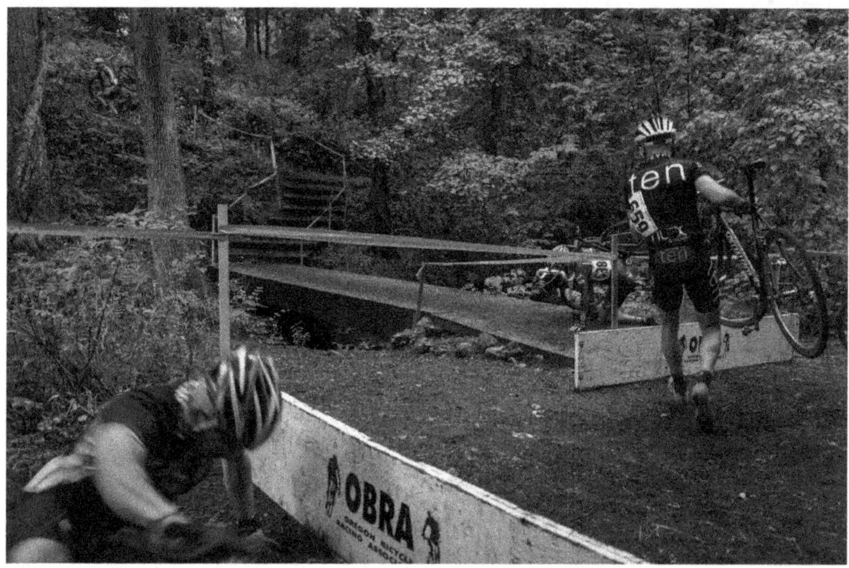

Photo 2.36 Challenge your centeredness by building a composition that isn't dependent on the middle and wait for the frame to come together. Sometimes photographs that reward exploration are the best.

you're not composing your pictures, you're photographing everything similarly. Do the same for splitting the frame and building from an edge.

2 **Triangulate:** Intentionally compose by connecting three aspects within a setting that are at different depths and heights within the scene. And stay out of the middle.

3 **Let the camera take the action:** Compose an active scene and then focus your attention on carefully maintaining the placement of aspects that are not the main, active subject as you repeatedly release the shutter. You're letting the camera capture the action within a fully realized frame. The goal is to produce more fully realized frames.

Section 3
You Make Photographs Engaging

Section 3.0 Introduction

A common compliment is for someone to say, "Wow, you make great pictures. You must have a good camera." As if the camera is what makes photographs interesting. That's silly. All ranges of cameras are used to produce photographs that hang on the world's museum walls and are celebrated widely. Daido Moriyama uses a point-and-shoot camera and usually black and white film. I worked with Wes Pope on a book about Route 66 where he turned aluminum pop cans into pinhole cameras to make every photo.

Back to the notion that something has to be interesting for resulting photographs to be compelling, if you describe what's in many of those museum-quality photos, what is pictured wouldn't be considered interesting by this way of thinking. Photographers standing next to each other in the same photographically target-rich environment can produce photos that are either boring or fascinating or somewhere in between.

Choice of the medium can be a powerful expression, but it is not the camera as a mechanical apparatus that makes photographs worth looking at; nor is it the subject matter alone that gives merit to photographs. It is who you are and what you do that elevates photographs to a higher state. Reference Don Weber's *War Sands* in which he uses a variety of mediums as the best choice to convey aspects that traditional social documentaries alone could not.

My first realization of this came from working with Mike Gallegos on a little story on just about the most mundane thing possible: lap swimming. Mike came back from an early morning assignment for The Albuquerque Tribune to photograph someone swimming early in the morning. A few frames had magical light, so I challenged Mike to return and make photos during those few magical-light minutes every day until he'd built an essay about what it's like to lap swim. He photographed for about 15 minutes every day for 3 weeks and what a set of photographs he made. Then I realized it's not what you photograph but *the why* informing how you make photographs that creates magic.

In the last section, I talked about using the photographic toolbelt to create more dimensional work. Now let's talk about what you can do from behind the camera to increase the power of your photographs and your storytelling.

DOI: 10.4324/9781003287544-3

Section 3.1 You Are Your Photographs

Who you are as a person affects every aspect of the making of photographs, which really are expressions of your self. It's not what is pictured but why and how it's depicted that will make photographs sail out of the visual doldrums. Personality plays out in what you decide to photograph, how you engage in those settings, how you make pictures and what those pictures convey.

We are our photographs, and they are us. If you are warm and ebullient, so will be your photos; if you are introverted and address the world cautiously, so will be your approach to making photos and the photographs that you make. The notion that we are or even can be objective in this process is naïve. That photographs present truth is equally ingenuous. At best our work presents our truth, which will likely be different from others.

By extension, get beyond the notion that there is a single standard that you must achieve, that says here's what a good photograph is. Trying to make yourself adhere to a perceived standard likely robs you of a more refined and individualized creative process. Just watch a competition judging and you'll see this dynamic at play as each judge favors a specific range of imagery.

Albert Watson and I were among workshop teachers in West Palm Beach not long ago and I happened to be next to him in the breakfast

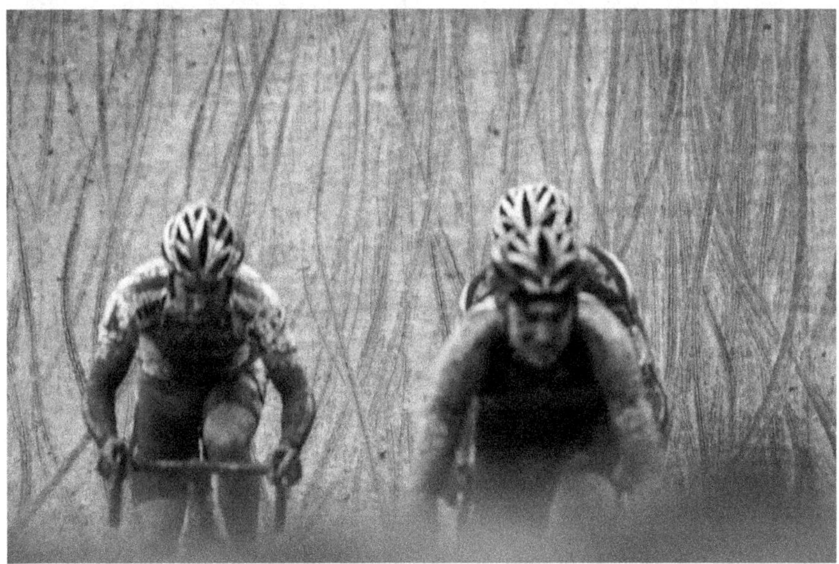

Photo 3.01 Each time I've worked with a new photographer or taken on new topics with my own photography, the goal has been to expand vocabulary. That means striving to create images that hadn't been made before in the service of saying ever more.

buffet line at the hotel one morning. We started a conversation that lasted an hour and a half. Among the most salient things I remember him saying is that he knows whether someone is going to succeed as a photographer – or as one of his assistants – within minutes of meeting them based on their personality. Your personality determines whether you'll succeed in the business as you want to, he said.

How do you know if you will? A starting point is to consider if your personality is contradictory to the types of pictures that you want to make. Many students in courses I've taught entered thinking they wanted to be conflict photographers and yet don't like to engage with conflict or destination photographers but don't really like to be in unfamiliar places or want to focus on portraiture but don't really like people. Each of these specializations requires a specific and dynamic set of personality traits to be successful. How do you know if you have the kind of personality that can produce the kind of work that you want to make?

First, learn what it really takes to make that work and then ask yourself and the people you trust if you have what it takes. If that's not conclusive, try producing that type of work. Was the experience one you'd want to repeat, endlessly? What aspects of it were good and what did you not like?

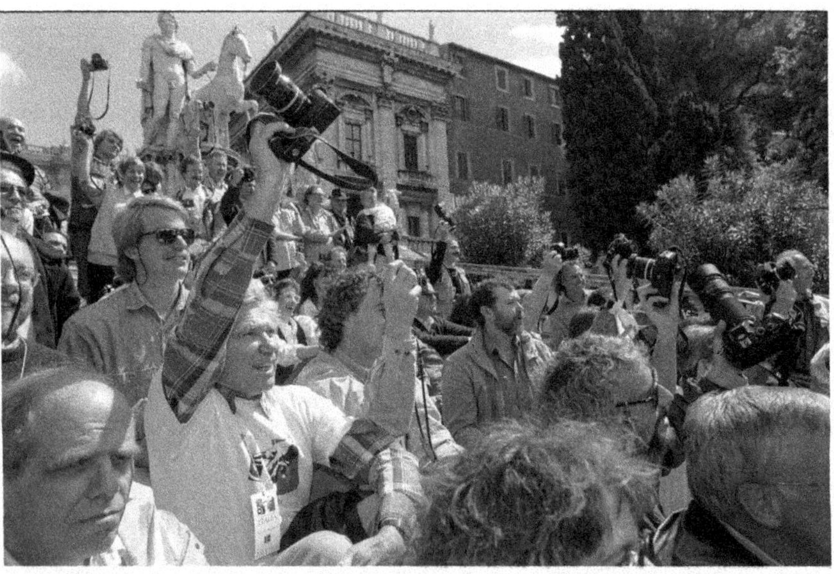

Photo 3.01.1 It can take a while to ease into your best path. It took me 13 years after graduating high school, spending time in the U.S. Air Force, undergrad school, working at a small daily newspaper and then graduate school, where I realized that being a visual editor was my path. That led to Rick Smolan choosing me to join 100 of the world's leading photographers and a cadre of the best editors in Rome for *A Day in the Life of Italy* book in 1990.

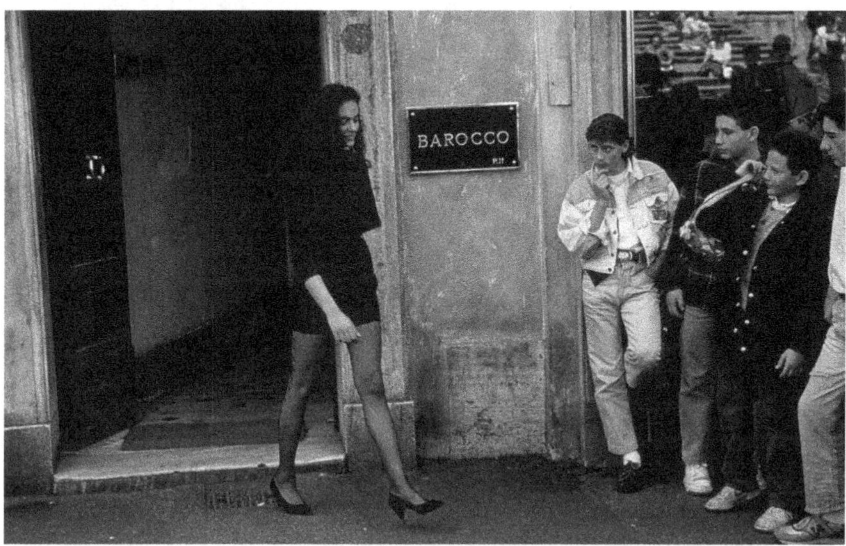

Photo 3.01.02 *A Day in the Life* books were just that. Photographers fanned out across the country to render its essence in one day. I made pictures that day, too, including this one that became the book's back cover photo.

Is the work you made worth a toot and if it's not why not? If the work is good or at least shows promise and the experience of doing everything it took to produce the work was enriching for you, then maybe that path is a match for you. It could be that some aspects were good for you, others were not, then maybe some variation or refinement of what you did is a better path.

The critical thing is to put choices in front of yourself. This is how I think of every aspect of teaching a course. I put choices in front of students in the form of assignments, with enough flexibility for each student to determine how they will approach each assignment, uniquely. And I create a range of settings where students have to define and express their values, speak to what matters to them, say why they chose to photograph what they did, what they sought to say and why they chose to create narratives as they did.

This series of decisions is like defining a path with a destination that's only discernible once it's reached. Sometimes the path is straight – we know what we want and each decision is a step further toward that destination. Sometimes one choice shows the next one, or, nope, that was not a good step, so I'll try another direction. It is the cumulation of these choices based on your personality and how it responds to producing work that determines your path, what you'll be good at.

Here's another way to think about this. Ask yourself if you have personality traits or tendencies that keep you from accomplishing more successful work – as you define success. I've found that all people who stand behind a camera can be self-limiting, whether they're just starting out or have been making pictures for decades.

Some examples of what I'm talking about:

There are people who put so many layers of expectations on what they want to happen that they'll not move forward because what they're doing doesn't meet those expectations. It's a self-limiting process that protects that person from failure and precludes success.

At the opposite end of the spectrum are people who have little or no clarity of why. Everything is equal and therefore nothing rises as being important or better or worse, efforts meander aimlessly.

Another representation of lack of clarity of why appears when people focus on the minutiae, the detail level of things. It's a bottom-up approach that dooms the doer to small thoughts and acts. This tendency manifests itself by not having a clear plan for your path that helps you determine a hierarchy of what to do to advance your livelihood. This shows up while working on projects or assignments, if you find yourself photographing a lot of situations for a project but they don't hold together, there's no narrative, as if you've bought something from every aisle in the grocery store but can't make a meal.

Then there are people who self-limit by putting roadblocks in front of themselves: "Oh, that'll never work, that's been done before; my boss would never buy that approach; they would never let me photograph in that setting; it won't be any good so why should I even try; I don't have the right equipment to do that …"

Contradict these tendencies by first identifying and addressing them. Ideally, you know someone you respect and trust who can help you with this piece. That person will likely only be honest and forthright with you if they think you will act upon their perceptions and suggestions – the notion that why should I be honest and forthright if I know you won't do anything, or you'll deny what I'm saying about you. Ask someone to help you only if you are willing to really listen to what they say and take actions based on their advice.

A parallel is when a white person asks a person of color to tell them what they do that might be racist or biased or at least inappropriate. Why would there be an honest and full answer unless the person of color thought the white person might respect and fully respond to their offering? It is the white person's responsibility to learn, not be told.

If you are someone who has trouble creating priorities, if everything seems equal so starting any one thing seems as important as every other, then creating meaningful work isn't likely. Some call this an inability to manage time. Managing time is a less fruitful way to think about this than if you instead think of it as managing your priorities. Of what needs to be done, which are the most important, second most and so on. Then spend the appropriate time to accomplish things, in the order of their priority.

The first step is prioritization. Make a list of what you need to accomplish. This can be an all-encompassing list or be specific to a project you're working on. Just spew, let it out.

Then create a hierarchy of what you've listed. You can do a numeric, 1–10, or whatever works best for you. Then rewrite the list – or use a to-do app or database or spreadsheet – with the highest priority items first. Different efforts will take different durations of time to accomplish. Factoring between priority and the time it takes to accomplish a given effort in the context of all others will help you decide how much time to devote to each. That'll mean either not doing some things or giving them short shrift. Not everything deserves a 100 percent effort.

I used this approach while working at the White House. There was always more to do than I could get done so I kept a running list of tasks with a clear sense of which were most important. Some never got done. The important thing was having a grander plan, a wider set of goals by which to measure the value of each of the efforts. Tasks that helped meet greater goals moved to the top and we created tasks to achieve those goals – our why.

So, the critical things are learning to what type of work your personality is best suited, knowing what things prevent you from achieving that work and figuring out how to overcome those limitations.

Section 3.2 Know What Precedes You

I mentioned in the last section that if you create a photographic library in your mind, then you'll make more informed pictures in the present. You learn by knowing the antecedents of the type of photography that you want to pursue, for sure, and even more so from a deeper understanding of the history of image-making.

There are two ways to think about this: learn as much as possible about the history of the medium; see as much work as possible on the setting that you're going to photograph. Use both as an inspirational springboard to create entirely new approaches. Go beyond what precedes you, knowingly.

Know also that your work will reflect your societal references, which include biases, clichés, how you understand color, light, history, religion and values of all manner. Steep yourself in other societies' norms to expand your vocabulary and what you're able to address.

The best all-encompassing book on the history of photography that I know of is Naomi Rosenblum's "A World History of Photography," fifth edition, which will likely be the last edition, given her death in early 2021.

To understand the antecedents of your type of work, look for the earliest iteration or effort that is like what you are taking on and march through the decades to learn how each person touched the topic with their camera. Develop a greater understanding by delving into what in those times affected the making of images – the music, clothing, food, architecture, literature … I require students to cite five such examples in my project development courses. Assess the strengths of each iteration and think about how the work has changed, or not, over time. Ask yourself how you could advance your understanding of the topic through a heightened notion of why you're producing the work and then apply your aesthetic and technical approaches to realize the work in a new way.

One example is the use of miniatures, or toys, to craft a narrative or essay. Matthew Callahan, a military student at Syracuse University in 2016 made a set of pictures of miniature ™Star Wars storm troopers by creating real-life combat environments. My visual library was empty on the topic so I looked for antecedents. Paul Outerbridge was sort of photographing miniatures – mannequins – in the 1920s. Most noted are David Levinthal's multiple series of miniatures using the 20 × 30 inch ™Polaroid starting in the 1970s, and Hank Willis Thomas' powerful series "Winter in America" in 2005. Many others have used the approach since. There's even a ™Toymaster War Photojournalist miniature or the ™Barbie version of a National Geographic Photographer.

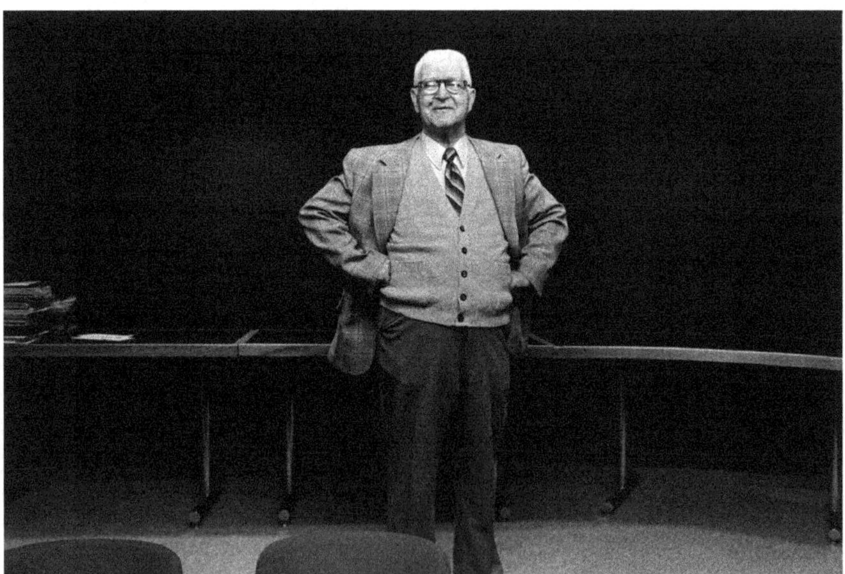

Photo 3.02 This is Cliff Edom, in 1986. I learned a lot of antecedents from Cliff while I was a graduate student. He founded the University of Missouri Photojournalism program, Pictures of the Year competition and The Missouri Workshop. You can learn as much by connecting with the people who have been instrumental as by spending time with current and historical work.

Learning what you don't know is the starting point. Constantly ask yourself if you know anything, or enough, about new things as they come across your transom. Do the same for things you think you know enough about, and you'll keep yourself fresh and continually grow your awareness and understanding. File this under curiosity and inquisitiveness.

Speaking of learning what you don't know, any discourse about visual narratives would be lacking if it excluded Eugene Richards – not that Gene is done producing work. His collective body of work spans more than 50 years and includes 16 seminal books, films, plays, receiving pretty much every substantive award and grant, gallery collections and published work throughout the world. If you are going to produce work about lives unfolding before you, understanding Gene's work is essential. From his work, you'll come to see that he is incredibly compassionate, empathetic, direct, understanding, compelled and humanistic.

Section 3.3 Step Away from Your Comfort Zone

The intention of this book is to introduce a different way of thinking about your professional life. You're likely comfortable with many aspects of how you now approach making pictures and the rest of your professional life. The longer you've been doing it, the more ingrained your way becomes.

What if that comfort produces pictures like an assembly line, repeating what worked in the past, regardless of what's in front of you? You can redefine success by leaving behind some practices and ways of thinking while embracing new ones. In other words, leave your comfort zone in the pursuit of making photographs you've never seen before. This dynamic is at play whether you've worked for years or months.

(Diagram) When first engaging with a class of students I present a diagram that outlines how to leave your comfort zone. It's a series of expanding circles:

Easy Peasy Zone

You're here if you are fine with who you are now, what types of photos you're making now and how you're making a living. Chances are you and your work will stay where you are professionally. You are left behind when your branch of the profession changes around you.

Yes, But Zone

This is where you might want to change but hear yourself uttering excuses that are used to keep you from stepping outside your comfort zone. "I can't do it. It's already been done. Somebody said it wouldn't work. I don't have the right gear." All of these justify inaction.

I Think I Can Zone

This is where you have committed to change. The first step is to define what impedes your forward progress, understanding what matters to you, then devising a plan to move through or around the impediments, learning what you need to know to accomplish forward motion and then acting despite whatever roadblocks you face. Finalize this tier by recognizing what you've accomplished, knowing how you got to a deeper understanding so you can repeat that going forward. All of this can happen by taking on a project or defining a goal for your photography that is greater than what you've tried before.

The New You Zone

Having succeeded in the I Think I Can Zone, you will have accomplished something beyond what you've been capable of, you will have expanded your visual vocabulary, your work will have reached a new plateau and your sense of self will be deeper and richer. Your income possibilities will expand. Your next steps along a path that you can more clearly define will be clearer.

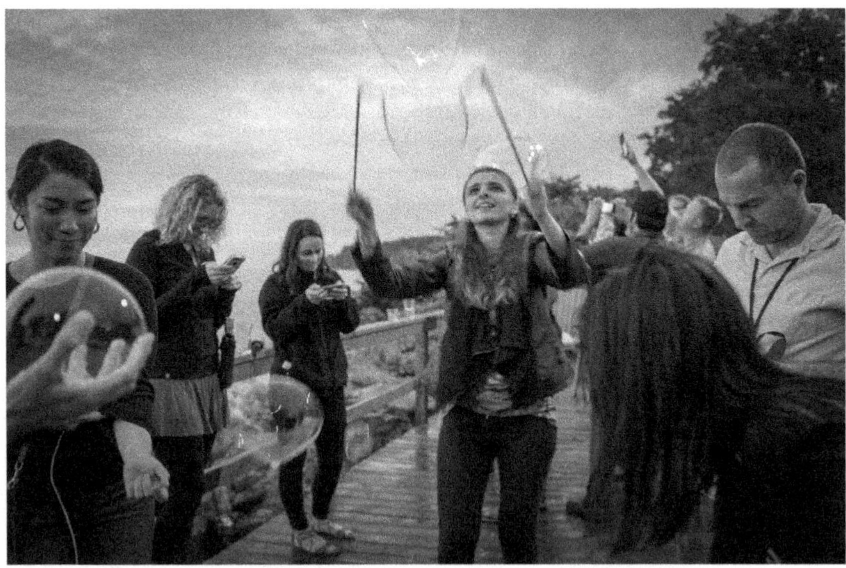

Photo 3.03 One way I try to continually get out of my comfort zone is by making photographs in settings that wouldn't seem to produce photographs. This setting was during the Kalish Workshop in Rochester, New York.

Let me go into greater detail:

There are two ways to think about leaving behind what's familiar. Grow as a person, and leave behind comfortable practices as you redefine more productive approaches. Neither of these is easy.

I've seen this play out when teaching courses with active-duty military students at Syracuse University. They come to the school for a year after having been full-time military photographers for several years. The military is usually their primary experience in the world. I joined the Air Force out of high school so that's how I started out, too. They arrive at Syracuse knowing how to make pictures in a way that satisfies military criteria. For them to grow as photographers, they must first realize, or admit, that how they've been making pictures isn't the only way and likely not the best approach, if the goal is to make engaging, substantive, emotive and compelling photographs. They have to expand their knowledge of photographic approaches by increasing their awareness of what can be said through their photographs. They must grow as people and learn new things to move beyond the Easy Peasy Zone.

How do you grow yourself? Step one is beginning to know what it is that you don't know. If you've learned to make pictures through a given set of circumstances, then your understanding is limited to that experience. We likely don't know what we don't know until we're exposed to different ways of thinking, perceiving and creating. Actively put different things in front of yourself.

The premise that why we make photographs determines every other aspect of the process of making photographs applies here, too. If you want to grow, change your why. Strive to say more, to convey more and you must change every aspect of how you're making photos. You'll quickly start to realize that what you don't know is what's keeping you from making more compelling images.

Figure out what you don't know, and rather than fearing it, embrace learning, expanding your understanding. Keep repeating this process, endlessly.

If a week goes by and I haven't felt stupid for not knowing something, then it wasn't a good week. Ignorance is not bliss, it's a reason to become informed. And I'm not talking only about things photographic. One value of a liberal arts education or learning a language is that they expand your understanding of how people relate, how that has changed over time, how that varies from place to place. Learn a language, read about something new to you, do a deep dive somewhere you've never been, learn from other media. Do anything to place yourself in unfamiliar territory.

Laurent Ballesta said it this way: "How big is your unawareness." This was during the 2022 National Geographic Storytelling Summit. Confucius said: "Real knowledge is to know the extent of one's ignorance." A 1999 research paper resulted in what's called the Dunning–Kruger effect, which showed that poor performers tend to overestimate the quality of their performance while the truly competent tend to underestimate their abilities. Where do you fall on this spectrum?

Move up by learning what you don't know, even about things you're certain you know. Continually ask yourself how you know what you know; question your understanding. More informed and compelling photographs will result, given that we are the photographs we make.

Section 3.4 Achieve Substantive Work

Photography can be a time suck. We can become so enamored of the gizmos that the photographic pursuit puts in our hands or so mired in learning the minutiae of all things digital or spend endless hours pondering what we might photograph. And there we are either not having gotten to the making of pictures or wading endlessly through hundreds of photos that say very little.

If this describes you, what's missing is meaningful substance and the clarity required to achieve it. *The why* of your making photographs is neither clear nor dimensional.

In one of many debates going on within the photojournalistic genre of image making, one person was complaining that the profession is evolving in a way that is leaving him behind. So, I went to his website and was not surprised to see that his approach to making pictures was dated. Each photo was so similar one to the next as to be indistinguishable except for the change in settings, regardless of how long ago the photos were made. You could layer most of his photos on top of each other and discern little difference in their structure. Nearly every photo was composed with the primary element in the middle of the frame, there was no foreground, and the background was scarcely considered. Photos were engaging only if what was depicted interests the viewer.

No doubt this person had a clear but limited reason for making the pictures: His intention was to show what was happening in front of him. The assumption was that the news value of what is pictured would make the photographs engaging.

What's the adage? "The road to hell is paved with good intention." It's only when intention, your why, has substantive clarity that reflects perception on the photographer's part that it has value and results in photographs that compel a response from a wider audience than those who are interested in the topic depicted.

"The best pictures elicit empathic responses which hopefully linger on long enough to encourage a form of engagement," Lucy Conticello said in a 2019 Lensculture interview about the editorial portrait. She's the director of photography of *M* magazine.

Circling back to the notion that why you make pictures informs how you'll make them, if the why is dimensional and has a clarity that informs the making, then the resulting photographs will more likely be compelling.

It'd be easy to overthink this notion, like the Tin Man in the *Wizard of OZ*, you could think big thoughts through your photos, for sure. But it can be much less complicated. You can respond to a setting more experientially, a pure response to what's in front of you. Recognizing the beauty or sadness or sense of achievement or failure or the connection between two people are among the infinitesimal starting points for the compelled intention in the making of a photograph.

Whatever you're responding to, ask this series of questions: Where are the qualities in the scene in front of you playing out, how much of the scene do you need to put in the viewfinder to convey those qualities; from what angle does the light most imbue each of the qualities; are there colors that add or detract; will there be things happening that are the essence of what you're trying to say and if so, when do those things happen?

Or this can be an instantaneous response. You're in a setting and the voice in your head starts to respond to the qualities of settings and says, "Oh, that's so sweet or chaotic or sad or lovely ..." Then fully engage with the scene to convey those qualities. Once you switch to striving to say more than merely being descriptive, you'll see settings differently, you'll become more and more agile in responding to making photos more dimensionally, as an extension of your compelled intention, which is a combination of perception forming your impression that you express through the camera.

What's joyous about this approach is that every setting you photograph will have different qualities, which means you can approach the making

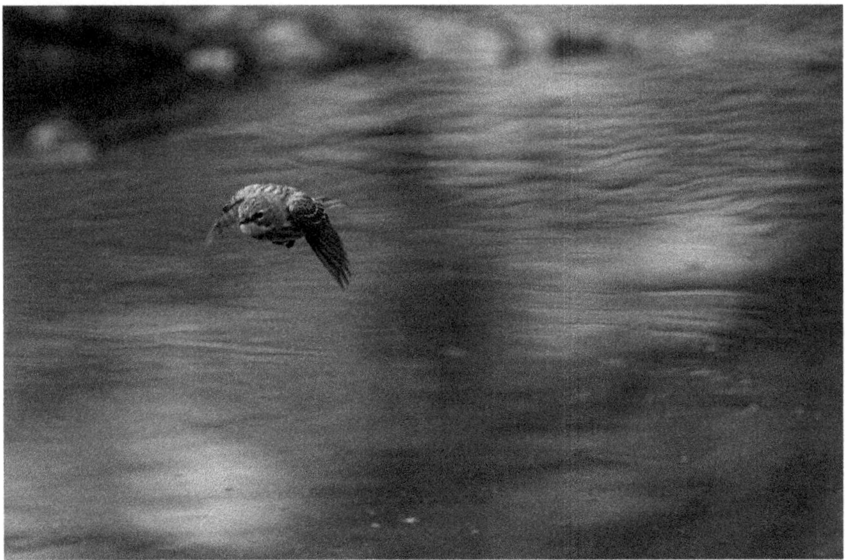

Photo 3.04 I set out with several intentions in mind when beginning to photograph wildlife: To get out during the pandemic, to learn new things, to challenge myself to make photographs that went beyond showing birds.

of photographs uniquely in every setting. You won't be able to layer your photos on top of each other with little difference one to the next.

I'll say more about this in the next section.

If you use a disciplined approach that works for you and you evolve that approach with the intention of continually responding to scenes more dynamically, your seeing will grow, your photographs will become more compelling and engaging. Discipline in this sense means using a consistent approach every time you approach the entire process of making pictures. It's only by being consistently disciplined that you will learn what is working and what could work better. If every time you go out or take on a new topic or scene you use a different approach and sometimes powerful photos result and sometimes they don't then you'll be less able to know why.

It's also important that you be as efficient as possible. Don't get mired in the gadgets and take every lens and gizmo to make pictures. Use only what you need to achieve what you're striving for.

Likewise, be efficient in what you photograph, both in individual settings and as you assemble a set of photographs on a topic. If you enter a scene and strive to photograph everything, that's the opposite of efficient and likely won't produce a successful picture. The take will be so frenetic that not a single picture is fully realized.

If on the other hand you pause and consider and get to know and come from an informed why starting point, you'll narrow and elevate the range of what you're striving to photograph. You'll be able to give a deserved level of attention to explore aspects of the scene to fully realize photographs more often. Creating more of less is usually the path to a defined narrative.

Section 3.5 Enmesh Yourself

Once you've elevated your why, engagement is what puts the effort in gear on the road to achieving high-moment value photos. Think of engagement in two ways: What you choose to put in front of your camera and the act or process of making photographs.

On What You Put in Front of Your Camera

The best photographers are considered the best because of their uniqueness. They've worked hard to achieve expertise and a way of making photographs that only they can realize. They are in demand for their specialization.

That's different from people who photograph some of this, some of that and use one approach for this and another for that. They are generalists, like having to be the pitcher, catcher and first baseman. Being a generalist used to generate a decent income. People were paid because they knew how to run the cameras and make acceptable images of what they were hired to photograph. Given that everyone everywhere has a camera that virtually runs itself, everyone is now a generalist photographer. People who specialize from behind the camera in some way are now the most successful in the business.

Your specialization can be topical or because of your unique way of creating images, the latter of which tends to be more conceptual or created photography, as opposed to captured. Topical specializations can really be of anything. For me, it's been food, bicycling, people getting together and now wildlife. You must be passionate and absolutely devoted to whatever that topic is. I usually ask students who haven't figured out their specialty: "If you had a month to spend with anything you choose in front of your camera, what would that be." Some iteration of the answer is your specialty, assuming there's a market, someone wants to pay you to photograph that.

If you are exceptionally able to convey ideas and concepts through your photography, that too is a specialty. Lynn Johnson is one example. She's able to create visual narratives of the most conceptual notions, such as lost languages, pain, autism. Her interpretation is why she gets hired and not surprisingly her work is an expression of her personality. She is perpetually curious, driven, personable and brilliant.

Enmesh completely with your specialty and that will propel your career.

On the Process of Engaging While Making Photographs

Popping the cork and then chugging a nice bottle of wine would be a waste, a lost opportunity. There's a process to drinking good wine that enriches and draws out the experience by tapping all of your senses. There's an equivalent in photography.

Matt Black calls this engagement a *photographic dialogue*, in the film *Unamerican Dream*, referring to his years-long revelation of California's central valley and whether what he'd seen there was an anomaly or is reflected throughout the United States "The question I was seeking to answer was a personal question, which is: How to make sense, really, of what I had seen and experienced in the central valley all these years."

Here's how to engage in an intentional approach to making pictures, presented first by what you can do before you're in a setting and then once you're in a setting.

The before-making-pictures engagement in photography varies depending on how long you're going to be photographing a given situation. If you're not yet in a setting, such as photographing on assignment, as a self-generated idea of short duration or will be going somewhere, first learn about what or who you'll be photographing; call the person or people who know the person; see what the setting will be like; figure out the best time to be there based on activity or quality of light; see what kinds of photographs have been produced in that setting before – though some

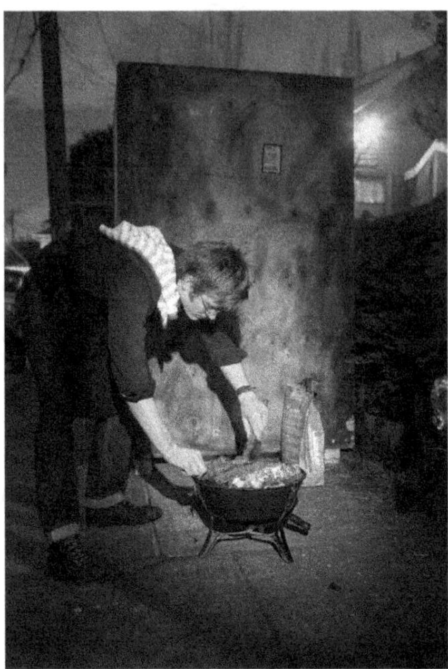

Photo 3.05 Once you engage fully with one thing, that can lead to other connections. After engaging with cycling I realized how connected food and cycling are. So I began to photograph that intersection. Here, Matthew Card makes a meal at Vanilla Bicycle Company in Portland, Oregon.

more experienced photographers advise against this, saying it corrupts their approach. The alternative is to show up and start making picture intuitively.

Longer-term efforts generally require further engagement upfront. More learning, more understanding, more awareness, more clarity in determining what the narrative should be, all of which lead to a greater degree of clarity of how to approach making photographs once you're in settings.

If you're already in a given setting, first figure out how much of what's in front of you inspires you to make a photograph. Sometimes we make photos of a setting and miss the fully realized image because we focused on too much or not enough of the scene, instead defaulting to a view that allows a simplistic presentation of what's happening – our mind's eye was not focused; the photo is an unrealized idea.; it's not a full frame.

I advise, metaphorically, that if you have five minutes to make photographs, spend four of them getting to know the setting and person or people or activity. Then you can spend a relative minute making more informed and dimensional photographs.

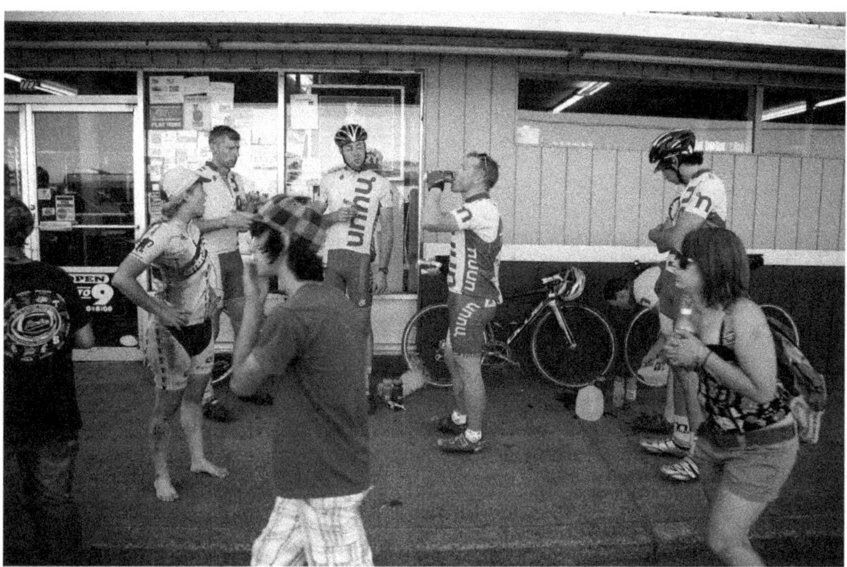

Photo 3.06 Further connections happen once you've fully engaged. We started to get commercial and editorial work related to cycling. Here, we were hired to photograph Rapha's Gentleman Race.

First, start to get to know the setting and its inhabitants. Come to understand and inform impressions of what will happen, what motivates people, what qualities you could speak to. If you're photographing a person, talk to them. Learn and understand how you can use the medium to convey the qualities of that person. Equally important, get them comfortable with you by sharing something of yourself. Photographing people involves creating a relationship, a connection, in whatever time you have with them.

Then inform your eye by reading the color and light, what you could speak to from what distances, what technical considerations would elevate your photographs.

Once fully engaged you can make informed decisions about where to place the camera in the pursuit of a range of qualitative photographs.

When you have a sense of what you want to achieve but don't know how to move forward, it's usually because you don't know enough. Move forward by engaging more completely. Expand your understanding and learn.

Section 3.6 Earn Trust

What has trust to do with making photographs? Early in the learning process a lot of people have the notion that you can surreptitiously make photographs, as if you were invisible, can step into settings and make magnificent photos without people even knowing you were there.

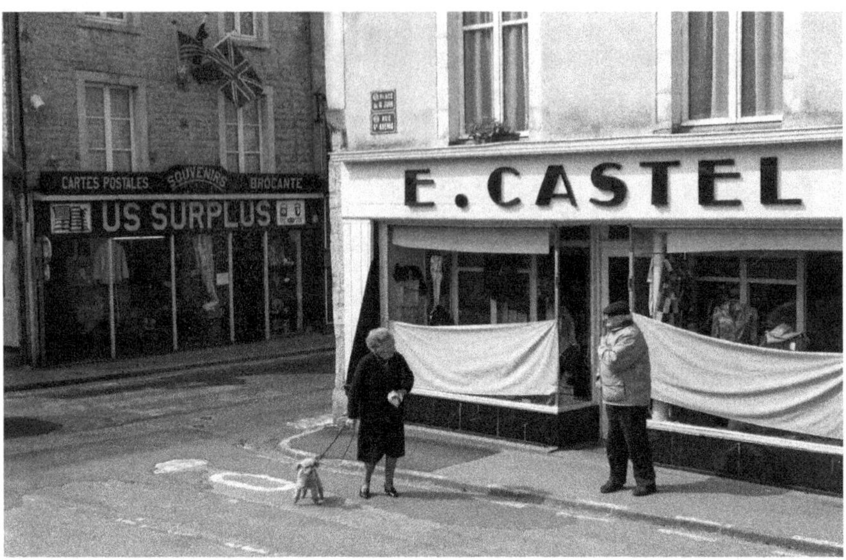

Photo 3.07 Trust happens in many ways in this profession. We had to earn the administration's trust when working at the White House, even we picture editors, who were tasked with going on advance trips to make pictures of where the president would go, in this case St. Mere Eglise in Normandy.

That's often called being a fly on the wall. Maybe that works for street photography, but that's about it. You might have some photos in your archive that you like that were made without talking to the person or engaging more completely with the setting, but they don't come close to what would have been possible if you had engaged, I'll bet.

High-moment value photos most result from the relationship that you create with who or what you want to photograph. Getting to be a fly on the wall of someone's life requires that they trust you to be there. This richness comes from people knowing why you chose to photograph them, why you want to make pictures and how the photographs will be used, what kind of person you are. Similar dynamics apply to getting permission to photograph places.

It is a two-way exchange to achieve trust and the level of trust you achieve will parallel the depth of the work that you produce. The longer you want to spend photographing someone or some setting, the more rounded a relationship you'll have to establish – it's not unusual to maintain lifelong connections with the people you've photographed deeply.

Danielle Villasana says in *Authority Collective* and *Photoshelter's Guide to Inclusive Photography*, "Building and maintaining trust is paramount and being trusted by someone to photograph them is sacred and should be honored and respected. …it's incredibly important to abide by people's wishes and clearly communicate your intentions." Danielle encourages photographers to share their work with people they photograph, to make your understanding and therefore your work grow through increased trust that comes from giving, not just taking.

Most successful photographers who photograph people's lives are good at engaging with people in a way that allows entry into their lives, whether for a few minutes or years. Reference the lists of agencies and grants in the resource guide appendix to see the work of hundreds of photographers.

How do you go about establishing trust? It's really a matter of the people you want to photograph getting to know you and your motivations for making their picture – and I say make instead of take because taking implies a one-way exchange whereas making implies a more interactive, creative process. Take, shoot and capture are colonialism's sibling expressions applied inappropriately to photography.

Start by introducing yourself as a photographer and expressing interest in aspects of the lives of people you want to photograph. Break the ice by telling them your impression of some aspect of what they are doing or of their setting; ask questions, to show that you are interested, curious. Be respectful. The goal is to establish a connection. They should know that you are interested in what they're doing by what you say and the questions that you ask.

It'll be appropriate to share something about yourself as the conversation progresses. That can come before or after explaining why you are interested in photographing the person or the setting. Unless they know you at least a little bit or if it's not clear why you're expressing interest, they likely won't let you into their lives.

Who you are, your personality, is the biggest determinant of whether you will gain entry. However, you present yourself is how you will be perceived. If you are nervous and lack confidence or the opposite and your ego drives your boisterous actions, you're not likely to be allowed to enter into people's lives or be granted access to places you want to photograph.

If you are not humble by nature, develop that quality. It'll go a long way in trying to connect with people. If you are not confident in approaching people, get there. Don't act like you deserve to make pictures, earn that right through connection, respect and expressing your intentions.

Make sure that they know how the photographs you're making will be used going forward and have a conversation about how that usage might affect them, whether in potentially positive or negative ways. It has been my experience that people allow you to photograph them if they have something to gain from the experience or nothing to lose.

If just approaching people is a challenge for you, do the exercise of connecting with five people that is in the self-assignment Appendix.

Once you have crossed the threshold to making pictures, I suggest making pictures as you want to from the outset, to get people used to being photographed in the way that you make pictures. Some people start shyly, by making pictures only from further away. Those being photographed get used to that distance and will likely balk when you move in closer. From the get-go, get close when what is happening is best photographed from nearby but then move out as that activity passes. Make photos from different distances so they get used to you being there in a variety of ways. Use the motor drive sparingly. The sound of the camera shutter flapping can be off-putting.

Most people wonder how much they should talk to the people they're photographing. There's no right answer. Your personality will guide you to the right level of interaction with the people you're photographing. You can set aside times when you're engaging with the people you're photographing and times when you are only observing and making pictures. Saying "pretend I'm not here" usually doesn't work, it makes people more conscious of what they're doing in your presence.

Some people show photographs on the back of the camera as they're making them, as another way of elevating trust. Be selective in what you show if you do share.

You can also promise to send a certain number of photos to people. Stipulate how they may use your photographs – usually for personal use only and on social media if with your permission. Making them prints of photos you think they'll like is a nice thing to do.

As you establish a relationship, become an ingrained presence in the lives of the people you want to photograph, they will feel more comfortable going about their lives. You'll never achieve fly-on-the-wall status, that truly is a myth. Your presence will always affect their behavior.

Section 3.7 Incorporate the Universal

Mindfully photographing activities and things that all people share will elevate the universality of your photography. We all eat and spend time with others and earn livelihood and wear clothes and live in spaces and travel from one place to another and relate to people. Every occurrence of the universal is distinctive, yet we can all relate because these aspects are all part of our lives, too.

Universal qualities are what is in each setting that we all can respond to either because they are familiar or unfamiliar. Photographers tend to either not consider those aspects important or exclude them because they clutter the frame.

By responding to the universality of each setting you photograph, you're responding to how the universal aspects play out uniquely in that setting, which means that the experience of photographing every setting and the resulting photographs will be unique, even if you've made pictures there many times before.

And if you've not photographed in a setting before, it's your responsibility to understand how the universal is expressed uniquely. Something

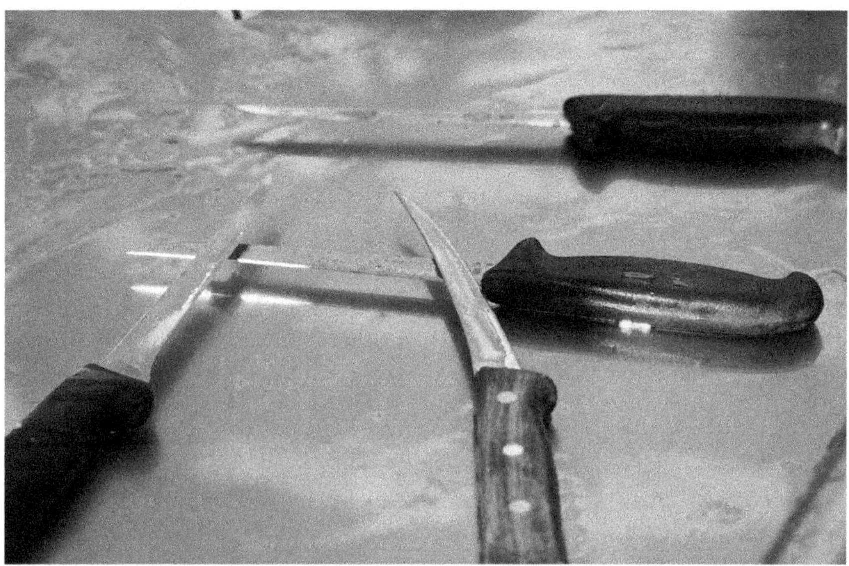

Photo 3.08 Strive to make engaging photos of the ordinary in settings and you'll add considerable dynamic to your photography. Here are knives resting at Afton Field Farm in Oregon after butchering their first chickens in a new building.

as simple as the color yellow has different meanings in different societies. How and whether people touch each other varies widely throughout the world. How personal space and architectural spaces are created is equally unique to each locale.

Yes, we all bring ourselves to the making of photographs but it's on you to expand your understanding beyond its current state every time you make photographs.

This idea didn't fully occur to me until I worked at the White House as the lead picture editor, with the responsibility of assessing every photograph Eric Draper and three other photographers made of the president, first lady and general happenings – about a million photographs in the nearly four years.

The same relatively limited range of things happen (the verbs of the White House) in the same settings with objects that don't change in those settings (the nouns). Varying numbers of people sitting or standing in rooms or outside, talking, or not talking, signing, holding or looking at pieces of paper, eating or not eating. Occasionally the main dude would play with his dogs or jog or ride his bike.

If photographs were going to be engaging beyond the day, if the moment value was going to rise above what was shown, photographs would have to tap into something more than the verbs and nouns of what happened.

Enter the notion of universality: What are people wearing and how precise, classy or sloppy are they and the settings; what are the food and accouterments like; what are people's body posture and personal space; how do people look at each other; what does the whole scene look like; what's the color palette; how does the choice, quality and placement of objects express qualities; how did the choice of setting relative to what's happening offer visual expression. There are so many things to engage with beyond showing the verbs and nouns.

How do you approach the making of pictures in settings to make universal aspects elevate what the images convey? Universal aspects can enrich parts of the frame, they can become the critical foreground element or that part of a background that adds another element or that little, bonus element in the corner of the frame. Or they can be a quality, such as color or light, that pervades the photograph. Incorporating the universal intentionally requires thinking about and being aware of aspects of a setting that you likely haven't thought about as separate aspects before.

Eye contact is one of the most universal aspects of humanity so waiting for people to look at each other itself introduces something all our brains will relate to.

Considering the universal aspects of settings equal to what is happening is the challenge. It comes down to deciding what else to include and expanding the times when you're there to make photographs so that you see and photograph more of the world.

Look at your own photographs and assess whether you've engaged with the universal to express the uniqueness. As with so much of what this book speaks to, addressing the universal involves flipping the hierarchy of what you thought was most important.

Section 3.8 Anticipate or Miss It

Someone asked me during a workshop what camera she should get. The one she had just bought wasn't fast enough, it kept missing the picture, she said. She apparently would see something happen and raise her camera to "capture" it. But, dang, the camera was just too slow.

I suggested that her camera might be fine but her approach could use some refinement. Not waiting for things to happen to try to make a picture is the trick.

Fully realized photographs, especially of active situations, occur because the photographer anticipates something notable happening and they begin to create the photograph before they occur.

That means the photographer has at least minimally read the light and color, determined a distance from which to begin making pictures and started to build the composition and then waited for all those decisions to come to fruition by making pictures of the flow of the setting. All of these decisions can happen on a spectrum, from taking seconds to several minutes, hours or days.

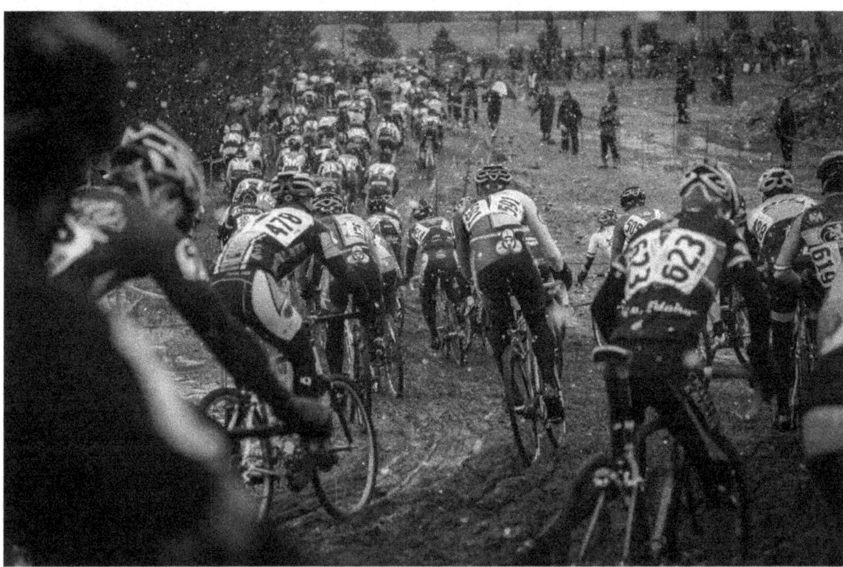

Photo 3.09 Anticipation can be as simple as knowing when something will happen, building a composition that considers how the frame will be filled and then waiting. Here, the National Cyclocross Championships in Bend, Oregon. I waited through three races for this to work out.

Being sensitive to what might happen is a professional trait that you can develop and hone over time, as is knowing what kinds of settings are likely to produce the most telling photographs and knowing when best to be in those settings.

There are two ways to think about anticipation: When you're already in a setting and knowing when to be in the settings.

The latter mostly comes into play when you are working on a narrative, you're producing a set of pictures on a topic and there are many choices as to where and when to make pictures. Learning as much as you can about when telling circumstances will develop tells you when to be there. Ideally, people you're photographing also let you know when important things arise that you couldn't anticipate. That's part of the process of building trust.

Once you're in a setting, happenings have a rhythm: There's the before-they-start, then they begin to form, rise to a peak and then descend back to nothing happening. The bigger or more complex a setting the more rhythms there will be.

What you're hoping to say about what's happening will determine what part of the rhythm is most telling. Sometimes the before has a strong sense of anticipation and that produces the most compelling photograph. Sometimes it's the peak moment that is richest. In other cases, the after is most telling. Or maybe photos from each of the phases are called for. Rare among photographs are those that incorporate a before during and after of occurrences. The value of photographing all phases of the rhythm is that you can't anticipate which of the phases will be most telling.

Anticipation, then, is the skill of knowing that which settings might provide the raw materials for a telling photograph and then crafting photographs before and as things happen in the settings you choose. I'm betting the photographer from the workshop started to make more telling photographs with just this bit of advice.

Section 3.9 Hello Serendipity

Serendipity became the focus of a conversation with Bill Allard when I worked at National Geographic as an illustrations editor. We were at a gallery opening of his work, talking about the magic of many of his images, which he says often comes from pure serendipity. They are photographs that by definition happen by chance, from settings that you can't anticipate would produce magical photographs, as are many of Bill's photos.

You might think that serendipity is the opposite of intentionality, engagement and anticipation. Things just magically come together in front of your camera and you make a perfect picture, unlike the person whose camera couldn't take a picture fast enough. In fact, serendipity is more likely to happen because of these three focused efforts.

One measure of photographs is thinking about what it took for the photographer to be able to make a given photograph. The more compelled the

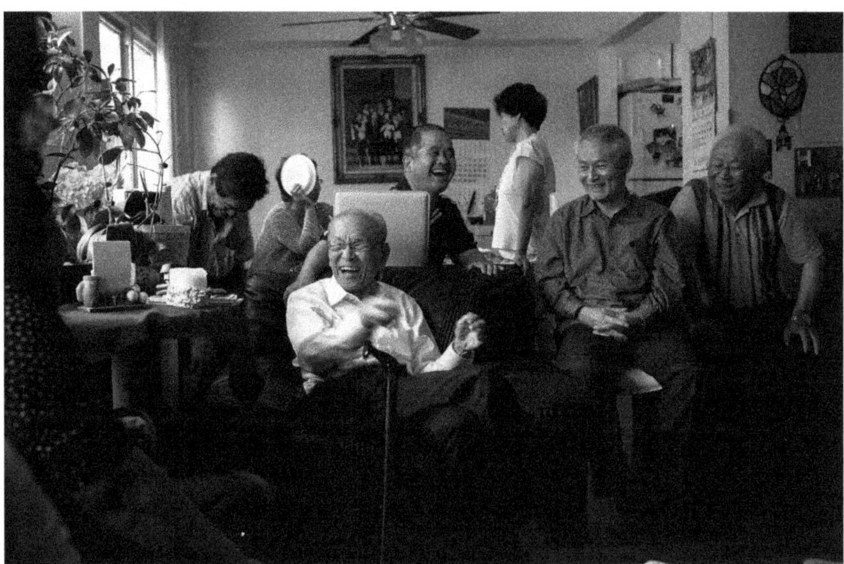

Photo 3.10 Being open to and prepared for photographs happening at any time is when serendipity happens most often. This is a gathering of my wife's family after a wedding. Photographing such settings is also a way to save time, addressed in the next section.

photographer's intention, the greater the degree of engagement and the level of anticipation – even if it's only momentary – the more likely the photographer will be in a position to make a photograph that appears to be serendipitous.

I realized that after editing several rolls of Bill's Kodachrome – yes, this was pre-digital. Frame after frame was incomplete, nothing held together, roll after roll and then one frame started to work, the next was almost there and the third was unbelievably powerful, subtle, nuanced, complex, amazing. And it felt serendipitous as if the universe coalesced just for Bill to make this one frame. Move back in time from when the photos were made and you'd see that Bill learned where and when to be in this potentially rich setting and didn't give up exploring with his camera until the richness dissipated.

As Bill meant it, serendipity is in part having the luxury of putting yourself in settings that you aren't certain will produce a memorable photograph. This was a time at National Geographic when time in the field was going from pretty much unlimited to being limited. His fear was that he wouldn't be able to linger in uncertain settings long enough for serendipity to bless his film through concentrated intention, engagement and anticipation.

Marvin Joseph describes the process in a Washington Post Magazine article as getting to a point of trust with the people he's photographing, "then playing with various props and concepts. I never know exactly how anything will turn out until I'm knee-deep in the process or when the photo shoot is over." Serendipity's first cousin, spontaneity, is both the goal and the result.

Time, trust and engagement are the magic-inducing components.

Section 3.10 Express Time like a Wizard

It was called the death check. Stories took so long to get in print when I was at National Geographic that we'd have to check whether people in the pictures had died by the time presses ran. Photographs had stopped time but time doesn't stop.

John Berger said that the true content of a photograph is invisible, for it derives from a play, not with form, but with time.

Photographs are time, but how so? Cameras stop what's happening in front of them but that by itself is largely a mechanical function. So many other possibilities manifest when you think beyond the process. Considering time as a variable is another way to expand *the why* of making photographs and in turn guide you to more dimensional expressions through the camera.

Here are several ways to think about and express time in your photography:

How Photographs Express Time

Spend some time looking at photos from the past. Curated anthologies organized through time are good for this. As you look at the pictures,

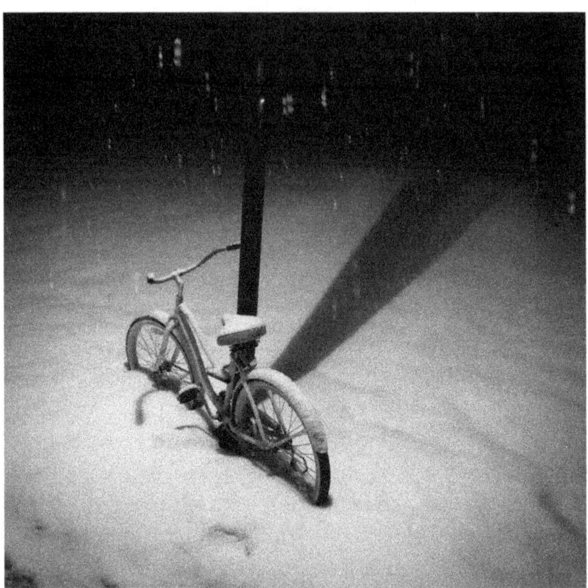

Photo 3.11 This bike was locked to a pole outside The Newhouse School at Syracuse University for several years. Making a picture that conveyed this longevity was the goal. Being there at the right time – when it was snowing and at night – with a quality of light and tonality that added to the sense of duration was the goal.

what are you responding to? That will include what people are doing, no doubt, what the scenes are, for sure. Chances are you'll also be drawn to what clothing they're wearing, hairstyles, the kinds of cars, dinnerware, food, things that are mundane, not the active parts of scenes.

If looking at older photographs triggers interest at what would be mundane in today's photos then that suggests that you should consider including that layer of things in your photographs now. (This is the universal notion addressed a couple of subsections ago.)

Time for Memory's Sake

Photographs do change as the time from their creation passes. The present becomes past as soon as the shutter releases. While I worked at the White House I thought of our work, our responsibility, as preserving history in the present tense. Thinking of how and what to photograph by considering how the passage of time might affect the perceptions of the administration added dimension to the visual archive of the presidency.

The immediacy of the moments and what we felt at the time fades or even disappears from memory with time. Photographs have the power to refresh what is forgotten, to remind us of the times and the people and the experiences connected to their making. If photographs freeze time, then they also can reconnect us with times past, from our current perspective.

It goes to follow that we should be mindful as things happen in the present tense of their potential to grow in value as time passes. If you make pictures of those seemingly mundane happenings and the people connected to them, you'll instill qualities that time will reward. As a professional that means photographing the edge of what you thought was the most important thing happening in a setting. Or think of settings as being more than singular occurrences and address as many different aspects as possible. Explore outside the core happening and you'll be looking time in the eye.

Maybe you weren't going to include that sign or that car in the background, instead choosing to simplify the scene. Rethink that, for time's sake.

Also, photograph the objects in settings because objects are reflections of the times in which they exist. People will relate now in one way and later in a different way to this aspect of your photos.

Photograph People before They Die

Whether you're a professional or not, above all, make pictures of people who are dear to you. They will die, to be blunt and sometimes unexpectedly. Going to visit a relative you haven't seen in a while? Bring your camera and make photographs of them going about their lives, of their settings, of things and activities that they care about. Better yet, schedule visits with that goal in mind.

Bring a camera to family gatherings and make portraits of everyone, as well as documenting the gathering's dynamics, intentionally.

I suggest this as I am gathering an archive for my children of the moments I've photographed in their lives. Though they may have complained once or twice about a camera always being present, they'll be glad to re-visualize their lives and be able to share them with their children.

Photograph the Quotidian

Another way to think about time is to photograph the quotidian, those things that happen repeatedly through the flow of life day to day. This is an assignment I give to students in the first course I teach. One of the students said recently that she didn't see the value of the assignment until time had passed. She said she realized that making successful photographs of the ordinary things in life informed and expanded her perception of what makes a photograph successful and what she could speak to. That seeing and understanding then extended to the making of more dimensional photographs in extraordinary settings.

Alejandro Cartagena is among the best at presenting the ordinary in extraordinary ways.

The Right Time

There's a perception that making high-moment value pictures requires massive amounts of time, having to linger in settings for hours waiting for things to come to fruition. That's true, and not true. The more important thing is to determine when the right times to be in settings are. That requires getting to know the people, the circumstances, the happenings and then being there when the most telling situations are unfolding. Unexpected, serendipitous photos result by lingering in settings a long time but balance that time expenditure with being there when you know things are going to happen.

If you're making a living as a photographer, you're no doubt often required to make photographs at a specific time. Sometimes that's the right time to make the photograph but often it's not. Do what it takes to change the system you work in and educate its decision-makers to more often be there at the right time.

Light has a right time, too. Know when the light will be most telling and be there then.

The right time approach is what differentiates vacation pictures from destination photographs. People who make a living as travel photographers make pictures at the right time; vacation pictures happen when you're passing through a setting.

Making Pictures of the Before, During and After

Time shows up in pictures in different ways. Peak moment photos tend to focus on the right now of what was happening. Anticipatory photographs focus on what is going to happen. Other photos show what has happened.

You can make photographs that present all three, the before, during and after. Such photos engage the viewer more dimensionally in terms of the passage of time that they express. Something will have happened, something is happening and there's a sense of what is about to happen.

How do you make this kind of picture? Engage the why first. If the why is to show all three, then in active settings anticipate something happening, begin to make photographs as the scene unfolds and continue to photograph, being mindful of multiple elements coming together and incorporating them into fully realized compositions as the scene rises to a peak and falls away. Somewhere in there will be photographs that express before during and after, with any one of three as the dominant quality.

A core dynamic is when the photograph expresses the notion that it took time for these elements to come together in the frame, for light to have a specific, dynamic quality that elevates this notion with the camera at a specific distance.

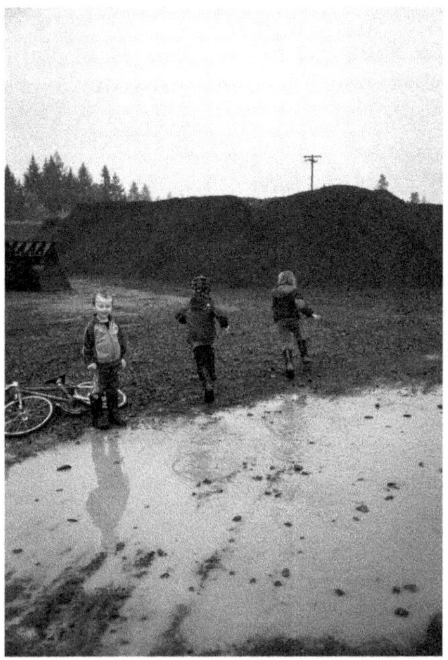

Photo 3.12 Photos that depict things that just happened and anticipate what might happen will engage in ways that photographing only the present tense does not.

If you focus only on the now when making photos, the less dimensional the experience of looking at your photos will be.

Time as Narrative

Time can be a powerful component in building narratives through multiple photographs. A typical iteration of using time as a narrative is by incorporating multiple seasons. Life unfolds differently with the seasons and showing that range decisively can introduce a dynamic that wouldn't be there if you only photographed during one season.

Passage of time is a common narrative structure for process stories: This happened, then that …

Another, more engaging, iteration of the passage of time is to photograph settings in the same way as time lapses, either by making similar photos as time passes or making unique photos in each new era. Which you choose depends on what you're saying about time passing, the why of the effort. Photographers have returned to photograph the lives of families through several decades. Others make daily selfies for years. Others find historic photos and return to those settings today. Possibilities are limitless.

Deanna Dikeman's 27-year body of work of her parents waving goodbye to her from their Sioux City, Iowa, home – 60 miles north of where I grew up – is one example. Jamel Shabazz's years-long photography in New York City's subways is another. Adam Magyar's subway motion work does the opposite by slowing seconds to minutes. Pablo Iglesias Maurer returned to 1960s postcard scenes.

More conceptually, a narrative can have underlying qualities that hold the piece together and time can be one of those. You can engage conceptually with the expression of time in a range of ways: Through the similarity or differences in the age of settings or people; in the balance of speaking to the past, present or future; by addressing history; by expressing memory through photographs …

Chris McCaw and Atta Kim express the duration of time in their photographs.

Play with time and it will reward your photographs.

Stop and Make the Picture

Ever have that dreaded, haunting feeling that you should have made a picture of something that you just passed by? Stop! Make the picture, now. Don't think you can come back to make the picture or let it pass by your view. There will always be excuses to justify not making a picture. Try instead to think of reasons that you must make the picture, now.

Sometimes there are settings that you think would make for photographs, but not now. Make note of those settings and when the right time to be there will be. I used to carry a small notebook and pen in my pocket for such times; now your phone can take notes for you.

Establish the discipline to stop, now or later.

Does Your Seeing Change Over Time?

Another way to think of time is as it applies to your photography: Does your eye evolve over time? Has your photography improved over time? Did you make photos in the past that you didn't think were good but now do?

I spent much of a recent summer scanning negatives that had been in the dark for as many as 30 years. Marks on the negative sleeves indicated which photos I preferred when I made the photos. My selections now were a lot different from then. So, what changed?

There are two functions to consider: the making and then the selection of photographs. Each incorporates different criteria, considerations and processes. Each is a different realization of your mind's eye.

If you return to your old images and choose the same photos you did when you made them or if you make photos in the same way that you did years ago, then both your making and selecting eyes are stagnant, they haven't changed.

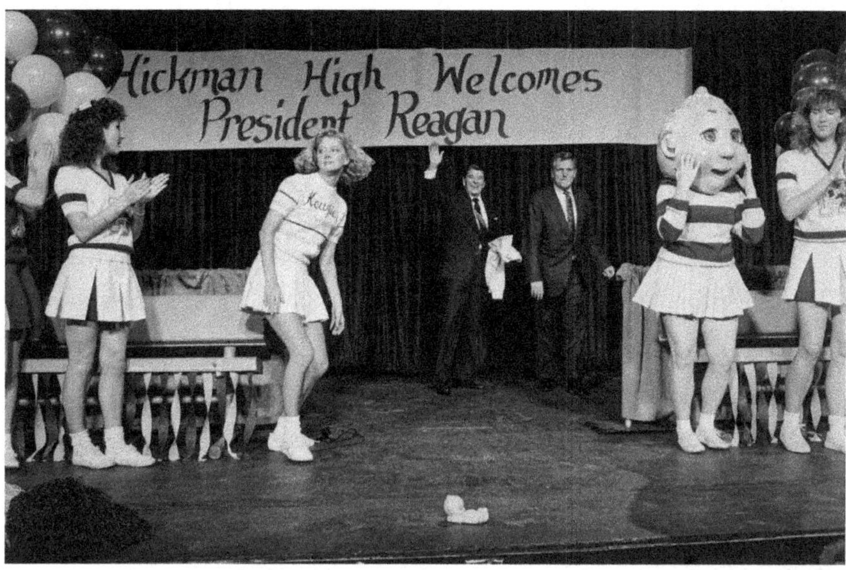

Photo 3.13 I went back into my old negatives as part of the process of writing this book and found this photo I'd made of President Reagan's visit to Columbia, Missouri, in 1987. Then, I chose a different frame from several of this happening and then cropped it. Now I appreciate roaming through the photo. There are several pictures in this picture.

If some time ago you made evocative, dynamic, complex photographs but didn't choose them then but do now, then your selection eye has grown.

If your photography was amazing then and it still is and you've recognized the strongest work throughout, you're an amazing rarity. Because rare is the person who can choose their strongest photographs. Artists and commercial photographers tend to be able to select their strongest photos – more so than those who photograph the flow of life – because they strive to make more specific photos and know when they've done that. That's why a lot of artists have never heard of picture editors.

Documentarians and photojournalists tend to choose pictures based heavily on the experience of making them, the richer or more difficult it was to make a picture the more they value it. Or based on the information that they think is important to present in the photo, with less regard for how strong the photo is. For their selection and seeing to grow, they have to expand why they're making photographs.

I've seen that some photographers make far more complex photographs than they choose. Once I've pointed out this discrepancy and described the difference, they'll tend to choose the stronger work going forward. The lesson is to be open to surprises, things you didn't intend to do that are boffo, whether you made the photo five minutes or five years ago.

Process as Expression of Time

The photographic process itself imbues photographs with a sense of time. Photos made with historic processes have a given color cast or tonality range that comes from both the time period and the process used to make the pictures. If you choose to use a historical process, do so for more dimensional reasoning than because you want the photo to have that old look – if that's all you instill, the resulting photos will likely be shallow. If instead, the topic you're approaching and the historical process you choose mesh to say more because of the combination then you're more likely to produce dimensional photos.

Section 3.11 See the Music

So many synapses happened when I first saw Roy DeCarava's book *The Sound I Saw, Improvisation on a New Jazz Theme*. I've been listening to jazz since I was 19 but seeing DeCarava's pictures made me hear it in a new way through his photographs. One of the enticements of jazz is that the best musicians interpret songs uniquely. Listen to Ethel Waters sing *Stormy Weather* and then hear Billie Holiday's rendition. DeCarava's photographs merge sound with image to interpret each venue as if his camera were riffing jazz.

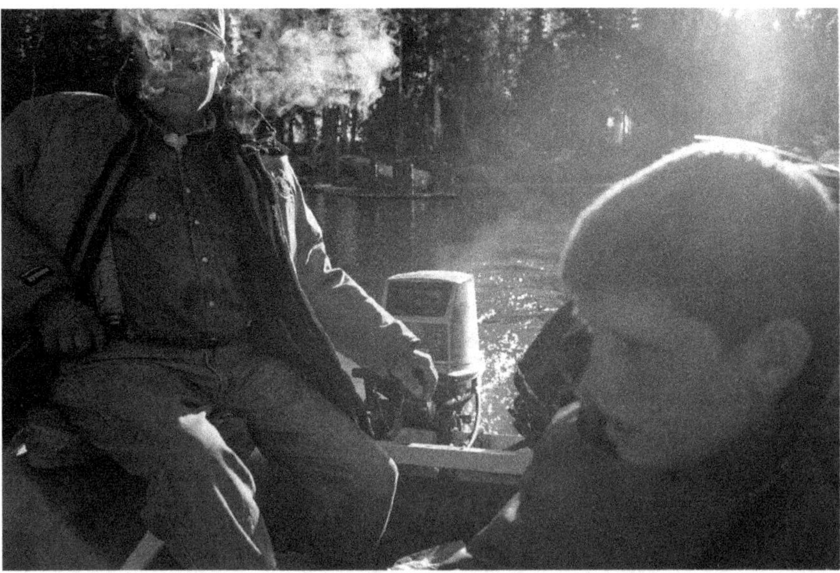

Photo 3.14 Here's a photo from 1999 that makes me hear the setting, a fishing trip with my son and dad in Canada – that's the guide on the left. The sound of the motor, the quiet of the water, the anticipatory nature of leaving the dock, the wafting smoke all combine to create a sensory experience.

He says in the book's introduction, "What is important are the ideas and experiences, what they evoke and how they're expressed. Their significance is relative and will depend on who you are and what you are. They will mean different things to different people, which is as it should be."

Wilson Hicks addresses the notion that photographs can engage sight and sound in his 1952 book *Words and Pictures*, a modest title for arguably the best book ever written about the craft of picture editing. (Not the type of editing that deals with digital post-processing of photographs, rather the profession of elevating visual storytelling by guiding photographers and working within publishing environments to awaken them to the power of visual content and developing all-encompassing approaches to ensure that compelling imagery happens regularly.)

Hicks used the term sound symbols that both words and pictures reference to elicit the experience of sound, meaning that words that describe a bell ringing or a photograph of a bell as it rings will trigger a sense of sound in the reader or viewer.

That's one way that photographs can create the experience of sound. Another is through the judicious and intentional reaction to and expression of the emotive qualities of a setting. You might have heard the expression, "Oh, that's just a one note photo." That's a musical reference that means the photographer's response to a scene and the resulting photo is one dimensional, a single note. If a one-note photographer produced multiple photographs in a setting, each photo would be like striking one key at a time on a piano, like playing chopsticks with one finger. It's a song but not a very engaging one.

If, on the other hand, your response to a setting were more dimensional, the making of each photograph could be like creating a set of chords within the frame – a chord is formed by playing three or more different notes together. The chords of a photograph could be pleasingly consonant or jarringly dissonant, or both within the same frame. Chords elicit emotive responses in listeners just as photographs that employ the visual equivalent of chords that are created to reflect qualities of a setting evoke those qualities in viewers.

Sequence a series of these dynamic images together and the experience of the sequence is like listening to music in terms of how your mind translates the experience.

Think of yourself as a composer when you have a camera in hand and you're engaging with a setting. Create visual chords that reflect the emotive dynamics of the setting and then sequence the photographic chords experientially to let the music play.

Section 3.12 What about Ethics?

What are ethics as they apply to the creation of photographs? That's a big question and one that doesn't easily fit into this book. Largely because ethics are as integral to the making of pictures as any other consideration.

Your answer to this question will vary widely, mostly depending on what type of work you create, who pays you to do that work and how that work is used. Each genre of work has its own code of ethics or none. At one end of the code of ethics spectrum is photojournalism and at the other is art, which isn't to say that the creation of art is without ethical considerations, just that there isn't a set of rules that practitioners must follow to be able to call themselves artists, as there is with photojournalists.

In between these two end points on the spectrum are documentary photography, broadcast, social media, blogs, advertising, commercial, not-for-profit and personal work.

Generally, ethics has to do with the realization of moral – and ethical – principles as they govern how you create, to whom you make your photography available and subsequently how and where your work is presented. In practice, it is the setting in which photography is used, published or displayed that determines what ethical principles apply to those images, from the point of their creation to their use and every step along the way. Words connected to images can and often do skew images to the unethical; it is the whole of how work is presented that you must consider.

It's important to understand where your work and its usage fits on this ethical spectrum because each use of your work will have different ethical standards. For instance, if you only controlled and manipulated the settings and people in your photographs then you couldn't sell those photographs to a journalistic publication as photojournalism. That same publication may have a space that would allow such photographs, though. If you had made some photos without manipulation/control, those photographs could be used in a journalistic setting and the entirety of that work could enter other markets, such as editorial, commercial, advertising, real estate, public relations and a gallery setting or book publication.

Photojournalism holds that its "primary goal is the faithful and comprehensive depiction of the subject at hand … we have the responsibility to document society and to preserve its history through imagery," quoting from the National Press Photographers Association code of ethics preamble.

The code itself includes the following aspirational points: Be accurate and comprehensive, resist being manipulated by staged photo opportunities, avoid stereotyping, be respectful of people in your photograph and your peers, don't alter or influence events, maintain the integrity of images' content throughout the process, don't pay people you photograph or accept compensation of any form, don't harass people. There's more but you get the point. Surprisingly unspoken, but assumed, is that you can't manipulate photographs in a way that alters the original physical aspects of a setting – that's usually done by removing or moving objects or people.

A thread within photojournalism ethics is the notion of telling the truth about what happened as if the truth were a singular, achievable expression. It's not. Just look at how different media outlets report on the same occurrences.

The American Society of Media Photographers (ASMP) has a similar code with categories that touch on the responsibility to colleagues and the profession, to subjects, to clients, to assistants and employees and assistant's responsibilities to their employer.

Ethical considerations are finally branching out from considerations of the creator to considering the dynamics of how what you do affects those pictured more completely, addressing everything from your motivations to how you engage to the story you're telling. Tailyr Irvine, in *The Authority Collective* and Photoshelter's *Guide to Inclusive Photography* says, you should "expand well beyond harmful and lazy reporting to tell a compelling, new and productive story." She was referring to engaging with indigenous communities. "It is our moral duty to provide context and take care not to oversimplify in our storytelling … Leave your preconceived ideas at the door and dip deeper to find stories that have purpose."

The Photo Bill of Right expands on this more humanistic practitioner perspective. https://www.photobillofrights.com The document's goal is to encourage the visual professions to be more equitable in how they treat independent "lens-based workers," specific to issues related to health, safety, access, bias, ethics, abuse and sexual misconduct and finance. (Tradition-entrenched practitioners objected to the term lens-based workers, which is a more inclusive way of saying people who make a living by creating images with devices that have lenses.) And the bill of rights describes a set of practices to do the same for people in front of our cameras. One among several significant takeaways from the bill of rights is that ethical practices are equitable practices. The bill of rights addresses more aspects of being a working professional than most codes of ethics.

The mostly traditional and white practitioners of visual journalism took issue with some aspects of the bill of rights when they landed, the largest being the suggestion that photographers speak to people they're photographing in public settings whenever possible. This was a suggestion in toolkits, one of the add-ons to the main document. Notable is that those who complained about this singular subset generally didn't fully acknowledge the great value and the wider scope of what the bill of rights put forth. This was during the time of protests and demonstrations related to the killing of George Floyd and many others by police so the context of the suggestion to speak with people you're photographing during active protests threw some people into a first amendment tantrum.

Photojournalists have the constitutional right to make pictures of people in public without asking permission and those people should have no expectation of privacy, of not being photographed, some argued. That's true but misses the point and took an extreme reading of the document as if it said you must get permission from people in all circumstances.

There are clearly circumstances where photojournalists can't even talk to people they're photographing, but yes, whenever possible, speak with people you want to photograph, regardless of the setting, and you'll make more informed and engaged photographs. Once you've engaged you can decide if your right to make pictures supersedes the consequences of their usage, or better, involve the people you photograph in the decision. A group of people are trying to ingrain this process into images, under the name, *Photo Fair*, which has its origins in *Fair Trade* commerce.

Most notable from this interaction was the contrast between the intention of expanding practices for the profession to be more accepting of a greater range of creators, more understanding of the implications of photographing people and those who would restrict and limit both of these intentions by adhering to aging principles and practices, largely because of the perception that being interactive would cost them time and money, though its expressed as limiting first amendment rights. (That's my opinion.)

Society of Professional Journalists added a "Minimize Harm" section to its Code of Ethics to address similar issues, including this statement: "Pursuit of the news is not a license for arrogance or undue intrusiveness."

The Native American Journalists Association offers helpful resources to curb stereotypical representations, including a Bingo Card of words, the more of which you use, the more you are stereotyping. Indigenous Photograph exists to "elevate the work of indigenous visual journalists and bring balance to the way we tell stories about indigenous people and spaces" and more.

Advertising, public relations and marketing communications codes of ethics outwardly express the same kinds of standards – minus language about manipulation – but I haven't seen that to be even close to universally achieved in practice. Advertising and public relations can use whatever visual approach to creating imagery that benefits their client, as long as the public lets them get away with it by buying the product or supporting the client.

Art practice addresses more universal aspects of ethics through what photographs express, such as right and wrong not in the context of what you can or can't do while creating a photograph but in what the photographer is addressing through their work. It's more about placing judgment on the photographer's intentions than restrictions on the making of images.

Independent of genre, the *Coalition for Content Provenance and Authenticity* – that's a mouthful that abbreviates to C2PA – has launched an effort to "address the prevalence of misleading information online through the development of technical standards for certifying the source and history (or provenance) of media content." In other words, the goal is to cut down on digital manipulations of images and misrepresentations associated with the practice. There's a 19-section site that explains the entirety.

Photography Ethics Centre encourages people to write their own statement of ethics, "a declaration of your ethical principles and a description of how you enact those principles in your photography practice." Learn more on their site.

A different way of thinking about ethics is to not think about it. Establish your way of working based on what you want to say and then find or create homes for that work. If you take this path, how you work is your ethical standard and you will be judged for that standard.

Regardless of your standard, it's important to question what kind of relationship the camera creates between you and who or what you are photographing. How are you accountable, who has the power and what are your and their responsibilities throughout the process? Talking through these considerations with people is important.

If anyone presents ethics as one standard, chances are they have limited professional experience or are wearing blinders. Do what is right, outside of your self-interest, and your practice will likely be ethical.

Try This

- Research and get to know the work of ten photographers whose work you respect and aspire to. Become familiar with them as people, not just their work. Never be at a loss when someone asks you whose work you admire.
- Photograph a person and a place you've never met or been and are outside your experience. Get to know them and make pictures. Return to that person or place three times. If you can't return three times, start over with a new person. Repeat until you've gained enough trust to stay in their lives.
- Make photographs that engage with and express time in three different ways, as described in this section.
- Confront your ethics. Talk to three practitioners in your field of photography and ask them how they approach their work in a way that is ethical.

Section 4
How to Select and Sequence Your Photos

Section 4.0 Introduction

Think of this process of creating work as being on an interconnected continuum, as opposed to each aspect being independent of the others. If why you create work determines how you'll approach the making of it, then that process continues through the selection and sequencing phase and concludes with the presentation of the work, most likely in multiple forms.

Selection includes creating a hierarchy in every group of photographs that you make – that means rating each image from not selected to the best, as in no stars to five stars. Higher rated photos convey qualities of what was photographed. Better photos elicit responses from the viewer because of the way you chose to make the photograph, not just because of what the photo shows or its informational content. (Let captions or other informational media present information and set a higher standard for your photographs.)

Sequencing photographs can play into the visual vs. informational dynamic as well. Many people sequence photos based on the this-then-that presentation of information to show a process or series of occurrences in their order of happening. It's a basic approach, the equivalent of *Dick and Jane* in the literary realm.

Journalistic settings tend to use this informational approach to sequencing because photographs are thought of in terms of the information they present. Confusion often results because it's not until you've read words that the information is apparent, unless the photos are literal/simplistic.

I've spent less time in commercial and advertising settings, but my impression is that the same informational criteria are often at play there, except in the more dynamic, less literal businesses and depending on their client base.

I've seen judges of competitions reject scores of entries because their sequencing was based on the information that each successive photograph presented. Judges couldn't discern the informational value from the photos, so the sequencing only confused them.

An alternative is to sequence photos based along lyrical, emotive and experiential qualities. Rather than sequencing based on what the

DOI: 10.4324/9781003287544-4

photographs show, build from one to the next based on the visual experience that the viewer has, without knowing the informational aspects that the photographs represent.

Approaches to sequencing can fall anywhere on this spectrum, from purely informational to purely lyrical. Why the work exists, what it speaks to, who the audience is and where it will live are among the variables that determine which approach is best.

It's also a personal choice. One photographer whose work I sequenced at National Geographic rejected my choices because she said she couldn't talk through the pictures in that order. Another photographer said he'd just make his words work with the sequence I'd created.

Now let's get into the how-to of selecting and sequencing.

Section 4.1 How to Select Your Best Photos

If all aspects of the photographic creation process are on an interconnected continuum, then the selection of your strongest work also falls on this spectrum. Picking pictures involves more than simply saying this photo is better than that one or this group is better than all the others; or only choosing the "best" photos that meet a specific need at the time of that need. Selecting your strongest work among all the photos you make or have made should provide the foundation for all possible uses of your photographs. In other words, you ideally could enter your archive and easily select photographs to meet a given need because you've created a qualitative hierarchy.

The goal is to establish a clear hierarchy of what you now believe to be the strongest or most successful photographs, second most, third most and

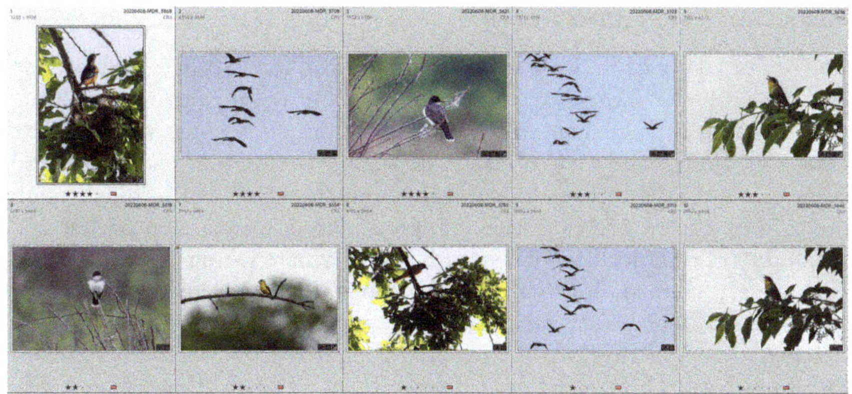

Photo 4.01 Here's an example of creating a hierarchy using stars in Lightroom, with four stars as the better rating and descending to one star.

so on, to at least a five-tier depth. And I say what you now believe because what photographs you value most can change over time.

Determining which are the strongest among your photographs is more likely achievable the greater the degree of clarity you have in why the photographs were made and the more depth and dynamic of that why.

If you invest the time to establish this hierarchical workflow at the front end, you'll save time and ensure that you're putting your best images out there every time.

Now, let's get down to the nitty gritty.

Selecting Photos, a Process

Here's a process to create a rated hierarchy when you have a set of pictures in front of you, whether it's from a day of making them, your inconsistently rated archive from the last 10 years or a project you've been working on for a while. The process creates a hierarchy by making several passes through the photos. No single step is overly judgmental; you're not trying to arrive at the best photos in a single bound. This allows you to gradually get familiar with the photos as photos and increasingly remove yourself from the experience of having made them.

This process presumes that you're using one of the image archiving software programs, such as Lightroom, Photo Mechanic, Capture One, etc.

It's good practice to caption and keyword your photos before beginning to create a hierarchy. You can start by giving all photos in a group a general caption and then going back to make captions more specific to each subgroup and individual photos. Same for keywording. Then when you begin rating, you'll be more familiar with the work and will have gotten through the tedious part of the process.

Pass One: Contact Sheet Review

You're not rating or making value judgments on the first pass, just getting familiar with the photos, what they show and how they were made.

Bring up a contact sheet, or grid, view of the photos you want to rate, with a medium-sized view of each photo, large enough to read but not so large that it'd take forever to scroll through the set. Then scroll through the grid of photos and note their range of compositional approaches and variability of distance from subjects. See how you're seeing light and color. Are there technical shortcomings that appear more than once that are worth addressing?

Recognize the rhythm of how many photos from each engagement there are. Most photographers make a certain number of photos of every setting. Five to ten is the most common. If you consistently make more than ten or so, that can reflect a lack of clarity in why you were making the photo, you're just hoping the photo would happen; or if you make fewer than five regularly, it may be that you didn't engage fully enough and may not have realized the potential of the setting.

It's typical to make more pictures when less is happening because you're hoping that if you press the shutter enough times, a picture will happen. Sometimes, you make just make one frame and it's magical but gets lost in the void.

Pass Two: Large View Review

Do not rate yet. Make the first photo in the set large. Then click through each photo, letting yourself respond to use of light, color, distance, compositional variability and degree of success. How much does your eye travel through the whole frame? This pass is the time to do the heavy lifting of getting over the experience of having made the pictures and starting to see them as photos. Let yourself mourn the failed photos that you hoped would work and start to recognize those that are working. Begin to let go of the middling and meager photos, no matter how important what they show is.

Pass Three: Large View, Rate 1 Star

Go back to the start of the photos at the large view and scroll through, giving your base rating to what you think are at least minimally successful photos. I use one star in Lightroom or tagging in Photo Mechanic. Some people use the select/reject keys in Lightroom at this point, but I think that muddles the process. Minimally successful means that of the five expressive means – light, color, distance, composition, moment value – a photo has at least some degree of success. You're setting a minimal professional standard for you work with one star. Another way of thinking about it is if this photo deserves to be seen ever again.

I respond to photos on a continuum. The first response is whether I feel anything from the photos or am engaged by what the photograph presents. I keep looking until I hit a fatal flaw, which is usually if more than one of the five criteria fails. If there are no fatal flaws, it gets a single star. A specific aspect to be attuned to is where your eye lands in each photo, the starting point. If it lands where you don't want to be the starting point, chances are that's a fatal flaw.

Don't agonize over giving similar photos one star at this point, include all photos that have some merit. That will give you more options when it comes to different uses of your work.

Pass Four: Large View, Rate 2 Stars

Now, bring up the photos you've rated as one star. If you can, take a break before jumping from rating the one stars and beginning the next pass; that will help further separate you from the making and refreshes your mind's eye. Go through the one stars large without judgment to assess what you moved forward.

Then, go through the one stars again and give two stars to photos that rise above others. Criteria are the same as those that made you apply one star, the standard is just higher. It's usually pretty clear which photos rise. Some will be hair-splitters; if you're not sure of whether a given photo deserves two stars, give it two for the sake of expediency.

Pass Five: Large View, Rate 3 Stars

Make another pass, this time rating better photos with three stars. Three stars is the level at which most uses of the photos you've produced will come from, meaning that you can sort the work to see three stars and choose from those to meet a given need. This is especially true of single efforts such as one-time assignment work. For ongoing projects or multiple-engagement efforts, three-star photos can be the base set to judge how the effort is progressing, what's working and what you need or don't need to photograph going forward. (More on the project-based aspects of selecting photographs later.)

Pass Six: Large View, Rate to 4 or 5 Stars

It can be helpful to sort to an even tighter, stronger set of pictures by rating the even-better photos with four stars. It's a good exercise to help refine your judgment of what qualities make for the strongest photos. If four stars still feels like a wide set, make another pass through the four stars and rate the absolute best at five stars.

It tends to be that the larger the set of pictures you start with, the more star rating levels, or steps, you'll have to pass through to arrive at the strongest set.

Pass Seven: Review Unselected Photos

Then go back through all the photos you gave no stars, to make sure you didn't leave behind gems.

Pass Eight (optional)

You can use the color ratings in software to further distinguish levels or categories of the work. (Some people use colors instead of stars in Lightroom as the base rating system so if you do, switch this step to using stars.) Colors can be helpful if you have rated to five stars and want to create the equivalent of six stars. Or if you have a subset of the pictures that you want to distinguish and be able to sort to, such as all the portraits or all the photos of a given aspect.

Once you have created a hierarchy in a set of photos, you can more easily assess what made the stronger photos successful and what kept the lesser photos from working well. It can be helpful to look at each of the four expressive means and how they play out in your strongest photos. From either single image view or a contact sheet/grid view, you can discern if the light is well seen, if color feels like it's an important element, if you've varied the distance between you and what you photographed, if your compositions vary and an overall impression of whether the set has high moment value. If any of the four is lacking, that tells you what you need to work on going forward.

One goal is to recognize what you are doing well now so you can repeat that going forward and understand why less successful photos happened so you can do that less often.

Inherent in this process is that once you create a hierarchy, you don't need to go back into the whole takes of photos, except to meet a specific need that the hierarchy won't fill. Over time, this process will build your selection skills and refine and expand your photographic skills.

If your entire archive is rated, captioned and keyworded, you'll be able to meet any future need efficiently by using search criteria that present your strongest work, the result of investing time in yourself.

Section 4.2 How to Sequence Photos

How photographs exist in relation to each other can be realized as an art form, by bringing to fruition visual raw materials into a form that elevates their creative, expressive process. Sequencing is usually thought of as one picture after another, and that is one form. A more expansive way to think about is creating relationships between a set of images. This distinction becomes more important as spaces in which images exist become less linear, and more three dimensional – the Van Gogh immersive experience is a pinnacle example, in this writing.

As with the entire process of creating photographs, the sequencing phase presents a spectrum of possible approaches, with the more informational/literal approach at one end and purely lyrical/visual/spatial at the other end. What the work is, who the audience is and where it will live determines where a given sequencing approach should fall on the spectrum.

Situations that tend to work better for informational presentations are those where you are talking as you present the pictures and the photos represent points you need to make. Chances are that in these settings, choices stem from some combination of what the photos represent and the quality of the photos themselves. Sometimes better photos are not included because they don't represent the points, the information, that you want or need to make.

Photographer presentations of their work at National Geographic fell on this spectrum – at least when I worked there. Some photographers determined what they wanted to say and chose photos to reflect what they were saying. Others created a lyrical flow of pictures that weren't connected directly to their words; others made the spoken word connect to the flow of pictures.

Another sequencing type is when you're representing a process or a journey. Sequencing tends to start at the beginning of what happened or the start of the journey and progress to the end. There can be magical connections between the pictures but making that happen is secondary to sticking with the progression of events.

A third type is when presenting more artistic photographs that are personal expressions, concepts or ideas. In those cases, I've found that the artist sees photos as what they represent conceptually, not in an informational way. Sequencing tends to build from one aspect of the concept to another. Sometimes I get this type of sequencing, sometimes not, because choices are as much about what's in the creator's mind as it is what the photos present.

My preferred form of sequencing is purely lyrical, letting the visually emotive qualities of photographs play into and against each other. When sequencing skews to the lyrical, other qualities of the set of pictures can influence the structure. Lyrical sequencing has the freedom to lean into the purely visual, tap the concepts and present informational aspects to make that third effect happen, creating more than the sum of the parts.

Nathan Lyons is regarded as groundbreaking among those who have taught and practiced the art of sequencing. As a photographer, curator,

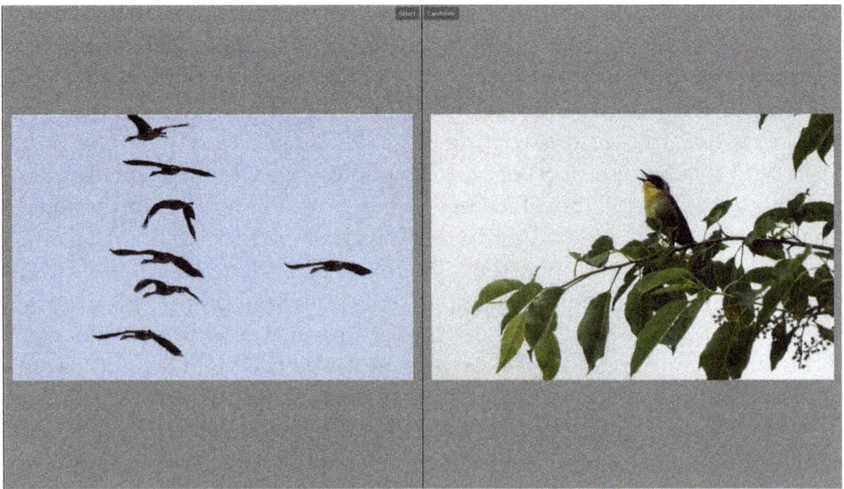

Photo 4.02 This is the compare screen in Lightroom. Move a selection to the left side and then scroll through the remaining selections until you see a compelling relationship between the two photos.

educator and founder of Visual Studies Workshop, Lyons explored the relationship between photographs, especially on the pages of books and exhibition spaces. I encourage you to learn more about him.

Three Approaches to Sequencing

A foundational sequencing form is placing photos one next to another and another... either successively, as in a slide show, or in a space, as in a grid or more random spacing. One or more aspects of one photo will typically carry forward or relate to the next. Elements that carry forward can be visual or what the photo expresses or both. The carry-forward can be similar – an aspect that picks up in the next – or opposite – something new – depending on whether you want a smooth, related transition or a contrast. (More on this coming up.)

Another way to think of sequencing is that you are creating a roller coaster ride for the viewer based on the experience of one image to the next. You can start with a set of pictures that build on each other and then slam people with a contrasting image, as if they were taking a dive on the coaster, then flatten out again and then a sharp left or right. The greater the range of photographs at hand, the greater the potential to create the coaster ride of your choosing.

Yet a third approach is to think of the sequencing as if you are creating a musical experience. If photographs can be musical notes or chords, then the sequencing of those photographs can be like creating a song. Some photographs will have a peaceful "sound" to them, others can be rowdy and noisy, some will whisper and others will blare, ad infinitum. You can treat groupings of photos as stanzas or movements that have their own statement within the piece, with either abrupt or smooth transitions to the next set.

Visual Variables of Sequencing

Here are some visual variables to consider, regardless of your approach to sequencing:

- How does the quality and direction of the light play from one photo to the next?
- How can you make color an important part of the sequence?
- How can you vary or keep consistent the distance from the camera to what is photographed, to convey a quality that is specific to the set of photographs?
- How can you make compositional aspects of the photos create an experience through sequencing?
- Can you pace the range of moment value in the photos to a desirable effect?

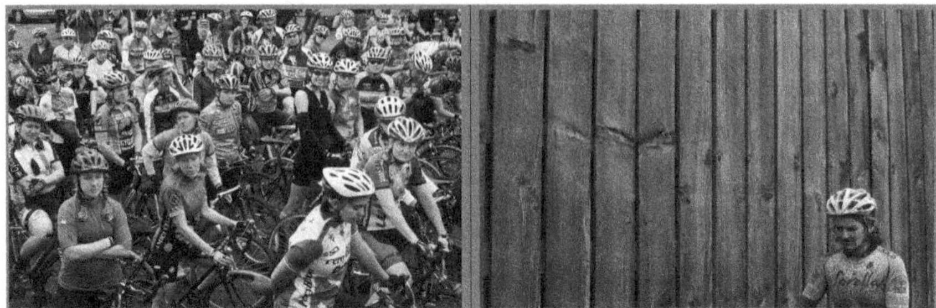

Photo 4.02.2 Tonality is the equivalent of color in black and white. Here, the contrast between the highly varied but repetitive tonalities on the left plays against the singular repetition of the wood on the right. The lone figure emerges from the right photo because of the contrast in tonality and because the idea of people was planted in the photo on the left.

Those questions come from the five creative means of photography. All five are in every photo, so while it's helpful to consider each separately, it is their sum expression that creates magical relationships between photographs. In the same way that it might have been difficult to consider all five as you were making photos, it takes practice to integrate your perception of all five as they affect sequencing.

Here's more on how each of the five plays into sequencing:

Light

Two connected dynamics of light that come to play in sequencing are its qualities and directionality. Quality of light is essentially the mood that comes from the image, emanating from the scene's light and how the photographer saw it. These are among the aspects of light that create qualities:

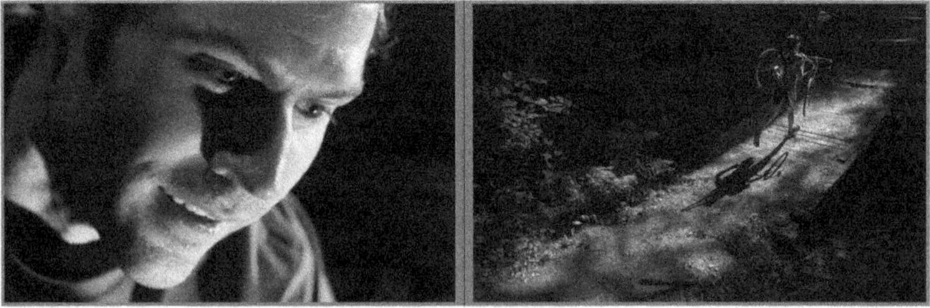

Photo 4.02.1 Directionality and quality of light can carry over one photo to the next or change. If light is the carry over, then, other means of expression generally change to create dynamic. In this case, distance and composition change.

Its intensity or volume; color temperatures that create unity or are jarring next to each other based on being warmer or cooler or by presenting opposing hues; high or low contrast; and high key versus low key. Directionality of light is an extension of presenting a quality in that you can keep the direction from which light arrives in the photograph consistent or change it. Directionality is an active process for your brain to engage with. The mind interacts with the spatiality that light creates, including its directionality.

Color

Color can create mood and spatial relationships and directs the eye within photos, each of which are critical to successful connections between photographs.

Mood from one photo to the next can remain consistent for a while and then gradually or abruptly change at any scale within a set of pictures, from dividing that set or flowing warm to cool to warm.

Playing the spatial sense that comes from the color layer of photographs can address a similar dynamic, going from consistent to changing with intention throughout the set.

Directing the eye through where color leads you into a photograph is one of the least considered variables yet has to the potential to create powerful dynamics. Making the eye travel to different points one photograph to the next can create a rhythm. At least be aware of how you're affecting eye travel frame to frame.

Sequencing considerations for color are as much about what you shouldn't do as what you should. On the shouldn't side, realize that if you put photographs next to each other that have a jarring or illogical color relationship, then you will deflate the power that sequencing offers, unless that's the point. This can happen if you put a photo with an abundance of bright colors next to one with muted color or a photo with colors that sit on one side of the color wheel next to a photo with colors on the other side, while your goal was to unify what the photographs convey. I regularly see sequences where the color just doesn't work. You can tell by looking at a contact sheet view of that set of photos and seeing no rhythm, consistency, or thread that the color creates. Instead of color unifying the set, it creates a sense of chaos and lack of intentionality when it's not fully considered.

Of note, a still photo sequence can use foreshadowing in the same way as films by putting a color or an idea or a quality of light at one point of the sequence and picking it up one or more times through the rest of the sequence.

Distance

Among the most powerful components of sequencing is the experience that comes from one photo to the next based solely on how far you as the viewer are from elements within the photo. That's why the more you stay

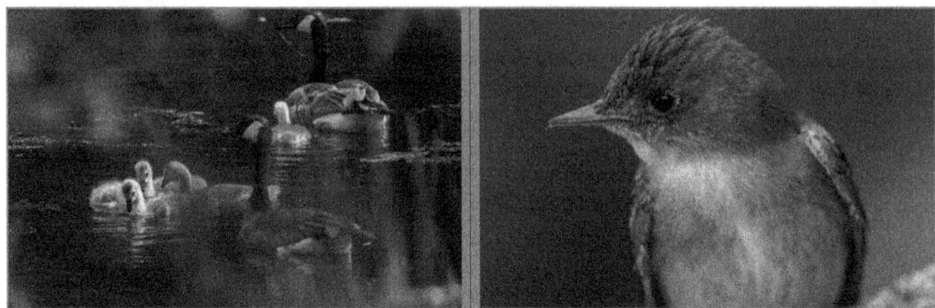

Photo 4.02.3 The photo on the left draws you into the setting while the one on the right comes out at you, because of how they're composed. Starting points and depths of space vary, too, to give a more dimensional experience going from one to the next. Though, both photos were made with the same long lens.

the same distance from what you're photographing, the harder it is to build dynamic sequences with your photos. If you do get close and further away and make photos from an observational distance, you can play those perspectives against each other during sequencing. Part of why varying distances creates varying experiences is that the size of objects within photos will vary, even offering the chance to see things larger than life.

Choices in sequencing based on distance are: Stay at a consistent distance for a few photos then change; vary wildly from one photo to the next; keep the distance similar throughout the sequence. Each approach is a choice you make based on what you're trying to say through the sequencing, whether it is to jar viewers or give them a non-confrontational experience or any other type of experience.

Composition

If composition creates a spatial experience within the photograph, then playing those spatial experiences from one photo to the next is a powerful tool. Among the experiences composition creates is a starting and leaving point within each photo, in tandem with color. Where you leave one photo is where you are likely to land in the next, so you can use this dynamic to direct people to where you want them to look throughout the sequence. Where people land can be the most important part of the photo, or the opposite if you want them to have to linger and find a new starting point. Varying the depth of the starting points within the frame from one to the next is equally strong. This plays on the variable of photographs either pulling you into them, jumping out at you or offering a neutral, observational experience. You can go along with a similar depth experience and then change dramatically, to offer a roller coaster experience or jerk people's mind's eye in and out to a dizzying effect. Or use any pacing to achieve the quality you want that aspect to convey.

Then there's the degree of complexity of compositions as a sequencing variable, from minimal visual elements to wildly full frames. Likewise, whether photos are spatially complex or work on singular planes and how varying that dynamic creates an experience from one frame to the next.

Keep in mind that how you sequenced a set of photos will not cry out or be apparent, the flow will just feel right and you'll get an experience that comes from the sequencing without even knowing it. That's the ideal anyway.

How to Build Sequences

Having a process in place to help you build sequences is critical and can help you consider all the variables. There's not one way to sequence and among the various approaches one might work for one set of pictures, and another might be better for a different set of pictures. Developing various ways and fine tuning them to match a specific group of photos is the trick.

Here are several ways that I've developed over the years to the best address as many sequencing challenges as possible.

Split Screen, a Lyrical Approach

The split screen approach works well for more lyrical sets of pictures because what puts one photo next to another is largely the visual qualities of each photo and how those qualities interact.

Here's the Process

Arrive at what I call a working set of photos for the sequence that you want to build. In other words, select what you think are the strongest photos worth considering to produce a sequence. I've found that number to be about twice what you want to end up with. So, if you're prepping a 12-photo contest entry starting with 24 is good; if you're editing a book sequence and you have a sense that it should be fewer than 100 photos then start with 200. And so on.

Choose an analog or digital approach, make prints or use software. With the working set in front of you, go through the photos and note which ones you think might work as the first photo in the sequence. Selecting the first photo is challenging; if the photo is too esoteric, it could confuse or put people off; if it's too literal or simple, it could invite viewers to leave. A middle ground is a photo that piques interest but also has context or is at least marginally clear as to what it conveys. W.M. Hunt, a collector, curator, consultant and teacher said during a PhotoPlus presentation that the first photo should both intrigue and inform, one without the other bores.

Next, put your choice for the first photo in the top left of the space you're working in – either digital or physical. Now, place every other photo in your selection next to that first photo and look for the third effects. Note relationships of the five things, how light carries over or picks up one photo to the next or the color plays off beautifully or contrasts or similarity photo to photo is magical or one leaps out and the next pulls you in… Create the second chord.

There might be several photos that sort of work in the number two spot, so set those aside and put just those next to the first photo in a second pass. Usually, one will stand out as the right one and there's a good chance that the contenders will fall in place soon after.

Move photo two next to one and start comparing the remaining photos to it. Determine number three and move it up. Repeat this process until you run out of pictures, the remaining photos repeat what you've already chosen, or you reach the number limit for this set.

Check the strength of what you've built as it progresses. Run a slide show after you have several photos in a row to see how that feels and then look again as it progresses. The larger the sequence, the more times checking the integrity of the edit in progress will ensure its strength.

Making the last photo in the set connect visually with the first one is an approach I call bookending. It's a variation of foreshadowing. Many settings where photos exist are looped "slide shows" so if there is a link between the first and last show the viewing experience will be even more complete and richer.

This approach creates a chain of linked photos – all these approaches do but this one is particularly chain linked. You'll find that once you've linked photos it can be difficult to add other photos into the group. It'd be like adding notes to a song that is just right. But it is possible to pull photos from the selections to get to a smaller number and still have the set retain the links if you have connected several of the variables with each of the links.

If you need to make several sizes of edits and you're using the split screen approach, it's most efficient to start with the largest set and then use it as the basis for the smaller sets – assuming each one exists to convey a similar narrative as the largest. It's better to pull photos from a larger group than it is to add photos to a smaller group because starting with a smaller edit is saying, "these are the absolute best photos," and you'd be adding lesser photos to the mix. In choosing photos, and sequencing them, it's an always-forward process that returns to lesser photos only for specific reasons.

Before locking into any sequence, return to the working set and determine whether any of those photos should be in the mix because they'd introduce something that isn't in the set yet or confirm that they're not necessary because you've hit their notes with your current selections. And let your sequence sit a while and then review it again to ensure you're happy with your decisions and selections.

Create Subgroups

For types of work that naturally form into subgroups, you can alter the sequencing approach by first pulling those groups together. Examples

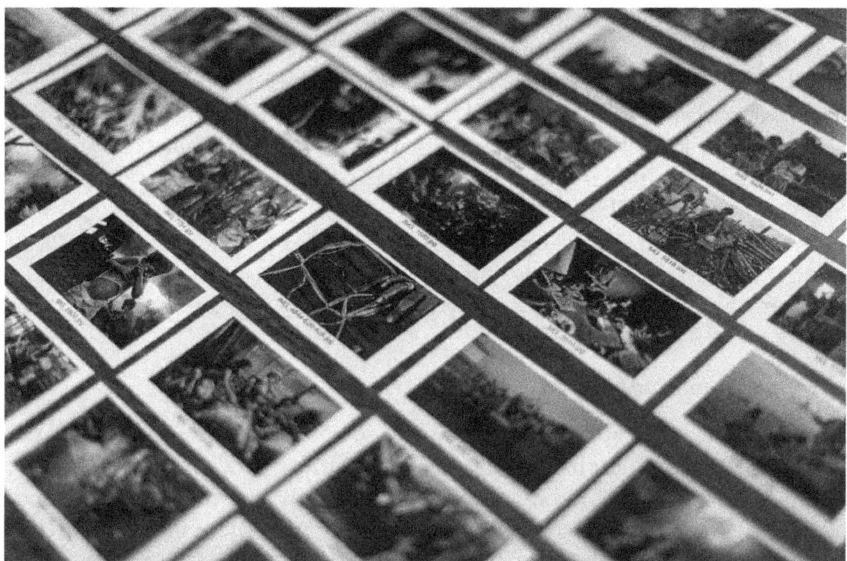

Photo 4.03 This is one way to determine a sequence, by laying out prints and seeing relationships. Photos by Lisa Wiltse.

of subgroups could be photos from a specific place, one person within a larger set, photos that share a quality, a time-based subset, a book or a presentation that breaks into chapters.

Once you've created the groupings, you can sequence each one in the same way as the split screen approach or anywhere on the spectrum between it and the informational/process approach.

Make Prints and Lay Them Down

Sometimes, it works best to lay down a working set of prints on a table or floor in no order – 4×6 prints are large enough, but some people use 8×10 prints if they have a space to fit them.

Start by looking for relationships, photos that cry out to be together. Use the same criteria of variables described above. When you find one or more photos that must be together, place them in order on another surface. Keep doing this until you either run out of photos in the working set or start to repeat what the selected photos say.

This process typically creates relational subsets of varying numbers of photos that work together well. The next step is to sequence the subsets. Inevitably one subset will flow well to or from another. Keep going until you've placed all the subsets. Sometimes, you will see better relationships as the process continues and can keep tweaking the overall sequence until it feels right.

Jason Eskenazi of Red Hook Editions told me this is how he edits books. He said he'll leave the sequence on the floor for a good while and may change nothing from the original choices or will change quite a few. It just depends on the project. He's among the best I've seen at this. So is MaryAnne Golon, director of photography at the Washington Post.

Some people tack or tape the working set on a wall but that tends to only work with smaller sets of pictures. It's too cumbersome to move a lot of pictures around like that.

You can do this spread-out approach digitally by bringing up a grid on the screen and moving things around but it is less effective because you can't see all the photos at once, unless it's a smaller set or a very large screen.

Create Columns and Learn

A more structured approach is to create several columns, or rows of the working set prints, each row representing some aspect of the work. How many rows there are and how many photos are in a row will tell you how diverse the group is and how much range of imagery you created. I'll also speak to using this approach during the creation of a project in the next chapter because it can be a useful tool to assess work as it progresses.

What makes for a row varies project to project, but rows can fall into photos from a similar setting, those of specific people, all photos that share a specific aspect of the project, photos made during the same time frame, or multiple photos that are nearly identical and need to be reduced in numbers. Many more possibilities exist; I hope you get the idea and can apply this notion to your project. You can split or unify rows as needed.

Next step in this process is to move the strongest photographs forward in each row. This helps you assess the strength of your work and creates a hierarchy in each row and, by extension, the working set. You'll most likely use more than one photo from each row, this just makes it easier to select only the strongest work for final inclusion.

Notice that there have been several steps in this process already and that each one was far from onerous. Like creating a hierarchy from a whole set of pictures, don't put too much pressure or try to go too far with each step. With the rows in front of you'll start to sense a structure for how to present the project and you'll likely see relationships between photos that you didn't before.

Next, start looking for relationships between photos that are in the same row and those that are in different rows, like pulling photos from the grid in the previous approach. Now move those connected/paired subsets forward and start to spread them out on another surface – I leave room directly in front of the rows so I can easily move photos about. Once you've completed your selections from among the rows and they're spread out before you, create a sequence from the grouped subsets, just like the grid approach above.

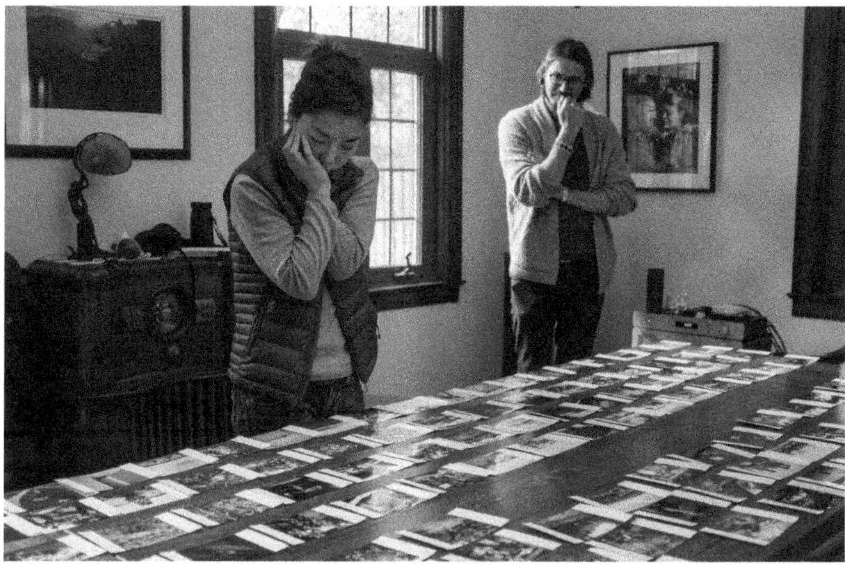

Photo 4.04 I worked with Aaron Elkaim to select and sequence his project about damns on Amazon tributaries into a book. Here, Deborah Pang Davis reviews our sequence. We started with about 250 prints spread out on the table and created a sequence of 64.

Regardless of your approach, a suggestion is to take a picture or screen capture as you think the sequence is complete, so you don't lose it or if you decide to change it but then reverse your decision. You can go back to what it was before you wiped out your brilliant solution.

You can mix and match these approaches to best fit a given set of pictures. For instance, you could open with a purely lyrical set of pictures that represent the range of the work and then drop into categorical or topical subgroupings. Processes are there to help you achieve a unique solution, not to be an approach applied.

Section 4.3 Variables for Different Uses

How you build sequences will vary with the type of space in which the sequences will live. The more complex the usage, the more variable the approach needs to be, and each use will require its own consummation.

Here are some approaches, based on several variables, including the complexity of uses.

You can sequence a handful of photos easily on screen just by moving them around and seeing relationships between photos and how pairings sit within the group. A larger number of photos takes a larger space and different process.

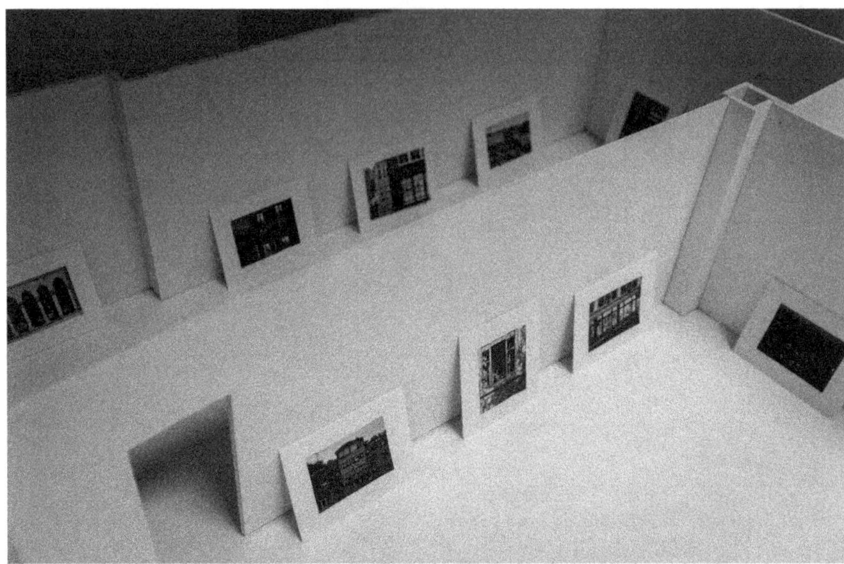

Photo 4.04.1 You can create a scale representation of an exhibition space and prints to work out how best to place photos, such as this at the Eastman Museum.

The space in which photos will exist influences how they're paired. Most of the examples in the previous section presumed a this-then-that relationship between the photos, like a slide show or spread of a book. If the space is physical, as in a gallery presentation, it's best to create spatial relationships within that setting.

I used to stop by the Eastman Museum in Rochester, NY, regularly and got to know some of the amazingly talented and brilliant people there. One day I met with Nick Marshall, the exhibitions director, and he was in the process of putting together an exhibition with Dr. Lisa Hostetler, curator in charge of the department of photography, in the main exhibition space at the museum. They created a mockup of the space using foam core pieces and small prints of the photos they were considering and had been moving them around in the space until they were happy with all placements.

For gallery presentations, I'd suggest narrowing your selections to a working set and then creating a scale of the space in a software program such as inDesign. That'll tell you how individual groupings work and how they fit into the overall space. It's easy to move photos around and change sizes, add more photos, or eliminate some. You can move to a three-dimensional mockup once you're happy with the digital version. To further refine the sizing and placement, you can make rough scale prints and place them on the gallery walls, if that's an option. Cutting out paper

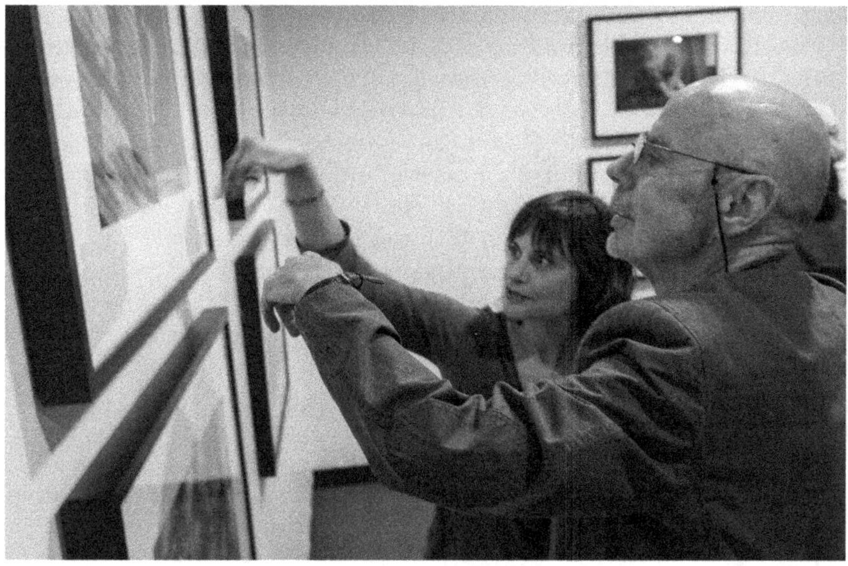

Photo 4.04.2 Eugene Richards and Dr. Lisa Hostetler talk about the photographs in his Eastman Museum exhibition in 2017.

or cardboard of the size of the exhibition prints and using them for placement and relationship refinements can be helpful.

Exhibition variables vary slightly from slide shows and books. You can see all of the work at once, generally, which allows you to create dynamics that viewers see only when looking at the whole exhibition. Equally important is how the photographs align on the walls, whether you use a hanging line, center or bottom-line alignment, or free form placement. Size of the prints is an equally powerful consideration.

Any one of the approaches described in the last section can be effective for book sequencing. And you can introduce more dynamic spatial relationships in books, as with exhibitions. Courses are taught about the art of creating books but let me mention a few critical considerations. Dimensions of the book are a starting point that you can determine by knowing how you want to present photos on the pages. If you want a photo to fill two facing pages, then the proportion of those pages combined must be the same as the photograph's format. Sizing the book is a function of the feel that you want people to have while holding it – and your budget, the bigger it is, the more it costs.

Decide how photos flow through the book by the experience you want people to have. Single images on a spread, either filling the pages or smaller, create a spatial feel, a pacing that is different from when photos face each. Facing photos play more directly against each other. Not all the photos have to be the same size or limited to a few different sizes. Being consistent in how you size and place photos on spreads is important.

Creating spatial relationships in a web environment tends to be either horizontal or vertical scrolling. Either of those can use one or more of the approaches described. More sophisticated renderings are happening, and those can be approached similar to an exhibition in terms of photographs being different sizes and being placed in different spaces within the web space. The web offers the additional tool of photographs emerging and fading at different times. What a blast to push the envelope.

It's exciting to see people who step out of platform-based presentations. High-resolution photographs projected onto the buildings or landscapes; large-scale prints being placed in a great range of spaces, multiple mediums existing simultaneously to convey more than either could alone; mixing historical processes with digital ones; playing with time and space and motion and stills to create truly unique experiences as expressions of what matters, oh my.

What is most exciting is that the approaches are becoming more varied to reflect ever more dynamic expressions. The medium may not be new, but the bar of quality is being raised by ever more dynamic forms of presentation as extensions of what's being said. People who can bring this greater range of creative expression to fruition are in demand more than ever.

Try This

- Select a set of photographs you've made but haven't created a hierarchy for. This is best if the photos are from a single session or from multiple sessions with the same topic or person. How large a set of photos you start with depends on the complexity you feel comfortable with for this exercise. Apply the hierarchical process described in this section.
- Take the upper tier of the hierarchy you just created and build three sequences with varying numbers of photos – one that is as large as the group of photos can sustain, one that is of medium size and one that is as tight a selection as possible that still conveys the essence of the set of pictures.
- Take the same hierarchy and build sequences that would live as a web presentation, one that would be in print form and one that would live in a physical space, such as a gallery. Then compare these sequences to the three you created for the second exercise.

Section 5
Creating Visual Narratives

Section 5.0 Introduction

People have been producing cohesive multiple image sets of photographs that represent and say things about whatever topic the individual embraced nearly from the inception of photography. Early on, documenting the Crimean War or the Pictorialist movement, which notably nurtured many photographers who were women, such as Anne W. Brigman, Doris Ulmann and Gertrude Käsabier. There are scores of notable, early practitioners but let me mention Florestine Perrault Collins, who depicted the lives of Black Americans in New Orleans and a specific body of work within the Creole community of New Orleans. I mention her because she was one of 101 women photographers who in the 1920 U.S. Census identified themselves as African Americans. And she was the only one in New Orleans at the time. Imagine what it took to go against those odds, then or now.

It's rare now that any paying entity requires producing a single photo to represent the topic or subject being photographed. Regardless of how you strive to make a living through photography, chances are that the people who would pay you to create photographs want at least a range of photographs, and, far better, a set that creates a visual narrative about what you photographed.

I was working with a photographer recently who does a lot of work for a major metropolitan newspaper, mostly photographing events, quick profiles of people, a set of photos about a place where something has happened, is happening or will happen that isn't tied to an event. Most of these happen with little advance notice.

The typical approach to any of these three types would be to photograph as many different aspects of what happened during the event or as many views of the place and person as possible so that the publication's editors could put together a selection of photos from what you've made that meets their needs.

Most photographers develop an approach that guarantees they'll make a range of photographs that "represent" what happened or who the person is in a way that primarily meets the needs of the person paying them

DOI: 10.4324/9781003287544-5

to make photographs. This is another form of default. Regardless of the event, place, or person this approach is likely to produce a similar range of pictures. Default event coverages tend to dwell on the "action" of the event, the perceived center of what is happening, by making several versions of informational/verb photographs of the core as the event unfolds. The resulting narrative structure is limited to process, a beginning, middle and end, or a straightforward representation of what happened. There's usually little variety in the photographs beyond the activity pictured changing.

When photographing people, default-approach photographers have a bag of tricks that they pull from to match the person and setting where photographs will be made. You can tell someone has a bag of tricks because no matter who they photograph, the set of photographs won't vary that much. When Hank Willis Thomas photographs people, he photographs each person uniquely and the underlying context of the set of photographs further elevates what we as viewers get from the experience of looking at them.

If you want to move away from a default approach change the why. Move beyond simply meeting the expectations of the people paying you to make pictures, exceed what they think they need and expand their impressions of your skills and what is possible to say. This is another form of elevating why you're making photographs to achieve greater outcomes, except now instead of striving to do that with the individual photograph, you're doing it with a set of pictures – and potentially other mediums – to say more. Expand what you want to say about what was in front of you by striving to produce a set of photographs that express a narrative as an extension of your informed, fully engaged, experience every time you go out with your camera.

That's what this section is about.

Section 5.1 What to Create, What to Call Them?

How people experience the whole of a body of work is the sum of all its parts. Regardless of how large that body is or how many parts there are, every aspect must contribute its own elements and qualities to the whole with the goal of creating third effects in a variety of ways. Sometimes that is a freestanding set of captivating pictures with no words, but the space in which the photos exist and how they're presented says a lot. Or the photographs might just have titles and/or captions. Other efforts may have words: Journal entries or short essays with titles and subtitles or it may be a set of associative words that sit next to images. Introduce motion and you further expand the experience by creating third effects.

A reminder that the third effect is the dynamics of when two or more images sit next to each other in a space, creating a relationship between the images that express more than either image alone.

Determining which media to utilize for a given project isn't an automatic process; that choice is an outgrowth of why you're creating a given body of work, with each medium there to convey specific qualities that add to the whole for a more dimensional representation of the why. In the same way that the making of images should be diverse and unique for every situation you photograph, the choice of what media you create should be unique to that effort.

The work of Geloy Concepción titled *Things You Wanted To Say But Never Did* is an example. Geloy started to embrace the idea of loneliness with his photographs – as reported by Picture Editor Michele Abercrombie, who was then at NPR and now works for the Wall Street Journal. At first, Geloy photographed his wife and daughter, then others, adding their handwriting to the pictures. He then expanded the project by presenting other people's photographs with their handwriting. The writing adds something unique and connects with the photographs in a way that enriches the experience beyond the separate parts, which is the definition of the third effect.

Josué Rivas' project *I Am A Future Ancestor* is another example of work that uses words imposed on images and more media to say more than photographs alone would have. (You might have heard the rule that says: No words on pictures. How absurd.)

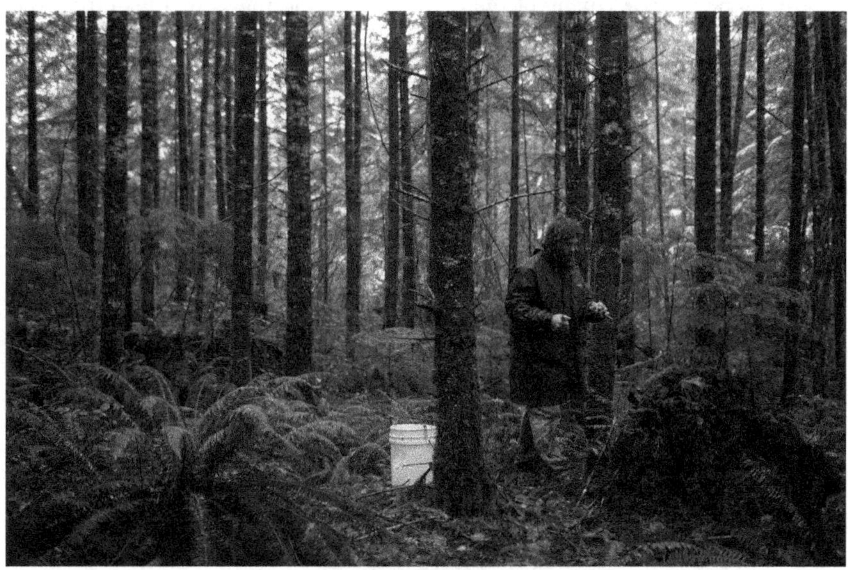

Photo 5.01 An interest in food grew to a passion for photographing all things food, for me, while living in Portland, Oregon. Each topic required a unique approach, but I saw the whole of work on the topic as being unified. Here, going wildcrafting, finding mushrooms in the wild with a family that gathers and then sells them at markets.

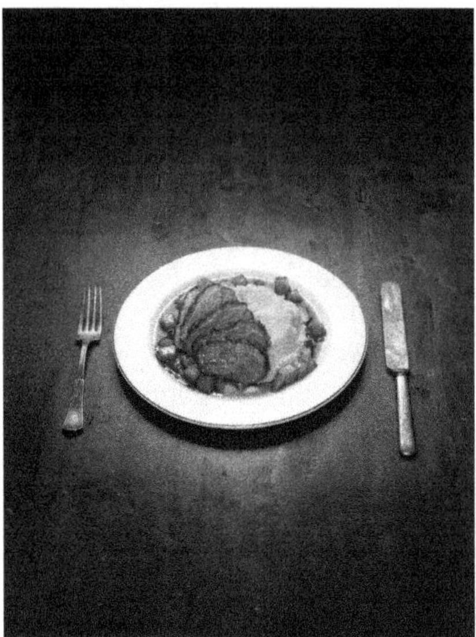

Photo 5.02 I chose to learn how to photograph food, here a soft box with snoot over the strobe from three-quarter back lighting position and a reflected light from the foreground for a story about holiday meals. The best part of many of these stories was working with a team that was often led by Martha Holmberg.

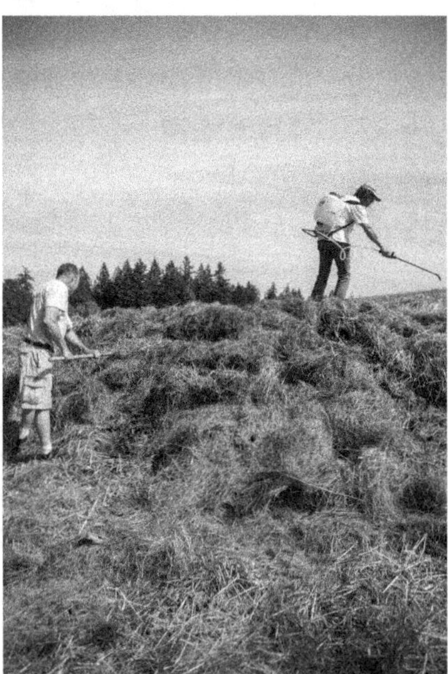

Photo 5.03 A story about biodynamic wineries proved challenging to convey what was unique, so, I tried to convey differentness through compositional tension. This is J. Christopher winery.

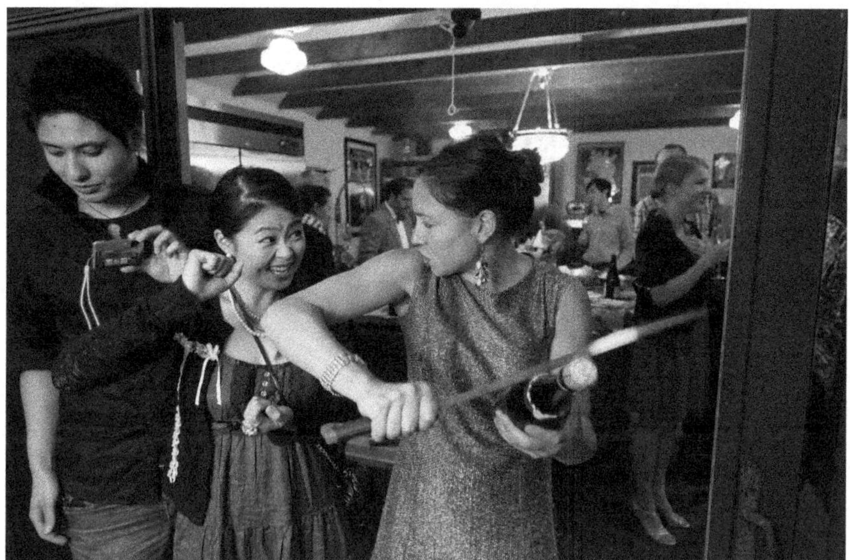

Photo 5.04 MIX magazine had a feature about people who host get togethers with great food. I jumped at the chance to photograph many of them. Here, Cheryl Wakerhauser, owner of Pix Patisserie, shows guests how to saber – opening a champagne bottle with a knife blade.

It's important to understand that choices of which media to utilize should not be genre specific. Medium choices don't have to be limited by the company that writes your check. Yes, photojournalism has traditionally been restricted to photographs with captions. Now, moving images are all but expected of practitioners, and as an extension, more people (probably) call themselves visual journalists instead of photojournalists. But still or video don't have to be the only choices, you can use other media as a visual journalist to convey what your photographs can't. You can write personal descriptions of what you witnessed and what it felt like to be there, you can collect freestanding quotes from people who were in the setting you photographed, you can create one-second video blasts that strung together convey the nature of what you photographed, you can write short word stories for posting to social media with your photographs. Whatever your creation choice, make it reflect the qualities of what you photographed and what you want to say.

I'll say it again: More and more people earn money from their work in more than one genre, they have multiple income streams. If you limit yourself to only producing photographs, then you also limit your potential income streams. The more imaginative you are in what you approach topically as you increase the diversity of mediums, the more homes that work will find, the greater the range of people who will want to hire you to create for them.

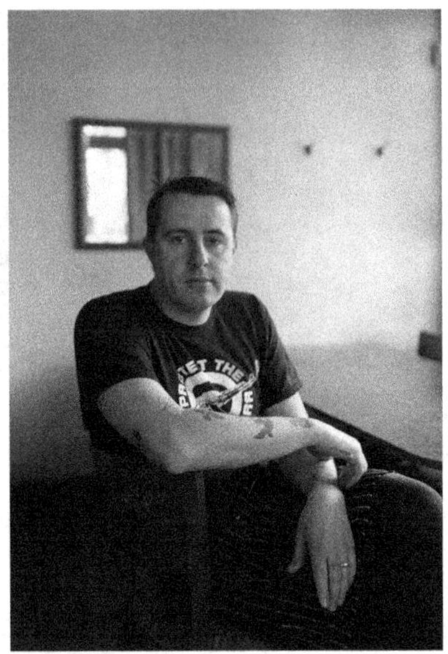

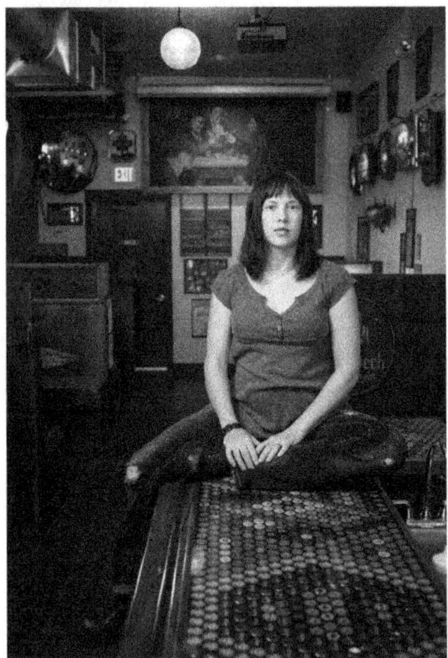

Photos 5.05–5.08 Portraiture was often called for as the best way to add to a story. Figure 5.05 is Gabriel Rucker of Le Pigeon, Figure 5.06 is Sarah Pederson of Saraveza Bottle Shop, Figure 5.07 is Carmen Feirano and Eric Ferguson, wife and husband owners of Fino In Fondo Salumeria, and Figure 5.08 is the daughter and father, Tahmiene and Moe Mombazi, winemaker and owner of Momtazi Vineyards and Maysara Winery.

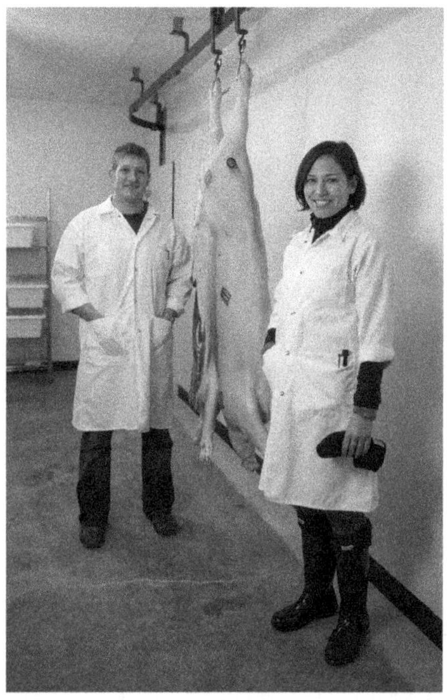

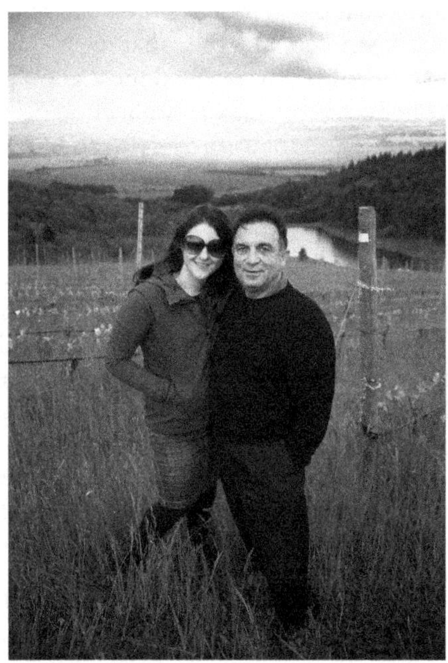

Photos 5.05–5.08 (Continued).

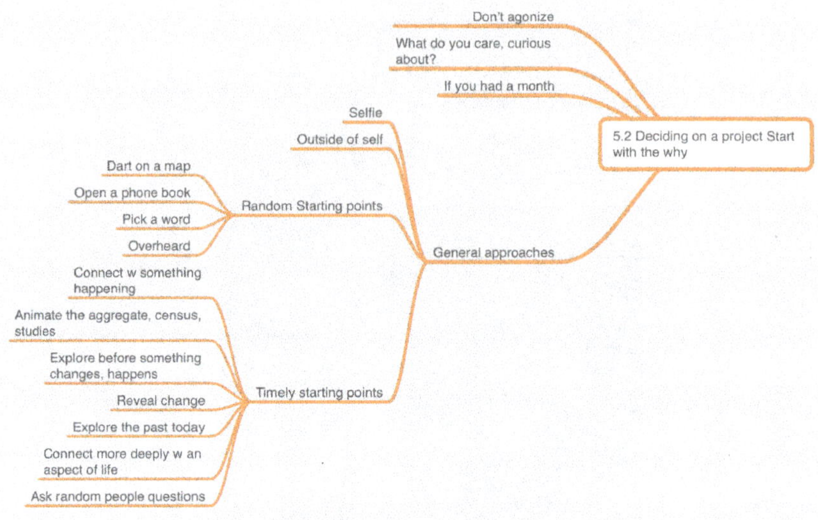

Photo 5.09 Here's the mind-mapped version of this section of the book, done in Mind Node.

This dynamic is why more and more people are also initiating bodies of work, based on the notion that if you produce the work that you care about – and it's good and has market potential – then that work will get you hired to produce more work like it, as long as you've done a good job of connecting with a market – stay tuned for more on that in Section 6 of this book.

With that framework, let me focus on a critical and often assumed or under-considered aspect of producing multiple image efforts: What do we call them?

What we call a given type of effort can be at least helpful, both for you as the producer, for those you're trying to sell the idea to and for those who will experience the effort. Your description of your effort sets everyone up for what to expect. Creating a description can also help you clarify what the work is about before and as you're producing an effort. If you can clearly, precisely and dimensionally describe what you're presenting, that's usually a reflection of the clarity you had in producing the work.

Descriptors can be a bridge, a welcome mat, that puts people in the right frame of mind to receive the experience. Or they can confuse, put people off or set people up with the wrong expectation.

There are two types of descriptors: There's the general term for the type of work you're producing and then the specific title for each body of work. Both should be unified in what they convey, one adding to the other.

Multiple image efforts have been called many things: stories, essays or picture stories, projects, bodies of work, portfolio, visual narratives, a shoot, my work, visual anecdotes, yarns, documentary and series. Stephen Shore uses the term serial imagery in his book *Modern Instances, The Craft of* Photography, citing the work of Bern and Hill Becher as examples. What you call your work reflects your personality, the context, scope and realization of the work and where it will live.

I shy away from using the words story or stories because they lean toward words as the primary medium, whether it's written or spoken. The descriptor *picture stories* was used to bridge between words and pictures in the same way that the word photojournalism did when it was created and now I've only heard picture stories used in a newspaper or wire service setting. Picture stories present a smaller set of photographs that address smaller topics, generally, and employ photographs and words to tell that story.

Project can work well to describe a specific, contained effort.

My favored term is narrative, with or without the word visual in front of it, to describe the result of the act of creating. If I said: "I'm going to tell you a story." Would your mind immediately think that I might show you pictures? Whereas if I said: "I'm going to present you with a narrative," you'd likely expect something more than words. Some people believe that the word applies only to single photos, so they prefer the term narrative series. For me, narrative means that you're creating and presenting multiple images and often several other mediums on a topic. The term speaks to the whole of an effort and its presentation.

A good source is the book *Telling Tales, Contemporary Narrative Photography,* especially the essay by Gregory J. Harris. You'll learn many things, including that historically not everyone believes that photography can create narratives, or stories.

Now, the NFT world is creating new dynamics in the selling of work and assembling communities, essentially new publishing environments that create their own nomenclature that is evolving day to day, such as the term contiguous experiences, to describe narratives created within NFT platforms to enhance the sale of the digital NFTs. Emergence of digital communities is in a sense a revolt against gatekeepers who increasingly took more livelihood from creators. Zun Lee: "At best, it galvanizes or coalesces a community around shared meaning. At worst, it becomes an extension of increased tribalization and dogma."

Similar considerations are happening in other evolving disciplines and their communities, including AI (artificial intelligence) and VR (virtual reality) and whatever metaverse means. When you read this, the metaverse won't be what it was when I wrote these words. Narratives will no doubt be a critical component of the metaverse as more and more of world experience becomes digitized into communities. There is great potential for those of you who are forward actors in this burgeoning marketplace for visual storytellers. (Thanks to Zun for helping me try to understand this.)

When I entered the profession, desktop publishing was brand new and those of us who embraced it were able to move the profession forward by leaps. You have the same opportunity today by learning about and adapting to new technology-driven possibilities, where you have the greater potential to own what you produce and introduce than giving your content for free to platforms such as Facebook and Instagram.

Visual realms will continue to expand, it's up to you to be aware of how you can be part of the evolution. One example you can see is at LDV Capital, a venture capital company that Evan Nisselson created to invest in nascent businesses that are exploring, creating and expanding new visual technologies. I've known Evan for nearly 30 years, and he has always been ahead of the forefront of ideas and technology that create new possibilities.

It's up to you to choose the terminology that best expresses what you're producing in whichever of the environments you place yourself. Better yet, create your own terminology that reflects your unique creative voice. How you describe what you're doing is not the goal, it is the outcome of achieving clarity in what you're doing based on why you're doing it.

Beyond brief descriptors, it's important to create several scales of pitches, from summary to fully realized representations. Regardless of scale, it's best to create written and verbal forms, freestanding delivery methods and those you present in person, with and without imagery.

Back to the spectrum approach to offer extremes of how to do this: At one end, you can simply say who or what you're photographing, why you're photographing it and why that's important, without embellishment; at the other end is the statement that tends to be simultaneously so esoteric as to be ungraspable while striving to be universal in a way that everyone should understand and the creator's motivation usually supersedes what or who is depicted.

A short example at the more straightforward end of the spectrum: I'm photographing x person because they are the last one alive who is x. Photographs were made over a period of x months. The project also includes journal entries and video snippets in a web-based presentation.

An abbreviated example at the opposite end of the spectrum: My project addresses how human anxiety is overwhelming our society. I've photographed the human condition as I perceive it to be in x countries. Each country is presented as a separate narrative. My opening, a written essay, gives context to the work.

You can use either or something in between, such as an anecdotal summary, but my suggestion is to shy away from the latter, the esoteric version. It sets up such a far-reaching parameter for the project that viewers may not comprehend. And why set people up to be turned off. Understatement with the certainty of why the engagement might interest a viewer and what they can expect is more likely to produce a positive response in the same way that more people are likely to respond to humbleness than boastfulness.

As you'll see in the section on grants, I suggest that you don't pontificate or preach or offer your opinions in presenting the focus and scope of a given effort – unless your personality is such that you can get away with this me-centric approach. Instead, be creatively straightforward and clear.

Tell them what your effort addresses, why that's important and what they'll see (which is the same as telling them what you've produced.) The scope of the descriptor can expand to match its reason for existing, to get support for the work. More on pitches in the coming section.

For you to get to a point of clarity in describing your effort, its focus has to be clear in your mind. It's not easy to create such a summary and chances are it will evolve as the work progresses. It is important to be as precise and focused as possible while being completely open to scrapping some or all of it as things move forward.

If a title for the project comes to mind at this point, write it down. But don't expect it to remain as is any more than the summary will stay in its first form.

Section 5.2 Setting an Effort in Motion

A lot of people struggle with starting an effort that leads to a complete narrative. With seemingly infinite possibilities, how do you even begin to choose one to lock onto?

You can start by asking yourself why you're doing a project, what's driving your narrative, what are your motivations, expectations, hopes? If you're a student and your answer is that you have an assignment that requires you to do one, then figure out a better answer and think beyond meeting the requirements of the assignment. If you're a professional and you know that you should be generating a self-initiated project but don't know where to start, stay tuned for more advice on how to define and get started on one.

What does it take from you to create a powerful visual narrative? They require a commitment on your part, don't go half-in. Curiosity, knowledge, understanding, desire, persistency, compassion and passion are among the qualities that will help propel your effort. If you don't feel committed, then you probably haven't defined a project worthy of your time. How do you get there?

Well, don't overthink this, or put such a burden on your expectations that you'll never even get started on something because there are so many layers to penetrate. Redefine the why of creating a project in a way that lets you engage with something you can be passionate about and committed to. Knowing why you are the right person to take on a given topic is a starting point.

Ask yourself what having a completed project could accomplish for you and let that direct the focus of an idea and its creation. For instance, if you know that you want to work for a specific entity, then developing a project that would appeal to that entity is a good starting point. If you are passionate about experiencing the outdoors in a particular way and always wanted to work for Patagonia because you respect what they make, for example, then you'd start by learning everything possible about Patagonia: What the company values are, what kind of work they present, who is in charge – Heidi Volpe is their director of photography at the time of this writing – and what's her background/taste/personality, look at who they hire now and connect with one of them to ask how they connected with the company. That will help you shape an idea and define what to create.

You can also approach something you've always been curious about or something that you care about or wondered about or revisit something you passed by that piqued your interest but didn't stop for at the time.

Levingston Lewis was struggling with what project to do for a visual storytelling project development and editing class I taught at Syracuse, as did many students. Lev was among the active-duty military students who get to spend a year at Syracuse to elevate their skills and then return to active duty. So, I asked him: If you had a month to spend however you wanted, how would you spend that time, where would it be and what would you be doing? It was as if he were 10 years old, and I had said he could have anything he wanted for Christmas. Flyfish was his answer. Flyfishing was full of memory and tradition and passion for Lev. His project idea was clear; he was freed from the burden of expectations and limitations.

We Are the Work We Create

The underlying notion is that your *why* can be to use narratives/projects to define your professional self. If you are the work that you create, then let the work you create reflect your self and what you value.

If you're a professor and you're creating course assignments – beyond the basics – that require everyone to produce the same kind of work, then you're not allowing students to achieve their potential; the assignment is more about you and what you think is important for you to teach them than it is allowing students to learn and develop uniquely. Assignments should help students define their professional values and path by allowing them freedom in the choice of what to produce. Learning that results is deeper and wider because it will be self-motivated, not stipulated.

If you are a student, then go beyond meeting the requirements of your course assignments; make your execution of the assignments rise above that to produce work that propels your unique voice and path into a professional path that you define.

If you are a professional, you can use this creation process to realign your existing career to connect with paying clients or employers that are more in line with what you value, as opposed to just doing work that pays.

If you are clear in what you want to accomplish through a project, and why you're doing one, then coming up with an idea will be much easier.

Other Starting Points – to Selfie or Not

Another way to think about ideas is that they are either selfie in nature our outside of self, meaning that ideas can come from your life directly or not. During the Covid-19 pandemic, proportionally more self-based projects have been done because it just hasn't been safe to venture into public spaces or other's lives openly.

Selfie doesn't mean that you're pointing the camera at yourself, necessarily. It just means that your own experience or life is the starting point of an idea. For instance, photographing your family members, such as Nancy Borowick's work photographing what became the end of her parents' lives as they exuberantly existed with cancer. Or the immense body of work by Dìana Markosian called Santa Barbara, a film, book and interactive presentation about her life growing up. Or when your work is about aspects of where you live, such as that of Alejandro Cartagena.

The value of doing such work is that you start from an informed place. The danger is that the work just becomes about you; the challenge is to express things from your perspective that others will find valuable. For example, there's a personal nature to the work of Sophia Nahli Allison that informs and guides her rich and provocative work but most of it is not of her life.

Random Starting Points

Put a map on the wall, close your eyes and throw a dart at it. Go to the place where the dart landed, find a phone book for that place and open to a random page, then close your eyes and let your finger pick one of the residents. Call or visit them and do a story on their life and/or where they live. Les Rose, now a professor at Syracuse University, said he and Steve Hartman used this approach for their years-long series *Everybody Has a Story* and not once were they refused.

Pick a word randomly out of the dictionary and illustrate what that word suggests or means or conveys.

Go somewhere public, such as a bus stop or a golf course or a high school basketball game or outside a courtroom. Listen to what people say and start a project based on something you hear, something specific or connect dots that from what several people are saying.

How about randomly asking strangers questions and seeing where that leads you? A version of this is to photograph someone and then ask them who you should photograph next, just to see how connections play out.

Timely Starting Points

Or, if you want your project to be more timely because that's more appropriate to your specialization, connect with something as it happens. This can be a news event such as a storm, but you stay connected with those affected as they deal with the storm's aftermath. Todd Heisler did this when working for Copley in Chicago. Among the memorable photos was a high schooler in a prom gown with her date stepping over the downed tree that fell on their house.

You can explore a place and become known in that area before something significant happens. Lianne Milton moved to Rio de Janeiro before the Olympics happened there, knowing that there would be heightened interest in the city. She started producing narratives that then got her assignments with a range of publications and organizations.

Noting change is another approach. This can play out in a great range of ways, either noting change as it happens in the short or long term, using historical images compared to today's circumstances, or starting today to engage with something that's going to change in the future.

You can aggregate and interpret data and studies. Read the census, and you'll learn that two-thirds of minimum wage earners are women. That's the starting point for a project.

Try exploring the past. I remember a New York Times story where they found all the living *Marlboro Men.* Not surprisingly, some had died of cancer.

Connect with an aspect of life, such as manual labor or street fairs or cosplay or medical school, suburbia, athletics …

The *est* is another. Meaning that you can look for extremes in each topic: the biggest, oldest, longest, most important, groundbreaking …

Or you can read *The Photographer's Playbook,* an Aperture book edited by Jason Fulford and Gregory Halpern. There you'll find 307 assignment ideas.

I also find Claire Rosen's book *Imaginarium* fascinating as she talks about how she comes to ideas and executes them as bodies of work.

Section 5.3 How to Know If It's Worth Doing

How do you know if a project is worth doing, whether a narrative thread has enough substance?

Questions are helpful: Will anyone care, beyond you, about what you produce? Another way of asking this is, will there be a market? Will anyone pay you for your effort? (Stay tuned for more on market variables in Section 6.)

Another expression that can help: If this were a movie, would anyone buy a ticket? The movie reference is real. Projects should have many of the dynamics that make movies notable. And more and more photographers are producing feature-length films. I mentioned Dìana Markosian's *Santa Barbara*, another is Janet Jarman's *Birth Wars* and Jimmy Chin's academy-award winning film *Free Solo* and, more recently, *The Rescue*.

Is there present-tense dynamic to the scenes and the people you'll be engaging with? Usually, that's considered as a factor of whether enough is going on that will produce compelling imagery and other mediums. Another way to say this is: Did everything that makes a topic interesting happen in the past, and there's not much to photograph now? The past aspects might make for a great pitch but lousy photographs in the present. You can overcome the lack of present tense by using an illustrative approach, portraiture and other mediums. Books that deal with non-present-tense-based approaches include Álavaro Laiz's *The Hunt*, Amani Willett's *The Disappearance of Joseph Plummer*, Pascual Martínez and Vincent Sáez's *The Tree of Life Is Eternally Green*, Christian Patterson's *Redheaded Peckerwood* and the now-classic *Kitchen Table Series* by Carrie Mae Weems.

Another way of gauging worth is considering whether there is enough change or conflict within the topic, setting or lives of what you're approaching. Some people begin and end with this notion and say that stories must have conflict and resolution, that there must be transformation. That's certainly one approach among many possibilities. A variation of that notion is whether there will be uncertainty or surprises during the flow of what you photograph? If everything is predictable, it's less likely to be compelling, whether you are using a documentary or illustrative approach, fiction/non-fiction, or some combination.

Above all, you must be passionate about and committed to what you initiate.

Section 5.4 Considerations of How to Approach Creation

A given visual effort sits at its beginning with infinite possibilities of how to approach the topic, place or people. Though specific genre has codifications or automatically limits approaches in some ways, it's still better to expand the scope of how you create work so that it will have more spaces in which to live and can appeal to a wider market.

Combining multiple approaches in one project can be as simple as photographing things as they unfold in front of you and, in some cases controlling a setting. The latter can be to try and represent something that isn't possible through documentation. LaToya Ruby Frazier uses a variety of approaches in her multi-year body of work, *The Notion of Family,* with portraiture, documentary, controlled settings, aerial and landscape imagery. Students in courses I taught would sometimes mix captured and controlled image-making with powerful results. One was Laura Oliverio, who was inspired by Julia Blackmon's work. Laura photographed the life of a girl over several months. Most of the photos were of life and interactions with people and settings as they happened, but sometimes Laura would be struck by something she understood about the girl and she would create a setting to express that quality. Her work can be published in a variety of settings because of the combination, though in journalistic uses, she'd have to limit to submitting *documentary* photos.

As an artist, what you're expressing drives how you'll produce the work, without limitations.

Approaches and Forms

Though there are infinite possibilities to a unique approach to your project, there is a pull-down menu of sorts that offers a starting point. In the broadest sense, here are the primary three again: place, person and idea/concept.

Within the three, here are some more ways to think about the approach:

Essay involves creating a series of images and other media on a theme, where each image or subset of photos contributes to the overall idea, concept or quality that you're conveying. That can be as simple as photographs of people who share a quality such as height, or address loneliness, or the loss of agricultural land. Will Matsuda utilizes the essay form in much of his work. As does Erica Deeman in her *Brown* series.

Then there's flow of life. You enter people's lives or stay connected to a place long enough to create a complete narrative. The more dynamic the lives of the people and the more qualitative the settings, the stronger your pictures are likely to be. Regardless of the setting, it is your ability to produce compelling photographs and weave them into a tapestry that determines the strength of each image, each medium and the resulting narrative.

KayLynn Deveney's *The Day-To-Day Life of Albert Hastings* is a beautifully lyrical set of pictures made in the apartment of an elderly man, hardly an inherently compelling setting.

How many mediums should you utilize, beyond making pictures in one or more ways? Why you're creating each effort will determine whether photographs alone accomplish your intentions. If photographs aren't enough, think about what you are trying to address or speak to and what would be the best way to convey that or those things. I'm thinking of a project that Josh Ives accomplished while in one of my classes. Josh retired from the U.S. Navy after 24 years and then returned to get his undergraduate and then graduate degrees. To fulfill one assignment, he returned to the thousands of photos he'd made while working as a supervisory medic in Afghanistan. He was trying to express and resolve his personal experience of war and realized that photos alone didn't impart the whole, so he also integrated his orders, the daily agenda notes, poems from an Afghan poet he'd gotten to know and other missives from that time. The whole was greater than its parts. *NPR* (National Public Radio) published his piece.

Rather than suggest mediums for you to use, just know that you can devise your own that are specific to what you want to say. Give yourself permission to explore without feeling cajoled by the rules of a genre.

How Many Versions?

You may be able to produce one iteration of your project. Increasingly, people are creating multiple versions, each to work in a specific platform or environment or unique expression of the topic. Knowing what kinds of spaces, you want your work to exist in can help determine what mediums to develop for each use. Start by clarifying what the grandest expression of the work would be. Maybe that's a book, a website, an interactive presentation in a three-dimensional space, massive prints displayed publicly, leaflets you hand out, postcards you mail to people to engage and connect them with what you're working on. That last approach is one Anastasia Taylor-Lind used for her *Donetsk* project. Then consider what other, smaller expressions would be venue-specific, add to the effort or be helpful for promoting the project.

Working with two photographers to select and place photos for their gallery exhibitions made me realize anew that what drives decisions, the real goal, is to fully realize what the work speaks to in the spaces where it lives. That might seem obvious but so often we go into production mode with preconceptions of how a given medium looks and we plug our work into that mode. Achieve higher states by making your version unique, specific to what you want to communicate. A helpful way to think of this is to separate the purely process aspects of producing a medium from creative decisions. Every way of presenting narratives has inherent physical processes that you have to learn to be able to use that space. How you use the space is the creative process, which has to consider the limitations and possibilities of the physical processes but is also separate from them. This dynamic is like knowing how cameras work in the service of making more creative photographs.

Questions to Ask Yourself

It's important to know whether the project or narrative you're creating has been done before – chances are it has. But how many times? Is it to the point of being a cliché? If so, then how will you create your work in a way that rises above the standard set by the cliché?

One way is by researching the topic generally and the specific aspects that you'll be engaging with. Become an expert on your topic and create work knowingly. Your effort should involve more than just looking at other people's work. It can rise to the level of actual research by doing formal or informal surveys on the topic that asks for people's understandings or practices, or opinions as they apply to what you're taking on. Learn about your topic deeply, not just how others have photographed it. That was one of the joys of working at National Geographic. Both photographers and picture editors had to become "experts" on the topic being photographed. Look beyond visual disciplines to those that have been addressing your topic for decades – visual approaches tend to develop as responses to current conditions.

How do I challenge myself to say more than x, y and z happened in front of my camera? In other words, the burden of going beyond presenting information through photographs is even heavier for projects than it is on a single image. It's easy to produce a set of photographs on a topic that don't say much in the same way that you can go to a grocery store, by a bunch of ingredients and then not be able to make a meal from what you bought.

Should I partner with other people to make this effort happen more completely? It's becoming more common for there to be multiple authors and contributors on efforts of all sizes. So don't think of creating a team as a shortcoming on your part; there's no way any of us can be proficient in creating work for all media and all aspects of its creation. The nature of your project will suggest who could be an additive voice, what medium would enrich the result. Build a team as needed, from those who join the team at the beginning to later in the creation process or in the post-production phase.

Who would pay you to produce this work? Or, if you are planning to produce the project without support, who would pay to publish or present or support the work after it's realized? Knowing where work might exist can help define, confine, or expand the creation and production process. It's like knowing where you're going can help you prepare for the journey and take the best route to get there.

Kainaz Amaria, the national visual enterprise editor at the Washington Post, offers these questions: Why should you tell this story? What stories have previous images told? Have there only been repeated tropes and if so, how can you approach the telling in a way that breaks the trope? Should you be collaborating with the people you're telling stories about, or other people who bring other skills and how can you do that in new ways?

"You must have a willingness to share your expertise, to collaborate and to grow to tell stories in new ways," Kainaz says.

Now, I hope you're ready to start making the work happen, thus, the next section picks up with creating the work.

Section 5.5 Creating the Work

In the same way that figuring out how to get going on an effort can be challenging, knowing the best approach to creating the work can be fraught. One default approach is to just start making pictures of whatever seems worth photographing and stop when you stop. But that's less likely to be successful for most people than a structured and defined approach will be.

The creation spectrum's end points are structured or unstructured.

Unstructured Approach

With the unstructured way of going about creating a narrative, you'll identify something you want to connect with. That can be as specific as the life of a single person or as general as the idea of home. You can choose to learn as much as possible or very little about what you're going to photograph. Your passion, interest, curiosity and personality propel you into settings. Once there, you make experiential photographs. Photos will tend to be as much a reflection of your personality as they are of what you photograph. Your camera is a shopping cart, the topic is the grocery store, and you wander the isles filling the cart with whatever looks appealing.

Resulting photographs from the unstructured approach will be the starting point for defining the actual narrative that you're going to create. In editing parlance, this is creating a narrative, or an arc, from the photos made, as opposed to doing it while creating the work. You discover the story within the photos, in other words. You may decide to add other mediums at any point and figure out the best way to present the work toward the end of the creation process. It's a self-revealing narrative process that requires you to completely enmesh yourself with what you're photographing. The engagement can be for long or short durations of time. By lingering in settings, the hope is that surprises happen while you're there. Or, if you have gotten to know the person or setting or idea that you want to photograph, you may learn when things happen, so only need to be there then. A combination of lingering and right time is usually best.

Structured Approach

Here's one way to help define the narrative that brings structure to what to photograph and how to photograph. Some people call this a shot list, but that derogatory term tends to apply to pretty simple topics and short-term efforts; a more complete terminology is calling this developing a coverage plan, a term with roots in editorial storytelling. Minus terminology, this is just a determined way to help you produce a more predictably representative set of pictures on a topic and consider alternative types of content and presentation earlier in the process.

Start by learning everything you can about what you're going to photograph. Learning happens before you start photographing, by reading and talking to people who know more than you do, by getting to know the specifics of what and who you want to engage with, whatever it takes to become familiar with the topic. This often breaks into things that happen or are done and qualities of person, place, or event. Learn the past, present and future, the good, the bad, likes and dislikes, personality traits. Know what's going to happen when, why things and people are as they are, what are the qualities that make them what they are?

I suggest writing down all that you've learned in bullet form, one-to four-word summations in a long row. Then look for connections between the items you've written down and literally draw connecting lines between them. You can use different colors of pens or markers to make it easier to recognize the connections. Most projects end up having three to five larger groupings that emerge from this connective process. You can call these themes, but thematic thinking can be limiting; just call them groupings for now and be more specific when you perceive what each grouping represents in the context of the whole, the actual narrative that you can tackle, which will reveal itself from the groupings.

Once you start to perceive the groupings, I suggest drawing a circle for each of them. Think of each grouping's circle as a pie, and the individual items from your original list will become pieces of that pie. Instead of photographing everything on the list you created, you'll choose what is more relevant and telling. Each piece of the pie is what you'll choose to photograph or qualities you're striving to reflect within the group of photographs. The grouping of the pieces forms a complete expression of whatever the whole pie is about.

If you have three or five different groupings that you've carefully considered and determined to reflect the essence of your topic, then it's likely that you'll be able to discern the overall focus of your project and the narrative approach to achieve its expression. This will evolve as you continue to learn more as you engage more.

I promised to say more about Levingston Lewis' fly fishing project in this section. His starting point was a narrative about the passion of flyfishing. Lev's research told him that the best place to photograph fly fishing in central New York was the Salmon River. He learned everything he could about the river's history, unique qualities of places people fish, who fishes, who makes their living from fishing, environmental concerns, where fish come from, what kind of gear people use that is unique to that area and on and on. That was his list. From that, he surmised that the groupings dealt with the Fishing Experience, the Culture and Business of Fishing and The River itself, as if it were a personality. This process also helped him understand the importance of depicting the river in different seasons, which introduced a much greater dynamic to the body of work and lead him to settings and circumstances that he wouldn't have gotten into by just wandering about. Lev was able to approach the making of photographs for each of the groupings knowingly. They gave him a clear starting point and context for how to make photographs in a way that went beyond simply showing what's happening. There were more dots connected.

This structured approach also helped Lev determine that the best outcome, or expression of the project, would be a book, which lead him to create a written narrative stream that flowed through the pages of the book.

It's important to note that this structured approach is focused on producing a dimensional, complete set of photographs and any other mediums you choose, from which the outcome or outcomes are produced. Knowing how you want the work to be presented can help inform how to produce more dimensional work, the end meets the beginning somewhere in the middle. This approach ensures that you have the ingredients you need to produce delectable results.

The selection and sequencing of the photos in Lev's book did not follow the groupings, it was a more lyrical sequencing that played the qualities of one image to the next, with some linked subsets.

I started to more fully understand how to approach topics while at National Geographic and continued to evolve my understanding and ways of creating ever since, exponentially in a teaching environment.

You can use this structured approach regardless of the scale of your effort or what you're going to address. Use a chunk of your time to learn things, then surmise what you can say. Then make photographs that express as much range as possible in the remaining time you have, knowing how that work will be used. Instead of the multiple pie groupings analogy, a shorter engagement is like producing one pie and you decide how many pieces of pie there are and what each one conveys.

Another historical reference for how to structure what you'll produce is Roy Stryker's Script For A Small Town, which he created to help guide Farm Security Administration photographers.

You can use mind mapping software to help create structure and see relationships.

Determining whether to use a structured or unstructured approach is an individual decision based on the combination of variables: Your personality, the complexity of what you're taking on, how much time you have, how many different aspects you could address, your hopes for how the work is expressed and what it accomplishes, expectations of the people who might be paying you to make the work.

A hope is that each successive project you produce is a greater expression than those before it, that you learn from each effort and apply learnings to the next in an endless stream of growth. By challenging yourself to produce ever-more prescient narratives, you can increase the likelihood of ever-growth.

Characteristics of Story

As Garry Winogrand said, "Story? Just get someone in trouble and get them out of it."

Think of the Cinderella story as the classic narrative structure. Her life starts out miserable, rises to a peak at the ball, crashes back to her awful life and then rises again when the valiant prince saves her. There they are, the most common traits of storytelling: A plot, a story or an arc where characters drive the narrative and a setting that provides a telling backdrop for conflict that does or doesn't get resolved; a moral or mores of social value presented as the overarching point of the story. I'd add universality to this list, meaning most people can find something of merit in either the topic or the approach to it. The narrative elicits responses from viewers.

The challenge is that this list can come off as a formula that you just need to apply to what you're engaging with, and it'll produce a successful effort. While this might be a helpful list, don't consider it like a formula, it's more of a reminder of things to consider. Your project can easily exceed or break from this form of storytelling.

In the non-fiction storytelling world, fewer stories have these narrative qualities, but the potential is there. Be aware of how situations and people might introduce at least some of these dynamics. Picture stories that deal with ill people tend to have these qualities, and among that category, the sick child is the most trodden. All of the above characteristics are automatically part of stories about ill children: The plot is that they recover, or not; the child is the primary character, and parents, caregivers and others are supporting characters; the hospital setting is loaded with known conceptions, and the likely moral is universal: love sustains, or the loss of a child is the deepest felt.

An exception to the sick child cliché is Deanne Fitzmaurice's long-term narrative about the life of Saleh Khalaf, whom she got to know with camera in hand starting in 2003, soon after 9-year-old Saleh was severely wounded while walking home from school in his Iraqi hometown. The depth and years-long duration of Deanne's connection with Saleh rendered a rich narrative. Her photographs tell the story of an innocent life forever changed by war. The immense sweep of what the work expresses, beyond his wounds and recovery, is what makes Deanne's narrative rise above cliché.

Types of Narrative Forms

I mentioned some of these in the last chapter but present them here as a collection of narrative forms so you can get a sense of the range in one place. First, understand that subject matter does not a story make. You may engage with something that appears to be fascinating and active and you throw yourself completely into the setting with your camera blazing but then come away with a set of photographs that says nothing beyond representing the activity. This is the danger of a completely unstructured approach. Know why you are creating the work, what you can speak to and determine the best form to weave that narrative thread into a complete, incisive form.

Here are the preset story forms: Conflict with or without resolution; process; character development; essay that presents an idea or concept or connected/shared/disparate aspects; a combination of these; an original form that is none of the above.

Section 5.6 Realizing the Effort, Start to Finish

Editing a photography-centric effort involves the whole of the process: defining the topic, what narrative form to use to tell a specific, dynamic story, figuring out what to photograph and how to photograph each aspect, creating a hierarchy of the work every time you've made a set of photographs and assessing the work you produce as it moves forward. Assessment is best when multi-dimensional. Here's a series of questions that help you assess your project as it progresses:

What can you do to increase the number of photos at the top of the hierarchy, those that are most successful? Determine that by assessing what you're doing well and what you're doing that keeps photos from succeeding. If you don't self-assess well, ask others for their thoughts and impressions, or engage a visual editor.

Is the work you're producing adding to the narrative completely? Is the work you're producing a complete realization of the thematic groupings that you created, using the structured approach described in the last section? Place selected images into those groupings as the work progresses and ask if there are still holes, things you need to photograph. I use Lightroom for this process, creating one collection set for the project and then collection sets that reflect the groupings and collection sets within each grouping that reflect the pieces of that pie and collections for each piece of that pie. I rate each of the photos with one to three stars, as described in the editing section of this book, so can then select or sort by any number of star rating for each tier of the project, from a collection up through the tiers of collection sets.

Is the narrative form you determined to take still the best approach? Have things changed in what you're photographing enough to warrant a shift in the form, or are you on track as is?

Should you consider introducing other mediums that could help elevate the narrative? Did some lightbulbs go off that suggest other things that you could speak to, but photographs aren't getting you there? If so, what mediums would allow the expression?

Should you bring others onto your team to produce the other mediums or help you edit the work you're doing? If you're feeling stressed or that you can't say what you want to say by yourself, get help and make a team.

Is the outcome that you had considered as the best way to present the work still the best way, and if not, what's the best way to present the work? This adjustment can be small or large, completely dumping what you thought would work, or simply tweaking it. Try building a sequence from each of the groupings to see if they hold together. Or build a sequence from everything you've done so far and see if the bones of the project hold together. You can see what's working and holes that need to be filled. These interim sequences are just that, discard them after they've served their temporary purpose and start anew the next time you want to assess where you are.

All these considerations are in the context of you producing a body of work unsupported. If you are trying to get someone to pay you to make the work, a lot of these are still at play, you'll just have to deal with the people who are paying you – or your professor if you're a student.

Are We There Yet?

How do you know when your project is done? How much is enough? Imposed deadlines often answer this question, you only have so much time to produce the work and however much gets done in that time is it. In those circumstances I'd suggest outlining everything that needs to happen by the deadline and establishing a timeline for those things to happen, whether you're on assignment or have a pile of schoolwork in front of you as a student.

Or there's the dreaded "No more pictures" when someone you're photographing leaves or says you can no longer photograph in a setting. Yow. Most of the time, these shutdowns come out of the blue. You can decrease the likelihood of being told no more by doing periodic check-ins with the people involved in granting you entry. Ask how they're feeling about how you're approaching making their photo or if any issues have come up about getting into places that you can help resolve. Showing people some photographs as you're making them can be helpful in circumventing shutdowns because they sometimes happen if people feel like the photographer is taking advantage of them, that they're getting nothing out of the experience. Remember that the act of making pictures is as much about creating relationships as it is pushing the shutter release button.

If you aren't clear about what story you're telling, then you'll not know when it's telling is complete. Revisit why you are taking on this topic, restate the focus, repeat your summary and assess if all parts of the pie you created are whole. Then you should know if you're done.

If that doesn't work, sometimes there are natural breaks in the flow of what you've engaged and they can provide an ending point. If you're photographing a phase of someone's life and that phase ends, then you're done; if the season changes and the feel of photographs shifts outside your scope, you're done.

You can also knowingly break the project into self-contained parts, knowing that you can complete the work in phases.

You're Done, Then What?

Time has run out, or you are patting yourself on the back for having completed the creation phase of the project, now what? The answer is much easier if you have been creating a qualitative hierarchy as the work progresses and you've been refining the focus and how the work will be presented.

Chances are you'll need to create multiple outcomes/versions of the project and each one will have specific considerations.

Addressing just the photographic aspect of your project, bring together all of your top-tier photos. In my workflow, that'd be all the three-star photos. If you know that there's no subgrouping of photos in your outcome, you can leave them in one collection or folder. If creating subsets is what your outcomes call for, then create those from the top tier. In Lightroom or Photo Mechanic, you can use color ratings to create these subgroups, or use folders if you don't use an app.

You might have to create a higher level in the hierarchy to reduce the number of photos you're working with to a reasonable number. I've found that starting to create a sequence with twice the number of photos that want to end up with is a good balance between having enough and too many photos to work with. If there are multiple sizes or uses, then start by creating the one with the largest number of photos required and then create the smaller ones.

The rest of the sequencing process is the same as the one described in Section 4.

If there are other mediums and/or other people involved who have been working on their components progressively, then you'll have to assemble the team and move the project to fruition as a group. Determine your role, if you're the "editor" leading the effort or you'd rather that the art director among you is taking the lead to create the fully realized outcomes, and your role is to respond to what the designer produces. Most projects should include the benefits a skilled designer brings to the effort, and ideally, you involve them as early in the process as possible. They will be able to present ideas and offer solutions that no one else would, way more than "designing" the completed work into something stellar.

Most projects take multiple versions to achieve their final form so don't go into the design process thinking it'll be one and done. Design is another space where project shortcomings can become obvious. That's a good thing. Welcome those, produce whatever is missing, re-work whatever isn't working. There will be a point where you're mostly happy with the outcome. Though you're likely to want to keep tweaking it endlessly, there has to be an end. Knowing when the presentation is good enough is similar to knowing when you can stop creating the photographs.

Once done, please do pat yourself on the back.

Section 5.7 How to Pitch Your Effort

Pretty much every way of making a living from photography requires being able to present your way of making pictures and the specific ideas you have for producing a set of pictures to whoever you want to pay you. Making a pitch is a universal term and process to sell yourself and your work. Yes, you are selling people on you as much as your work.

The previous sub-sections brought you to the point of having a project at some stage of development, which included having some idea of who might want to support the result. Knowing who might pay for your type of work can help you create work that they're more likely to pay you for.

This discussion is different from bidding for commercial jobs or developing a following for your fine art. Other sources could address those specific environments.

Who to Pitch to?

The first step of a creating a presentation is defining to whom you're going to pitch. That'll determine how to craft each one, though there are some parts of the process that can be easily adapted as needed, once you've created them.

How do you even begin to know who might be worth pitching to? Certainly, search engine results can start to point you in the right direction, but those results are just a starting point. From them, you can develop a list of potential entities that you refine by learning more about each one.

Many places will describe what they're looking for. Here's some of what ProPublica's visuals team says on its site:

> ProPublica is looking for visual stories that expose abuses of power and betrayals of the public trust by government, business and other institutions. The most successful pitches will be for stories you have begun photographing, so you can demonstrate access and approach, but we are open to well-researched pitches that you have not yet begun reporting.

Here are some ways to develop a potential client list:

- If you want to find publications, go to bookstores and libraries that have the biggest selection of magazines you can find and rifle through them looking for matches.
- Your specialty likely has a business type associated with it. Learn what those businesses are and consider whether they'd respond to your work. Chances are there are trade publications associated with your realm, too. Search for trade publications in your specialty.
- If your specialty is more topical, then find organizations and entities that touch on that topic. Look for lists of not-for-profits. As you find groups, see who they're connected with, it's usually a web-like, interconnected world.
- If you are known for a skill or personality trait that produces unique work, it's equally productive to search for people who would respond to your work, based on their tastes. Search for organizations and events where such people gather, look at who is judging competitions

and presenting at workshops that recognize or speak to what you do. When you've identified people, track back to their sites or where they work to learn more and connect.

- Develop a list of photographers who touch on the same topic that you are going to pitch and see who pays them – most people have a client or tear sheet section on their site. You can find these photographers' work in the settings listed above.

How do you confirm if your pitch is a match to an entity or organization? Look carefully at the work they've supported in the past, who they've hired, the approach to the photography they present, the language they use in presenting topics. Are the topics they address and the style of the work in the same ballpark as yours? If your approach to the photography and narrative form are in line with theirs, you're at a good starting point for reaching out.

In some cases, be sure that the point of view of your pitch is in line with who you're pitching to. If you pitched an idea about Antifa, it would be different if pitched to FOX News than it would to MSNBC or The Independent vs. The Daily Post.

Ask, Specifically

Know what you want to get out of the interaction with a given entity. Pitches can be for different outcomes, whether it's an initial query to establish a relationship, publishing existing work, asking for support to produce a project or to join the roster of people they hire. Each one is a different form of engagement.

When pitching a project, a challenge is finding the balance between presenting a clear idea and approach and being open to hearing how that entity might want things to be different. You might as well pack your gear and leave if you're not open to alternative notions, instead responding defensively.

Tell Them

No matter who or what form it takes, the pitch has to let them know that you have done your homework, that you know who they are and what they care about. Dig deep enough to learn who specifically you pitch to and what their background is. Convey enough about you for them to know that you're worth engaging with, that you have enough experience and knowledge to be able to accomplish what the pitch is about.

What Form?

Develop more than one way to make a pitch and various versions of different durations.

- Marvi Lacar of Lowy + Lacar is masterful at creating pitch decks, which are PowerPoint of Keynote versions of her pitches. Pitch decks work best in person and through interactive, remote platforms. Or you can create a video version of your pitch deck and share that.
- Create a teaser iteration in a postcard format.
- Make a formatted email with a base pitch that links to a private page on your website.
- PDF versions with images work in some settings.
- Imagine your project as a billboard if that's a space where it would connect with the result.
- Presenting a set of impeccably made prints in person while talking about the work is another form.

The easier and more enjoyable you can make it for people to understand and appreciate, the better. And never rely on internet access to make an in-person presentation.

Further thoughts from Marvi: Luck is what you make for yourself; always be empathetic and kind in how you present yourself; make it clear that only you can off the talent your pitch involves; demonstrate and emanate passion; connecting with people personally, directly results in creating a network of people who will support you, the pitch is just the way to make that connection; measured risks are healthy; use your free time productively; experiment; finding your narrative voice and aesthetic style takes time and requires trust in the process; envy will distract you; opportunities are either given or made.

Have More

Presenting just the right length of pitch for each format is critical. But they might ask to see more of your work on the topic, so have that available in a way that's easy to access and is structured appropriately.

Leave a Gift

Definitely have something that you can leave behind after your pitch, no matter how you've done it. If in person, one idea is to immediately after pitching, sit nearby and write a thank you on the back of a small print of one of the photos you showed that day and give it to the person you met with – even if it means leaving with an assistant or in their mail slot. Follow up remote presentations with something similar, but mailed. There is great power in the hand-written, sincere, personal note. I've kept many of them through the years.

Update Your Site

A lot of people will go to your site before or after meeting with you, so be sure it is current.

Photoville creates some of the richest experiences you can have as a photographer. Among them was a presentation about making pitches. Here are some additional thoughts from a couple of those sessions: It's good to pitch smaller ideas when you first want to connect with an organization so they can ease into you; pitch a story, not a topic; always carry a notebook to write ideas and thoughts down – though I suppose a smartphone could work for that; get used to hearing no but don't give up.

Questions

Here's a set of questions that I've been asked regularly:

- Is it better to not have the work you're pitching published before? Yes; maybe; no. It depends on the entity, but more publishing realms prefer content that no other entity has published. A given pitch's content that hasn't been published but is part of a larger project that has been published in some form might be acceptable. A lot of people have long-term efforts that tend to be on wide-scope topics that take multiple efforts to accomplish, and they'll get each one supported independent of the others. Not for profits care less about whether work has been published, while commercial and advertising entities care more, generally.
- How much of the project should be done before seeking support for it? If you have a relationship with an entity, then you're more likely to succeed in pitching a project that you haven't started. If you're just connecting with an entity, then it's probably better to pitch them a completed project or an idea that can be accomplished easily, which has the added benefit of creating the relationship that you can then build upon.
- What if they take my idea, give it to another photographer, and use it? This does happen, and it's infuriating. What you do in response depends on how formal your proposal was, how complete the work you showed them is and their response to your idea. If you've presented a massive effort, they say they're interested, and you've agreed to some extent on a relationship, but then they back out and give it to someone else, you probably could ask for a kill fee. If your idea was not super specific and you mention it in passing, then you probably have no recourse. Regardless, it's a good idea to talk to the person and raise the issue as non-combatively as possible; or you can hire a lawyer to go after the publication if you think it's justified.
- How do you know if the scope of what you present is too broad, too narrow or just right? The more you know who you're presenting to and the more clarity of purpose and intention you have with what you're pitching, the more likely you are to pitch the right scope to that audience. You can also ask for feedback about scale after you've presented, which helps refine the pitch going forward.

- How do you know how much money or support to ask for? Most entities pay a certain range for work, they have budgets, but rates are dependent in part on your status in the profession. Uniqueness of what you're presenting can also raise what you'll get paid. That's why it's important to know antecedents and the intricacies of who you're pitching to.

I'll mention Todd Bigelow's business practices book again as a source to answer this question and a suite of software called fotoQuote and fotoBiz.

Don't

Knowing what not to do is as important as knowing what to do. Don't: over explain; be preachy or didactic; explain the process of getting to your idea; present a process idea; explain what you're not going to do; don't present an idea until it's fully formed, though you can use the pitching process to bring clarity to your effort. Find the right balance between telling a story through the pitch and presenting too much data and information. People should enjoy engaging with what you put in front of them.

Ways to Engage

The goal, in most cases, is not just to get them to buy into this one project but to create a connection, a relationship that leads to you working with an entity repeatedly. That means connecting personably, directly, and specifically with the people who make decisions, as opposed to thinking that the process is generic.

How to connect with someone you don't know can seem tricky. Understand that a big part of a visual editor's job is to know about good work and who is worth working with. Same for art directors, art buyers, directors of photography at brands, etc. You do have to penetrate their busy worlds to get noticed. Sometimes email works, sometimes a phone call will do. Even better is to connect through a shared acquaintance. Or meet people during reviews or workshops (see a list of those in Appendix C). Having a pointed social media presence compounds the chances of connecting.

In-Person Presentation

If you do get in the door, physically or virtually, here's a way to approach the connection. The pitch should take at most 10 minutes unless it's an exceptional circumstance. You should be confident and enthusiastic but not bubbly or boastful. Introduce yourself and thank them for seeing you. Make the experience interactive, back and forth, ask them questions to ensure they're getting it, and to change the pace, so it's not you talking the whole time.

Start your pitch with a hook, something that's surprising or intriguing, to get their interest right away. Options include asking a question, telling a story that takes them to the heart of your project, or presenting little known information. Tell them why the project matters, why you're the right person to produce it and why now is the right time. Know how the project meets their needs and fits into their presentation platform, including describing projects they've done that you know they're proud of. Describe what you'd need from them. Close with a summary of your project and why it's a match.

Remote Presentations

Pitches by email are common, or you can schedule a phone call to make a brief pitch. In either, present a one paragraph summary of your project and why it's a fit. Include or tell them your website address to learn more. You can attach pdfs to emails, but that's not universally liked. Make the subject line count. Snail mailing them is a tough sell, other than to put your name in front of them with a promo card, so that when you do email, they may respond.

Practice, Practice

Regardless of how and where you make pitches, practice, and refine them. In academic settings, teachers ideally create situations where students present, get feedback, refine their presentations and present them again, repeating until they are perfected.

Now that you've crafted your path, created photographs and edited them and built narratives into complete forms and know how to pitch, how do you make a living on that path? That's next.

Try This

- Create the idea for your next narrative. This should be one that you can bring to fruition within a few weeks, not small but not large either. Define the market for this project as it progresses.
- Bring together a team of three to five people with varied skills and backgrounds who will respond to your idea, advise you as it progresses and potentially be involved in producing aspects of the narrative that you cannot.
- Move the narrative through the creation process.
- Select a final expression of the project. That may be more than one realization or a dimensional presentation in one space.
- Create a pitch for the market you've defined. Present that pitch to the team you've assembled, and then approach potential clients.

Section 6
What It Takes to Make a Living

Section 6.0 Introduction

I hope this section helps you move in a profitable direction, though it's not intended to touch every aspect of the business side. Instead, this section is about determining what your path is, making yourself known within that realm – what you can build, invest in and connect with to make a go of it. There are good business practices books that go into detail about how to run your business and budget and bid on jobs and the like. I've mentioned Todd Bigelow's *The Freelancer's Guide to Success: Business Essentials.* This section accompanies Todd's book nicely.

Section 6.1 Defining Your Path

How do you determine your occupational path? Your choices are working a full or part-time job or being an independent, which means running your own, solo business or one with employees. Next choice is whether you want to be behind an image-producing device or working in some part of the profession that doesn't involve making images – and there are many.

You may not know which is the better path for you. I didn't until I did. I've thought I wanted to be the one making pictures my entire career, since a staff sergeant sold me his 35-mm camera and two lenses when I was 18 and at my first station in the U.S. Air Force. Though I've made photographs with intention and been paid for that work for years, I've only been a photographer exclusively during a 3-month internship. I realized through a series of educational and occupational choices that I liked and was good or better at other things. I've been a writer and designed many efforts, but I figured out that being a visual editor leads to my greatest achievements and that's how I've made my living most of the years since buying that Pentax Spotmatic. I didn't even know there was such a job path until I did.

You may not know the answers now, but you can put yourself in settings and try different experiences to help yourself delineate at least the next steps of your route. There are no dead ends if we actively create

DOI: 10.4324/9781003287544-6

forward-acting opportunities that require choices. Try something and see if you like it. If yes, keep going, if no, make something else happen. The sum of how you respond to these big and small opportunities creates your path.

Building, launching and maintaining your career most likely take effort beyond your core skill. Someone said to Sara Naomi Lewkowicz, after an Alexia judging session a while back, that it was amazing how Sara had become an overnight success. Sara was winning many awards for her project about domestic violence. Sara's response: "Yah, it only took me 10 years to become an overnight success." Those 10 years included taking lots of different types of paying photography jobs and working other jobs part time to support life while she initiated projects. Sara is now phasing into more commercial work and producing motion pieces, on a continually evolving path.

The Visual Communications program at Syracuse was among many schools that left students short of understanding what they'd have to do to make a living, beyond creating work. How did we know that was a shortcoming? We asked and students told us. Unable to adapt the entire program to integrate livelihood as a fully integrated aspect, we added a new course that I designed to help students' understanding of what it takes. The course introduced outward-facing aspects of making a living – website, social media, promotional materials, photobooks – and producing another multi-medium project to apply in those settings.

Think of business practices as either being above or below the water line if your business were an iceberg. What I just described is above the water line, the outward-facing presence.

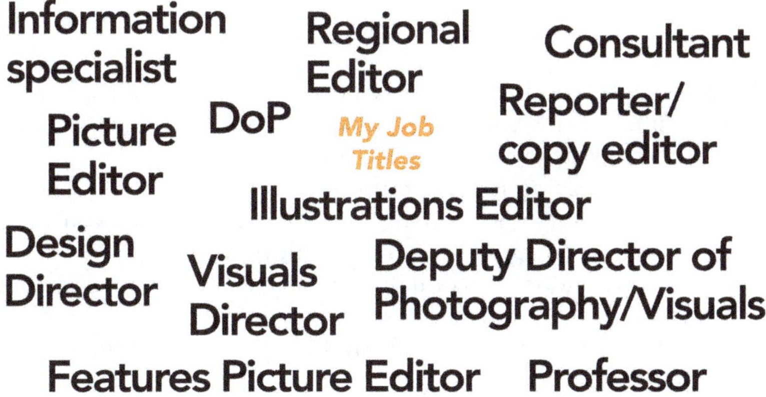

Photo 6.01 I've held many job titles through the years. In hindsight, they have all been on a path that explored ways to tell stories in different settings.

Academic settings fail on this front because if they teach business practices at all, it's typically as a separate course that teaches aspects that are below the iceberg's water line, from the perspective of the person teaching the course and whatever branch of the profession – if any – that professor comes from. How to run a business and create bids and copyright issues and accounting, insurance and all manner of necessities that fall below the water line is important but can vary widely depending on your branch of the profession. Developing a fully realized business around corporate headshots would be a different process from ones based on editorial assignments, advertising campaigns or studio-based businesses. A program would ideally incorporate making a living into every phase of the program that involves producing work and allow students to learn how to apply business practices in ways that are unique to their path.

I tracked where students in 9 years of courses I taught got jobs after leaving Newhouse – 90 percent got jobs related to how they spent their time in school, which means the work they produced opened the door to the jobs they got. Thirty percent created their own businesses as independent producers, 30 percent hold visual editor or hybrid positions, 20 percent produce moving images and 10 percent are "other" – educators, graduate school, assisting... Two people became newspaper staff photographers. Within these broad areas is an immense range of job types and settings, including six who got jobs as visual editors at National Geographic.

This section is a direct outgrowth of what worked and didn't work in courses I've taught, from working with photographers and working as a visual editor. It's weighted toward people who produce visual content through a camera but applies to most ways of earning a living in the visual professions.

Here's a series of questions I've asked students and professionals to help them determine or redefine their paths.

- What kind of working environment gives you the most satisfaction? Do you prefer being part of a team and if so, do you want to lead the team or be a team member equal to others?
- Do you favor having more control over what you do and when you do it or would you rather have the environment in which you work to create that framework and you do your thing within it?
- Are you pretty good at making images but feel like you are better at some other aspect of the profession?
- Do you prefer to – and can you handle – running a business and all that entails?
- Do you need certainty in your work life, or can you sustain periods where you don't know where your next paycheck will come from?
- How much of your life are you willing to dedicate to this profession?

How you answered these questions will put you behind the camera or in some other arm of this many-tentacled profession. It'll either point you toward a full-time job or working as an independent producer. It'll determine the scale of the setting you like to work in and whether you'd rather be in charge or work for others. Once you know these broader aspects of direction, it's easier to know how to focus your efforts in the most efficient and intentionally dynamic ways.

Other Ways to Make a Living

Ways to earn income fall into several categories: Full-time jobs; independent as a generalist (used to be called freelance but not so much now, given that free is what too many people expect to pay for photographs); independent as a specialist; passive/alternative income sources.

The distinction between generalist and specialist is notable in that far more people were generalists, those who could make photographs of pretty much anything to an acceptable level, versus those who specialize in some way. That change and the incredible expansion of job titles that don't involve creating images offer great potential.

Elizabeth Krist is among the founding members of The Visual Thinking Collective, with Sarah Leen, Lauren Steel and Shannon Simon, and a longtime friend. She offers this set of settings and job titles among the ways to make a living on the perimeter of making photographs – and I added a few: still and motion visual editing, curators, archivists, gallerists, corporate, university, government, hospitals, real estate, not-for-profit organizations, art buyers, a range of jobs with book publishers, master printers, as an archivist, digital post-production specialists, digital forensics, law enforcement, museums, motion producers to include casting/location scouts/stylists/editors, media managers, live event producers, foundations such as Catchlight and The Open Society, academic researchers, visual anthropologists and public relations companies, wedding, event and portraiture. Then there are groups that create workshops, competitions or reviews, pop-up exhibitions and events. And related businesses such as grant writers, copyright detectives, equipment technicians. And a changing but still present wing of the visual profession: agents, stock agencies, wire services.

"But we have no idea what kinds of roles will surface in the future. Who knew a few years ago that film productions would be hiring people to enforce anti-harassment of COVID-19 precautions," Elizabeth added. Or that Apple, Facebook, Flipboard, Nike, Under Armour, Patagonia and Amazon would all have visual content staffs, to name a few of the many.

It may not have occurred to you that most pursuits on the planet have associated businesses connected to them and that those businesses have their own media networks, generically called trade publications. Whether it be sailing or farming or skiing or woodworking or countless subsets of outdoor activities, connect with their media and you'll have an income stream.

As all things become more digitally and virtually driven there will be an ever-increasing demand for people who can produce and present the visually compelling narratives that others create. And as AI images become more and more integrated, a whole new avenue opens. An active learning approach in the classroom presents students with challenges that require learning what is new; not all of the burden should be on the teacher to know everything and give that knowledge to students.

Before getting into the sections, here are some more general thoughts on what it takes. First is a set from 2 years of presentations by Photo District News 30 New and Emerging Photographers' panel during LOOK3, which was a beautifully conceived and executed photographic festival held in Charlottesville, Virginia. It's sad that both PDN and LOOK3 no longer exist. I miss them. Here are perceptive thoughts from the 30 presentations:

- Personal work is the work
- Photographic equipment is useful only if you know how to use it
- Define your market as you create work and then connect with that market
- Always have something to share with potential clients
- Your personality is half of why you get hired
- Use social media: In the way that works best for you
- Use social media: To connect with others, build a community and create a network
- Paths you'll take are not straight or predictable and that's good
- Community is where you go and who you meet there, so go places
- Your career is the sum of the mountains you create, and summit
- Engagement outside your comfort zone produces adventure, experience, growth
- Visual editors will see your work, if it's good, and they can find it
- Everyone has to figure out the business side of the photography for themselves
- Be clear in your intent with reviewers, people who might hire you
- How you present yourself is how you'll be perceived
- Only making still photographs is no longer sufficient
- Learn that you have a voice. Find it by speaking with your camera

Here's good advice from Annie Flanagan, a New Orleans-based photographer who focuses on the environment and gender in the United States. They told students in one of my courses: "Create opportunities to connect with editors but know the intent of why you are reaching out to an editor so that your meeting has resonance. You will define yourself along your path; self and work are intricately connected."

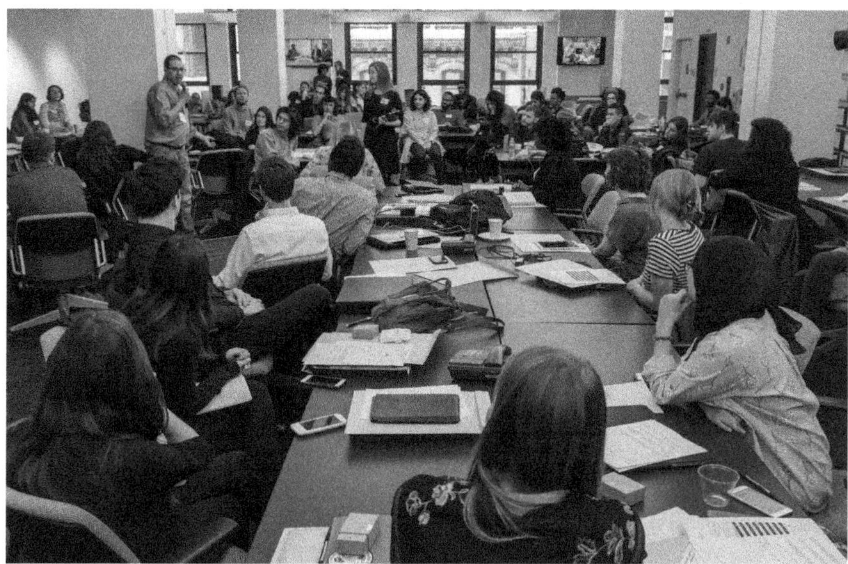

Photo 6.02 Getting your work reviewed in formal settings can help your career in many ways. Here, David Gonzalez explains the workings of the New York Portfolio Reviews, sponsored by the New York Times and the Craig Newmark Graduate School of Journalism in New York City.

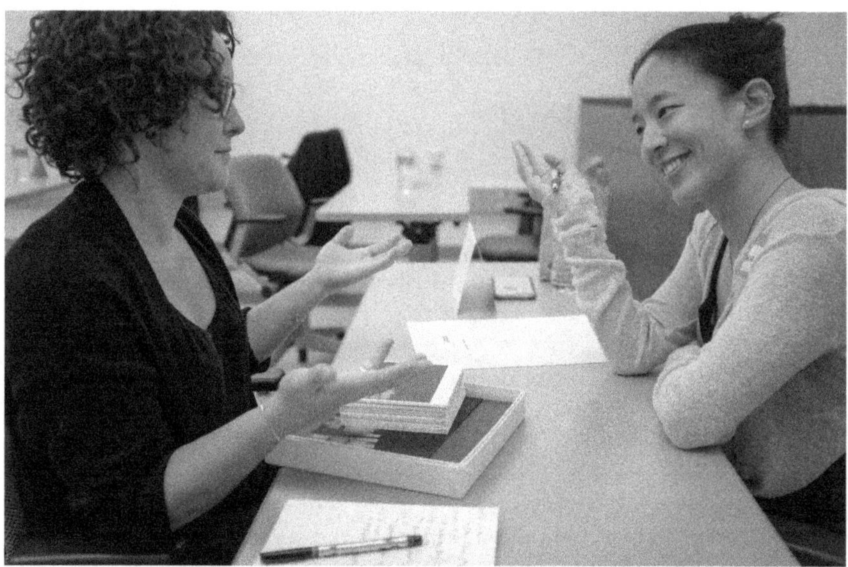

Photo 6.03 Pamela Chen reviews the work of Andrea Wise at the New York Portfolio Reviews. Reviews are as much about creating a relationship, a connection, as they are about getting feedback and direction.

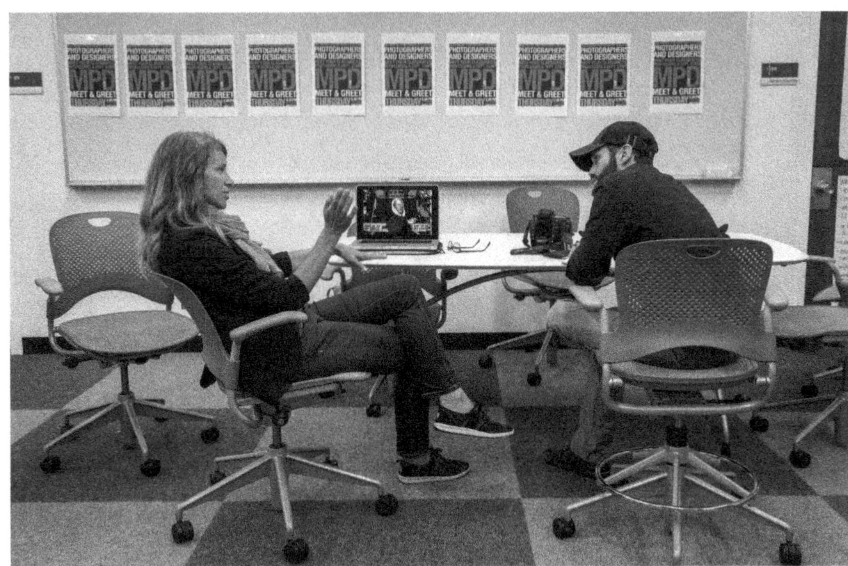

Photo 6.03.1 Take advantage of any opportunity to connect with people whose advice would be beneficial, and listen to them. Anne Farrar was in from National Geographic to judge a travel photo contest at Syracuse University. Grad student Todd Michalek asked her to look at some of his work.

Here's another list, one I made to share with students to tell them the kinds of things you need to have, do or know to create your own photography business:

- Business cards
- Stationary (digital and letter if you're going to physically write people)
- Leave behinds
- A newsletter and a service to distribute it, such as Mailchimp
- Promotional materials
- Web site
- Know what your cost of doing business is, to help establish your rates
- Return on investment to know whether the money you spent was worthwhile
- Ask every new client how they got your name. Track back to ensure that happens
- Know the cost of computers, software, the right camera gear
- Insurance for you and your possessions
- A place to work out of and a way to get around
- Relationship with an accountant, tax preparer and lawyer
- State business license and tax id number

- Register your company, most do this as an LLC
- Create a team of people who you trust and bring additive skills to your efforts, to include designers who specialize in your niche, visual editor, video and audio producers, animator, writer

More advice, from Holly Hughes, long-time editor of PDN and a perpetually curious person: "Shoot what you love. Hone your skills. Deliver something your audience can't find elsewhere."

Maren Levinson, founder of Red Eye Reps, offers this advice: If two people who hire photographers were riding an elevator and one of them mentioned your name and the other person interrupted with, "Oh yah, they're the one who …" You are responsible for creating the end of that sentence, through the cumulative effect of the work you create and how you put yourself out there.

In an article titled *Visual Storytelling in the Age of Posts-Industrial Journalism,* David Campbell, a communications, media and politics professional and now the managing editor of VII's Insider, offers a compelling perspective and this advice, paraphrased here: Have a responsive, fresh site; learn video, audio and other new skills to add to your storytelling repertoire; be an expert; innovate by creating unique story forms and expressions; collaborate with others to bring more skills to the telling; partner with sponsors, funders, organizations; connect like crazy through social media; diversify your revenue streams; tell stories all the time.

Another good source is *Photoshelter's* White Papers, which all address aspects of succeeding in the profession, such as *The Photographer's Guide to Branding and Marketing in a Distracted World.*

Master portraitist Yousuf Karsh said, at age 77, "I know what I want to do and I do it." Can you achieve that level of clarity and act on it? I had a lengthy conversation with Mr. Karsh in 1989 in Santa Fe that stands in memory as if it were yesterday.

Regardless of the work you want to do, chances are it's going to occupy more of your life than a 9 to 5 job. To succeed at the higher levels of this profession, no matter the branch of it that you pursue, requires immense effort. Count on the first few years taking many of your waking hours. Think of that time as an investment in yourself as you learn how to produce compelling work, establish a reputation, learn how to earn a living and move up the ladder. Maybe your work life will take less of your life, maybe you won't ever distinguish between work and personal life. Dispel the myth of balancing work and personal. Instead, figure out what works for you.

On to the sections that address putting yourself out there.

Section 6.2 The Mother Ship – Your Web Site

The Why applies to your website as well. Knowing why the site exists, what you want it to accomplish, will determine every decision you make about its look and feel and structure and functionality – yet another example of the milking stool.

A lot of photographers' sites have a general presence that reflects a lack of specificity in why they exist. Such sites present the photographer's work either well or not so well and the structure suggests what type of work they have done. Words that appear are for the most part descriptive of the work, as links to various selections; the photographer's name is the largest word presence. Photographic representation on the home page is either a single, large image, a slide show that most likely scrolls horizontally or a grid of photographs.

And that's fine, if *The Why* of your site is simply to say that you are a photographer and to present work you've done in a way that might be of interest to people in general. Ramp up *The Why* and your site can exist to get you the kind of work that you want to do going forward, to sell prints, to be an editing tool, or herald your specialty as a magnet to people who will then be drawn like metal to hire you.

Creating a clear mission for your site does not have to be limited to any one of these reasons to exist, though it could if that's the best solution for your formula. If you want the site to accomplish multiple missions, then be clear in the hierarchy of what is most important, second most and so on. Think of its structure as a spider web with the most important mission in the center and all others spinning off the center in a clear order of priority and scale.

Use words that punch the clarity of the central mission. Among my favorites is Boone Speed's website home page that has the larger words: *Boone Speed Gets It* imposed on one large photograph that advances to another and another, each photo of people doing out-there acts in the outdoors. The right combination of words and pictures in this context is another powerful third effect that delivers your message with greater clarity.

Whether you present one photo, a slide show, a grid or something freeform depends on what you want that presentation to accomplish and what the words that sit by or on the photos say. If, for example, you want people to know that you can make compelling, unique portraits of anyone, presenting a grid of range of your portraits might be the best approach, with words that compound the message.

Your web presence can include more than one site, or URL, each can address a specific client base. Some people create separate presences for their editorial and commercial work, others peel off wedding photography from other forms of lifestyle work and so on.

Melissa Farlow and Randy Olson have long referred to their home base as the mother ship, given that a lot of their work happens elsewhere but the heavy lifting of their photographic lives happens in their home spaces. Andrew Fingerman, CEO of *Photoshelter*, and Deborah Pang Davis – my wife, who works as a senior interactive designer for Disney – were the first people I'd heard refer to a photographer's website as their mother ship. It's an apt description, where all things you do professionally get better if you connect them to your website with clear intention and hierarchy.

Brent Lewis has offered insight on websites and many other aspects of the profession in a variety of settings, including my courses. Brent is currently a picture editor at the New York Times and co-founder of Diversify Photo, with Andrea Wise, visuals editor for ProPublica and a Syracuse University master's graduate.

Brent's advice: Keep it simple and easy to navigate with an informed awareness of who your primary audience is to help guide your decisions. Only include the type of work that you want to do going forward, with storytelling as an essential quality throughout. Specific to considerations for the Times, he suggested showing that you're a well-rounded photographer, that you can produce narratives in a variety of ways, make portraits and create a video. Use Instagram to represent your most recent work, with a link to your site from Instagram and to Instagram for your site. Update your site regularly.

Here's a collection of other considerations in creating or revising your site, once you have clarity on what you want it to accomplish. These come from the course I mentioned, advice from my wife, Deborah Pang Davis, who is an experienced interactive designer, and my own experiences:

Choice of typeface conveys qualities so choose one, or more than one, that aligns with your professional presence. Show your choices to people you respect to get their impressions of its efficacy. If you're not comfortable with making design choices, hire someone who is. They can help create a one-off site for you or guide your selections within pre-designed platforms. Your site must be responsive, work on all platforms and in all browsers. Photos should have titles or captions or both.

Commonly used options for pull-down menu fields include projects, stories, recent work, published work, clients, buy prints, about, contact, exhibitions, books and a set based on the type of work, such as editorial, commercial, advertising. Or a list of the work you've produced by the body of work. Which you use depends on The Why of your site. Locate your social media links as a group somewhere on your home page, often at the bottom of the pull-down menus, especially if they're on the left.

DON'T have a form to contact you. Give your professional email address that ends with @someversionofyourlastname.com Avoid email addresses that end in @internetcompany More people are using disguised email addresses and outward-facing phone numbers that connect with your actual number, to avoid spammers.

Contact and *about* can be one pull-down or separate ones. *About* should tell your story. People should get a sense of your personality. Say who you are, what you value, what you enjoy, what you care about and what type of work you do. Tell people where you're based. First person is better than third unless you want to come off as removed.

Please don't say that you are an award-winning photographer. That's like saying you've been bit by a mosquito living in Minnesota; if you haven't won an award, you probably haven't entered a competition. And using the words "at the intersection of" has become a trope; be more specific about the type of work you do and why you do it.

Farrah Sheiky's about is a good example: Arab American photographer, creative director and writer based in Washington, D.C. My work celebrates those who make and do in their element, subcultures and underrepresented communities, and those familiar moments that make you feel warm and welcomed.

Carlos Javier Ortiz' is another rich about the artist example.

More Dos and don'ts:

- Don't have the sound play automatically
- Don't use self-running slide shows
- Do update your site regularly
- Do choose type color carefully
- Do choose typeface to reflect your personality
- Don't use more than 20 photos in a slide show, unless there's a good reason
- Don't crop your photos into all kinds of shapes, unless that's the look you want
- Do select and sequence all of what you present judiciously
- Do use older work but only if it's still relevant to what you're doing now. Newer is better
- Do make your site responsive – it must work on smartphones and all browsers
- Don't be arrogant or boastful but do be confident in presenting your work and yourself
- Do check your SEO – search engine optimization

There's a list of website creation platforms in the resource guide appendix of this book. Variables between the companies are those that only present your work and those that offer or connect to other services or communities, services such as ecommerce, private sections, blogs and direct connections to those who hire photographers.

Section 6.3 To Social Media, or Not

Hate it, love it, become addicted to it or leave it in a rage, few people are neutral when it comes to social media. Should you be posting or differently from your current approach, or not at all? The answer again comes from asking why in this context: What could you accomplish through social media to elevate your professional life in a way that wouldn't otherwise happen? If the answer is nothing, then you're off the hook. For many of you, the answer will be something.

Backing up for a minute, what is social media, anyway? Just to be sure we're of a similar understanding. A rubber band ball of definitions include these bands: electronic communication that shares ideas, thoughts, information, personal information; communication tools that allow people to share and interact with each other digitally through a range of platforms in which you can create and join communities; digital tools that allow people to create and share content with people. Most discussion of social media is about how to use it, but there is reason to avoid using the mediums as a professional, greatest among them is that the platforms make money from your imagery and you do not. Read more broadly before committing.

Here's my understanding of how people use social media professionally, presented here along a spectrum: People randomly join the clamor to respond to other's posts with their opinion or experience or create posts that are personal opinions in nature; as a partial representation of one of their efforts to connect people to that effort; as a form of their project that is unique to social media platforms; to post for others, including clients or in support of their community; to create projects that exist only on social media; to directly promote themselves and the type of work they do; to create a social media persona, an outward extension of themselves as a brand and to which other entities want to pay to connect.

Which of these is your way of using social media now might be what you want it to be, or not. I'd offer that if you're using social media to get likes, to boost your ego and sense of self, or because you feel like you have to present, then you're doing it for the wrong reasons. They won't move you forward.

Ruddy Roye saw social media as one way to publish work that he thought was important, at a time when he struggled to get traditional assignments. And then as his following grew and the depth and breadth of what he was speaking to became fully realized expressions, media outlets started to hire him, he taught and inspired others and speaks regularly about what matters.

Pamela Chen advised during a class presentation that in your approach to social media you "build an appetite for it and a space for your voice to be heard. Make it feel like an extension of what you are in real life. People will respond to this honestly." This was when she worked for Instagram, after working at National Geographic. She went on to work for Apple.

Syracuse University Professor Jennifer Grygiel suggests approaching your social media model as if you were your own PR person. Learn to be in front of the camera, she says, sometimes physically so, but always presenting your unique self and the value that you bring to what's in front of you. And build a quality network; it's not about how many people follow you but how much those who follow you are in support of your professional life.

Think of social media as an investment of your time as opposed spending money for advertising of days gone by. And in the same way that the Black Book faded to black, specific social media companies and forms will quickly diminish or go dark. I read a survey the other day that said dramatically fewer younger people are using Instagram, preferring TikTok and, still, Snapchat. If you remember MySpace, you're showing your age. Don't even bring up Facebook, oldster. The value of advice that is specific to a given platform won't be relevant very long. Instead, here is some general advice:

- It's not how many followers you have, it's how many you have who are likely to support your work. Find those people, connect with them and those they support. That's one way to create your own social media community. You can join or create multiple communities that speak to things you care about.
- Separate your personal and professional social media accounts, though reflecting your personality in your professional usage is important.
- Post as often as you think your posts have value and achieve what you want to accomplish through social media. That number and frequency will change with circumstances and reasons for posting. You might have a flurry of posts surrounding the release of a new project or an extended series connected to supporting a book publication. It's best to avoid the feast or famine, to post at least periodically.
- You can create several tiers or types of posts: Those that support or present specific efforts you've created, your observations that contribute to the discourse on critical happenings within the profession, things that challenged you professionally, written from the perspective of how you addressed those challenges and periodic missives about things that you saw and appreciated, support and share the posts of others. The cumulative effect is for people to understand your perspective, your personality, so that they want to hire you for who you are as much as for the kind of work you do, which reflects who you are. Connect the dots for them.
- Keep politics out of your posts.
- Come from the perspective of offering positive contributions, of adding to the conversation in a way that is helpful or informative. That doesn't preclude being critical of things that shouldn't be the way they are but rather than bash or harangue, offer your thoughts of why that was wrong and suggest alternatives, to improve the situation.
- At this writing, LinkedIn is an underutilized professional platform, especially if you're looking for a full-time job. Activate the platform's looking for a job function.
- There are hybrid environments, such as Visura, that have some of the same qualities as social media platforms but have creation of and support for the community as its primary reason for existing. Visura

adds a substantial business suite and support to its platform, thanks to co-founder and CEO Adriana Teresa Letorney and her husband, Graham. Other community-based groups include Black Women Photograph, Women Photograph, The Everyday Projects, Natives Photograph, Diversify Photo, Kamoinge, The Photo Society, Girl Gaze, MFON, Women Focus, WeWomen.

No doubt the forms of social media will evolve and, I hope that as they move forward platforms will improve exponentially in what they bring to the planet. It's up to you whether and how to stay on top of this ever-changing part of your professional life.

Section 6.4 Promotional Materials a Must. Maybe

As I write this Sol Neelman just sent an off-the-charts promotional package to Rob Haggart at aphotoeditor.org. Sol bought and customized a 27-inch foosball table, including remaking the playing surface with one of his photos of soccer star Megan Rapinoe that he had made for a Clif Bar campaign. He packaged that piece with a box of the Rapinoe Clif Bars and a ticket he made to promote the ad campaign. aphotoeditor wrote about Sol's promotional piece – success.

Sol started to focus on photographing weird sports a few years ago and is now in the process of producing *Weird Sports III* – not that women's soccer is a weird sport. Another of his promo packages included Topps trading cards with bubble gum that he designed to promote his Weird Sports books, after learning that Topps will print trading cards on demand. Full disclosure, I've helped Sol edit all three books and worked with him while at The Oregonian.

aphotoeditor is the best place I've found to see photographers' promotional pieces. Get on their newsletter and you can receive regular examples and their pricing and bidding newsletter and others.

Should you make your own promotional bandwagon? Probably, in some form. Becoming known is the singular goal of whatever campaign you devise that is specific to your type of work. Sol works with commercial, advertising and some editorial clients so promotional pieces that appeal to those markets are the right fit for him and his work.

Your website and how you use social media can be a form of promotion for you and your work and maybe that's enough, for you. Time was that if you had a full-time job you didn't even think about having to promote yourself. Jobs were more secure and people tended to stay in one place longer. You could get away without doing social media or putting out promotional pieces if you're in a self-sustaining environment or you are in such high demand that people knock on your door without your encouragement. That'd be rarified air.

Making photographs and telling stories as an independent is a highly competitive profession; distinguishing yourself from others is where a well-considered and fully executed promotional campaign comes in. It's really a form of marketing but for a lot of people that's a less desirable word. To be clear, *the why* of promoting ourselves is to get the work that we crave. Every ounce of effort should be geared to and measured by whether promotional efforts achieve that goal.

Only you can answer the question of what approach is best for you. For me, when I'm actively involved in the independent editing aspect of my professional life, I write pieces on my website that speak directly to people who might want to hire me, with the intention of helping them improve their craft and edit their work. My goal is to provide useful information that in turn establishes my credibility. I post links to those written pieces on social media, pointing people to my mother ship, where they can contact me to query about working together. I also use social media to offer my impressions of things I care about and comment and share other people's posts that I value. My goal is to be known as someone whose skills and professional opinions people value enough to want to pay for.

Start your process by defining your goal. Then figure out who you need to reach to achieve that goal and what you want from them – to hire you, yes, but they have to know what you can do for them based on what you share with them – and determine the best mediums to achieve this.

Succinctly: Why are you promoting yourself, what's the goal; what's your budget; who are you reaching out to; what forms will be most effective for you; how often should you send each form?

A campaign could involve several types of presentations in a single effort, as Sol's soccer package did. He only sent it to one place because in the context of the pandemic, getting mentioned on aphotoeditor reached more people who might hire him than if he had done a smaller scale package and tried to get it into many hands.

Possible types of presentations include newsletters, postcards and packaged materials, from simple to complex iterations, either physical or digital. How often you send materials parallels the complexity and cost of the pieces. You can send newsletters out monthly – if you have enough to share that often – but most do quarterly. Craft your newsletters to telling a story about the creation of your recent work in a way that gives people a sense of what it's like to work with you, how you think and act while solving visual problems.

Postcards sent monthly or quarterly with handwritten notes that speak to the person you're wanting to work with can be effective. Susan Seubert told me that she sent postcards to National Geographic Traveler's editors for several years without a response. And then one day the picture editor and creative director walked to their mail slots together as they discussed who to assign to a particular story. They each pulled out Susan's postcard at the same time; Susan got the assignment and worked for them for years after that. And I later hired Susan because of my wife's connection to Traveler – Deb worked for the magazine then. Yes, it's a small world.

Larger campaign pieces can go out every year or two. People tend to produce this range of types of pieces: handmade or digitally produced books; a boxed package of a range of pieces, such as Sol's; zines; something between books and zines; pieces printed on newsprint, which can be larger and cost less; over the top pieces that you build by hand with a specialized case, such as the one Clint Davis produced in 2014. His package included a customized Pelican case, 20 5×7-inch photo cards, a personalized note to each recipient, a spiffy business card and most impressive a miniature zoom lens. The more complex a piece the more peripheral materials you can create, such as Clint's video of how he made his promo piece. That video has gotten nearly 20,000 views on YouTube.

Promoting yourself doesn't have to be so direct. Dana Scruggs created *Scruggs* magazine as a way to present her work. "I just knew that I needed to create something that was my own. My own vision and my own voice," she says in the introduction of the first issue. And there was income, digital and print versions of the magazine were available for purchase.

Possibilities are limitless. You could make a banner that a plane flies over an event where you know people you want to work with would be. Project a high-res slide show on a building that will be seen by potential clients. Plaster prints in valuable places. Offer to work with an organization that supports what you care about and spread the word about that work.

Vince Musi and Callie Shell make their livelihood making medium format portraits of dogs that present the canines as if they are kings and queens – check out their book *The Year of the Dogs*. They also volunteer to photograph shelter dogs and every dog they photographed has gotten adopted. CW TV network heard about their volunteer work so included them in the *Dogs of the Year 2021* program. That is a promotion you could not buy yet promoting themselves was never the intention in volunteering. Good deeds reward the doers.

You can also photograph events that you like. Five or six of us would photograph cyclocross bicycle races in Portland, Oregon, every weekend in the fall for several years. We branded ourselves as pdxcross with Deborah Pang Davis designing all aspects of our brand – definitely work with a designer if you don't have design chops. We'd post a selection of photos from every race that people could buy through the site. And we produced and sold a book through Blurb and that sold a few hundred copies. Our shared goal was to make experiential photos, not typical sports action or mug shots of riders riding. Commercial and editorial clients caught wind of the work and would hire us to produce work for them that was like our pdxcross work. (Another example of how doing the work that you want to do plays out.) Most importantly, we became part of a community and that felt good. I really miss those often sloppy, rain-soaked days of slogging through the miles of muck to create photos that conveyed even a little of the range of experience riders endured and enjoyed.

Here's the branding cycle in brief: Create your community through the work you make, conceive imaginative ways to involve people with your work, repeat those steps to sustain your professional path.

Section 6.5 Make a Photo Book?

Several hundred photo books are sitting in boxes across the room from where I write, waiting to be released from their year and a half containment as we moved from one place to another to another. I've opened a few of the boxes and set free some of the captives. I missed them. Each book reflects something significant enough that I acquired this collection that is unique to me. I know a lot of the books' creators so wanted to support them by buying their book, or they gave me one. Other books were created by people who I respect and wanted to support. Others still are benchmark bodies of work that set new standards for narrative storytelling of their time and therefore must be owned. A common aspect of this collection is my desire to learn from each book, from how the individual photographs were made, what they speak to based on the photographers' rendering of their perceptions, why each book is structured and presented as it is. I care less about the subject matter of the books than I do how the photographer created a narrative around that topic and then the book.

Those are my criteria. So, if you wanted me to engage with your book, you'd have to craft it in a way that appeals to me. Maybe there are enough other people who use the same criteria for your book to have an impact, an audience.

This is a way of backing into asking the question of why do you want to create a photo book and who is your audience. I've known people whose books are extensions of their egos and others who humbly create an experience for people who share their passion through their books. And others who believe that the book form is the best way to represent or realize a body of work and its realization is motivation and reward enough. And others who use their book as a promotional piece, hopefully to make people respect their work enough to hire them to make more of it. (Making money from the sale of a photo book shouldn't be your motivation, as few produce a significant profit.)

Know your why and begin. One first step is looking at as many photobooks as you can. One of those should be Darius Himes and Mary Virginia Swanson's book: *Publish Your Photography Book*. It's the best I found. They'll walk you through the entire process, much more so than this section is able to address.

Given what you want the book to accomplish and who the audience is, what type of publishing environment is the best match? Choices are on-demand digital or offset printers, small, medium, or large publishing houses that either charge you to produce the book or don't – most do. University Presses stand out from the crowd and might be a match if your work is regionally specific. Each type of printer or publisher has a different process for getting your book considered and published. (See the list in the resource guide appendix.)

Digital printing costs less per book for smaller runs but as the scale of the press run increases offset will cost less per unit. How many copies you want determines which is better for you, as one variable.

Finding the right publisher for you can start by looking at a lot of books and seeing which combination of style of photography, paper, printing quality and design aligns with what you want. See who printed it, the designer and consider if your book would be of the same standard to interest this publisher and designer. Range of designers' voices is limitless, from Teun van der Heijden to Alex Lin to Nontsikelelo Mutiti, to name just three.

Kris Graves Projects produces generally small-run books. Kris spoke to students in one of my courses and offered valuable insight. His approach is emerging as a viable solution to creating books that photographers, and hopefully others, value. At the time he talked to my class Kris had produced about 60 books. His market is specific: "We want books to be collected by the people and museums that like them and want them."

Knowing what kind of work a given publisher might respond to is important. Kris said he responds to work that is somewhere between documentary and art photography, a hybrid. If he signs on to your book, he'll require you to know you can sell enough copies to pay for the cost of producing the books. He'll design the book and handle the printing and some distribution. He advises photographers to offer limited edition prints with some copies of the book at a premium to generate more income.

For the self-funded route, you can use Kickstarter or other online platforms to garner financial support. It's a lot of work that requires being non-stop in getting the word out by producing videos and using various social media platforms and direct outreach and tapping networks of friends and asking them to spread the word. Plan on doing nothing else but promoting the book during the time period your book is open for funding.

Deb Pang Davis and I worked with Scott Strazzante to edit and design his *Common Ground* book. He also worked with a publisher but used Kickstarter to fund the printing. More than 760 people contributed more than $46,500 to support the book. Scott was cordial and relentless in creating this community of support.

Blurb offers an ecommerce option for printing your book with them. You can charge as much more than what Blurb charges as you want.

How do you take a set of pictures and mold it into a book? Section 5 presents my approach to selecting and sequencing a narrative. Doing that to produce a result at the scale of a book is just larger than most other forms. You can use the digital version of choosing a starting photo and using the split screen scroll to create a sequence. My impression is that more people create their sequences from prints, by placing them on a surface and moving them around until the sequence feels right. I've edited something over 40 books and have used both systems, favoring the digital for more lyrical sets of pictures and the analog when there are subsets or sections that become apparent only when prints are in front of you.

Working with a visual editor on the selection and sequencing might be better for you. The relationship and interaction can produce a stronger book. When Eric Draper and I started to work on his retrospective book about the 8 years of George W. Bush's presidency, bringing structure to that much work – more than a million photographs – could have taken forever. Eric, as the president's photographer, had hired me to be his picture editor. Our connection started a few years before, when I hired Eric as a staff photographer at the Albuquerque Tribune. We worked together well and I came to have immense respect for Eric's integrity and the quality of his photographs so when he asked me to join his team, yes was the automatic answer.

This long-term connection and a lot of advance work streamlined the production of his book. I was asked to give a talk about working at the White House later in my time there. I structured the presentation in groupings based on the various environments of the presidency – the West Wing, the Residence, domestic and international trips and the president's ranch in Texas. Eric has since expanded on that structure when giving talks. This gave us a starting point for the structure of the book, which we made better with continued refinement until *Front Row Seat, A Photographic Portrait of the Presidency of George W. Bush* was published.

Here are questions I regularly hear about producing a book:

- What text should be with the book? That'll be an outgrowth of what you're wanting to say with the book. Most books have an introduction, written by a photographer or someone who can speak deeply about the subject matter of the book, or both.
- Should there be captions or titles? Considerations of text are mostly a matter of whether the information or context that the words introduce is critical to or elevates the images and their narrative. Journalistic or more information-driven projects are more likely to have captions or titles that sit by the pictures and 'art' is less likely. An often-used alternative is to present thumbnails of the photos with captions in the back of the book. That presents the images cleanly in the body of the book while allowing additional understanding in the back of the book.
- Should there be mediums other than photos? You would have ideally answered this question long before this stage. If the photos and text aren't accomplishing what you had hoped, then explore other possible forms of expression. It's not too late until the press runs.
- How do you gauge how to size and place photos on the pages? Asking what kind of feel you want the book to have based on how images sit on pages is a starting point. How you place photos on the page is a creative choice. Regardless of how, treat facing pages as one space.

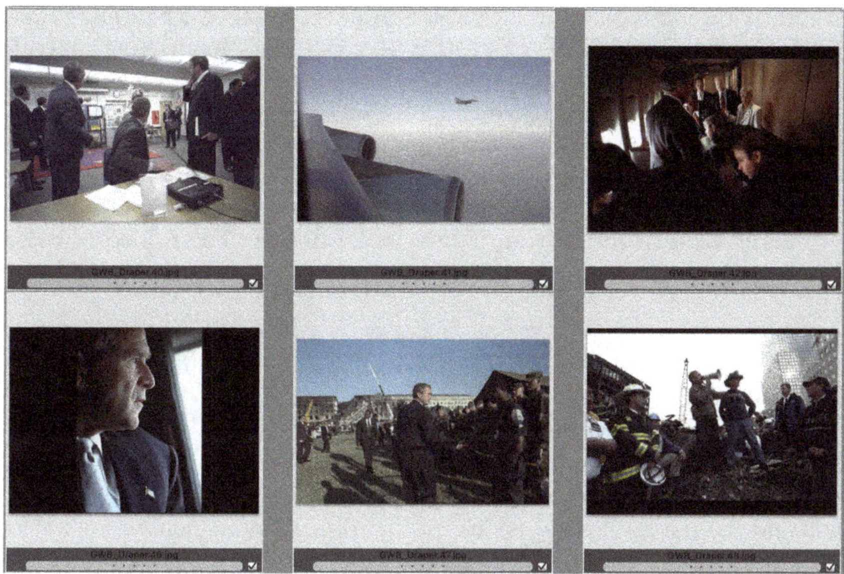

Photo 6.03.2 Here's part of the sequence for Eric Draper's book about the presidency of George W. Bush. These photos were all made on or soon after September 11, 2001.

If you want photos to be powerful and dominant, then size them to full bleeds or nearly so. If relationships between photos in a shared space convey the work with greater resonance, then place two or more photos on facing pages. People are increasingly placing different-sized images freely on a double page, with great effect. How you place photos within white, or negative space – that space not taken by photos – is a powerful aspect of your design decisions. Raymond Meeks does this effectively.

Placing photos on the pages of books is one way that photographers learn whether they've been centering the main element of their compositions too much. People who often build centered compositions must avoid full bleeds and size photos in a way that allows shifting the middle of the frame away from the gutter, to avoid key elements being obscured. Compositions shouldn't limit possibilities, they should present opportunities to expand the creation of third effects, which is the driving consideration.

- How do you decide on a size for the book? Sizing dramatically affects the experience of a book. Smaller tend to feel more intimate and personal, large books have a sense of self-importance and demand to be looked at. You can't just leave a large book sitting around without noticing it. Oversized books are hard to fit on most bookshelves and tend to cost more, so going big might diminish your market. There's been a trend toward smaller, more intimate books the past few years, in the 9 × 6-inch range or smaller. Nazraeli Press' has been producing its limited-run *One Picture Book* series since 1998, at 5 3/4 × 7 3/8 inches. In the 9 × 12-inch range is an average size. Proportion is a separate issue determined by how you want to display photos. Two examples: If you want to display photos full bleed across two pages, without cropping, then the spread will have to be the same proportion as the images; for vertical photos to be displayed as full bleeds, the single page size would have to be proportional to the photos format.

Try different sizing and placement strategies with your book and see which works best. Be consistent, though. Don't have a whole bunch of different sizes and placements, unless that scattered randomness is what you want to have come across.

Cover photo selection and display must work hand and glove-like with the book's title. The third effect should play strongly between the photo, title and the sizing of each. It's usually hard to know which photo works best for the cover until it's sitting there with a title.

Working with a designer is essential. Rare is a photographer who can design their book as well as a talented designer. A designer can also help guide the book through the printing process.

I initiated a 30th anniversary of The Alexia Grants book to commemorate the dedication of Peter and Aphrodite Tsairis, co-founders of The

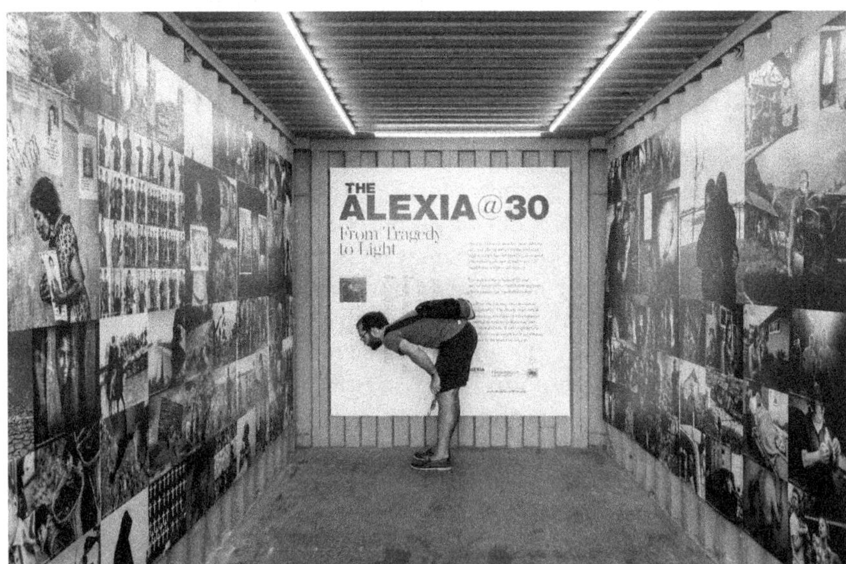

Photo 6.03.3 Bill Marr also designed a presentation for a Photoville shipping container to note The Alexia's 30th anniversary in 2019.

Alexia Foundation who I had the pleasure of working with for 8 years. Were it not for Bill Marr signing on as art director, the book wouldn't have happened. We went with a hybrid publishing form, where I worked with Syracuse University Press to help with logistics and connect us with a printer in North Dakota. We benefited from SU Press' rates but didn't contract with them for distribution. That was possible because I was on faculty at SU. Each 176-page book cost about $13 to print.

Aside from all these processes and considerations, making a book can be a blast, pure joy. What you learn from realizing that full execution takes you places you wouldn't otherwise have gone. And isn't that the point?

Section 6.6 Enter Competitions?

Should you enter competitions? The answer is another absolutely yes. Maybe. Why enter them, what is the value for your professional life? Do they mesh with and elevate your brand? Your answers to these questions will tell you if it's worth entering.

There are reasons beyond receiving awards to enter the competition fray. You can use the process of gathering work to consider for entry as an opportunity to assess what you did during the time frame of the work. If you enter and assess your work year after year it becomes an annual self-review. You can look at what you submitted last year and compare it to this year and evaluate the similarities and differences. Was there growth, did you produce work in the last year that you couldn't have a year ago and if not, why not? What made the best work happen and what kept you from producing more strong work? What will you do differently in the coming year to make next year's work another advancement in your life's work? Then instead of a painful burden, the entry process becomes a personal reward. Whether you receive an award or not, you've won. That is very different from thinking you've failed if you don't "win." (I disfavor the words win and winners, preferring awarded and recipients. You win the lottery with little effort, receiving an award takes immense effort so use terms that reflect the effort.)

Putting your work in front of a panel of judges has value. I've seen judges make notes of specific entries to be able to engage with the photographer after the judging. (Early on, I'd send a list of Alexia Grant finalist names and a brief description of their projects to a set of editors who I thought might want to work with those photographers. And later I revised the competition to publicly name 20 finalists, so their names and work could get out there.)

Name recognition that comes from receiving awards is a part of your brand. How many people's names changed from what they were to having a prefix of *Pulitzer Prize Winning Photographer* x. The Pulitzer is a big deal and receiving that recognition does change people's careers, if they capitalize on it. Some opportunities present themselves because of the award's recognition but most happen because photographers initiate subsequent efforts and are more able to get support because of the name recognition the award gives them. It's still hard work to get buy-in but maybe less so if one variable is people knowing that you're capable of producing compelling work.

Bill Kuykendall was the director of the Pictures of the Year (POY) competition and the professor I learned the most from when I was in graduate school at the University of Missouri in Columbia. We students got a front-row seat at the competition. Professor Kuykendall would tell us that he determined who was going to receive awards when he chose the judges because each judge would have preferences and choices of what types of photography to award reflected those preferences.

I had thought that there was some universal standard that judges responded to. Having been a judge in a bunch of competitions it has since been surprising to see what other judges did and did not respond to. I saw this even more firsthand during the 8 years I selected the judging panel for The Alexia Grants. I selected a panel by considering as many variables as possible: their viewpoints, varied personal and professional backgrounds, time in the profession and tastes. Most of the time the three-member panels ended up being split 2 for 1 against or vice versa. So I started to select panel members who were still diverse in their experience but were close to a shared perception of what strong work is. All members of the last year's panel that I selected had incredibly diverse professional experiences but all of them are Black. Noelle Thèard was one of the three and she noted that this was the first panel she'd been on where all members were Black. Their selection should be no more exceptional than it has been for all- or mostly white panels to be selected, for decades. I learned so much from that panel's conversations and what they considered and valued, and I hope the thousands who watched did as well – we posted a video of the judging to *YouTube*. Visual artists who are Black – Cornell Watson and Leonidas Enetanya – were chosen for the professional and student grants, respectively, that year, the first time in the history of the grant. What does that say about the consequences of deciding who sits on judging panels?

Representation in competitions is at long last a priority for more competitions. World Press Photo has new leadership and has revised its structure to encourage and increase entries from throughout the world by adopting a regional approach. POY is also expanding its international reach with POY Asia after years of partnering with POY Latam (Latin America), which was created by Pablo Corral Vega and Loup Langton. It takes more than just choosing a diverse panel of judges to make competitions represent populations more equitably. I spent a lot of time connecting with non-mainstream educational programs, organizations and individuals throughout the world as The Alexia director to increase participation; submissions more than doubled during my time, many of them from settings that were new to the competition.

It is astounding how many photography competitions there are. Every niche of photography has competitions, to the point that calling yourself an award-winning photographer is like saying you're an air-breathing human being. Who hasn't won an award? But not all awards are equal in stature. Knowing how a given competition is perceived in your corner of the image-making profession is an important consideration in knowing whether it's worth spending the time, and increasingly money for entry fees, to enter.

We've had to pay to enter some contests for ages but there have been increasing numbers of startup competitions over the past few years that exist to generate income for the creators – they make a living by running the competition. Other contests exist primarily to support an organization's members so receiving one of their awards has merit primarily in the context of that group and its members. There is still value in entering some of the for-profit and organizational competitions but not all of them. How to know which ones? Learn about those that you are considering entering. How many people enter, what does it cost, who runs it or owns it, examine the categories both for what they recognize and the number of them, ask around for people's impressions of the contest, look at who has won in the past and determine whether you think their work is worthy of

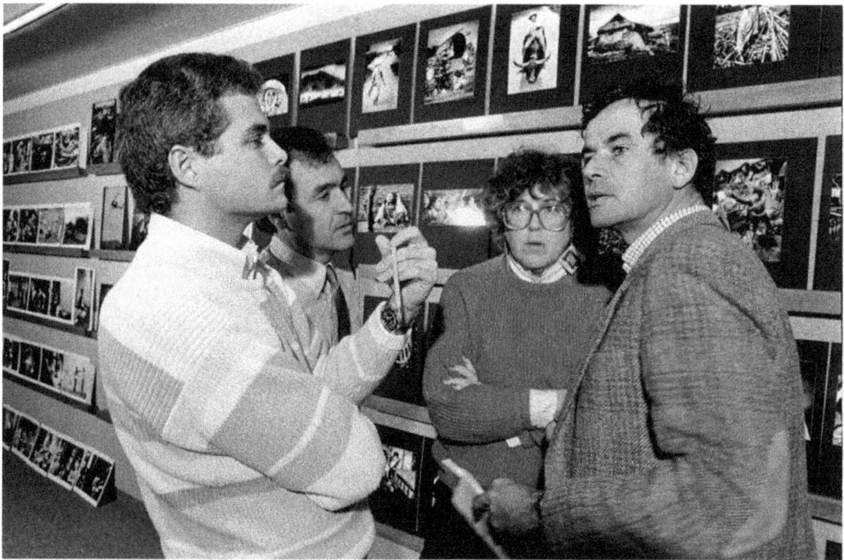

Photo 6.03.4 It's important to know the history of competitions you are considering entering, including what kinds of people are chosen to be judges. Pictures of the Year is the longest-running photojournalism competition in the world. Larry Price, Peter Howe, Karen Mullarkey and Bruno Barbey were POY judges in this photo I made as a grad student in 1986.

recognition, what businesses are sponsors of or support the competition? Look at the rules carefully, especially usage rights. Some contests want to be able to use your photos for anything and some can even sell usage of your photos outside their venue.

Another important consideration is whether the contest is more than the equivalent of a boxing match. Do they do more than put up a ring, let entries knock it out and hold up the winners' arm? Are there prizes that make it worth entering? Can you watch the judging? Do the organizers create an archive of recipients that is searchable? Do they write articles that inform beyond specifics related to the competition? Do they support recipients in ways other than monetary prizes, such as publishing their work with a partner organization, or making a book, giving feedback, hosting conversations? Are judges chosen and past recipients diverse? Do they create events associated with the contest that draw professionals of note, especially those who hire photographers? What press or trade publication traction does the contest get, if any? Who pays attention to them? In sum, what is the whole of the competition and what is its perception among the people who might hire you? That'll determine if it's worth entering for you.

Selecting, sequencing and placing photos in the right categories is a specialty. Part of the reason that Copley Northern Illinois publications won more awards than any other publication in the history of POY – 29 awards in 1 year, including first and second place newspaper photographer of the year – is that we knew how to enter well. Two important variables are matching photos and stories to the best category and taking the strongest photos from multiple-image entries and entering those in single-image categories. Sequencing for contests is similar to what it might be for your site or other setting but definitely make the first image compelling and clear as to what it's addressing. It's best to lead judges visually through the narrative, you don't want to be esoteric or base the sequence on the information the photos represent in this setting; judges should have an experience from the sequence as opposed to being told information or being left not knowing what your entry is about. There might be one judge who wants to read the captions but most of the time text in photos goes unread, given that most competitions have multiple rounds and caption-reading tends to happen only in the last rounds. Titles of multiple-image entries, on the other hand, are often read as the photos are being projected and some competitions also require reading summary paragraphs.

I've known a lot of people who say contests aren't worth entering. If your professional life is guaranteed to be stable, you're happy with doing things the way you are now, you don't reach out much beyond your own space, you don't care what others think of your work, then you're in a position to avoid competition. If this doesn't describe your working world, then it's worth engaging with this part of the profession.

Section 6.7 Apply for Grants, Residencies?

Grants, fellowships and residencies are like competitions on steroids. While contests can boost your career and lead to work, grants and residencies provide direct compensation and sustenance. Oh, well then for sure I should apply for some, you might be thinking to yourself. Hold on for a minute as we walk through some considerations.

The first question is: Should you incorporate grants and/or residencies into your professional life? Real question. Because applying for grants takes a lot of effort that would be wasted if the type of work you do wouldn't have a chance of being awarded. (I've paired grants and residencies here because there is enough of a parallel between them and in some cases, they are indistinguishable.)

You're likely to have a greater degree of success in the grant world if you are approaching topics that only you can accomplish and you're creating narratives that are unique to you. Another way of saying this is that you are the best person to execute this body of work and the work is a match topically and stylistically with the type of work that the grant supports.

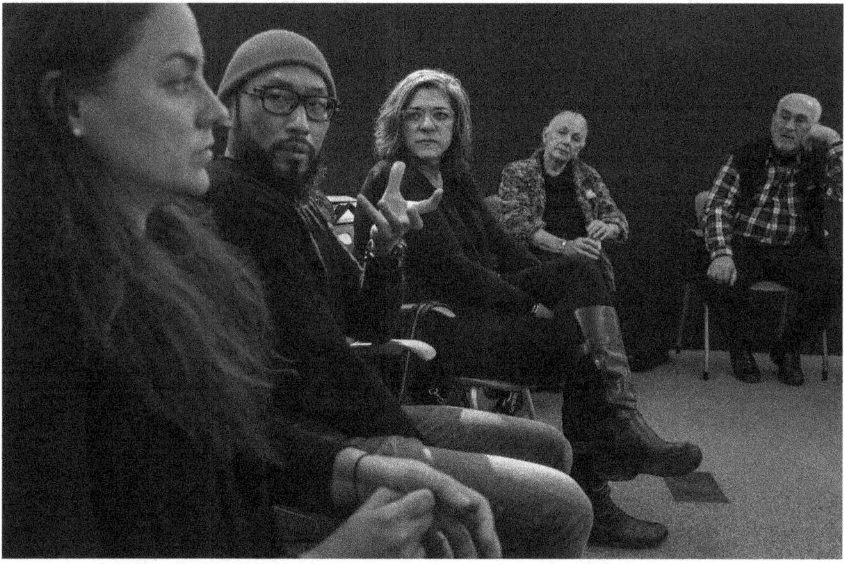

Photo 6.04 Applying for grants has many benefits, including getting your work in front of a set of judges. Here, Alexia Grant judges discuss entries with Alexia Foundation co-founders Peter and Aphrodite Tsairis looking on, in 2018. Judges are Adriana Teresa Letorney, co-founder of Visura, Zun Lee, visual storyteller, physician and educator, and Mary-Anne Golon, assistant managing editor and director of photography at The Washington Post.

A starting point is finding grants that are a match. There's a list of grants in the resource guide section of this book but it's hardly all-encompassing and leans toward documentary. How do you know a given grant is a match? Read their mission statement, what they want you to submit and what they expect if you receive the grant. See who has won the grant in the past and who the judges have been. Are you willing to go through the significant effort it takes to apply?

Some grants allow you to apply for other grants at the same time as theirs; some grants limit you in some way – you could not apply for an Alexia grant if you had won another major award in the previous year with the same project.

Here are some thoughts on how best to apply once you're ready:

Read the rules and submission guidelines carefully. They vary widely but most require a written proposal with or without a summary at the top and a set of pictures, typically 20 photos. Proposals are usually in the 500- to 800-word range. Brevity is appreciated, I'll tell you, from having read several thousand proposals. Some grants recognize work that is complete while others are looking to support work that is yet to be started or is in progress. The Alexia rarely awards a project that has not yet been started and most recipients have been at least half done with the work. Some will support paying to produce books and exhibitions, others will not.

The Proposal

I suggest starting to write your proposal with the summary first. If you can percolate what the project is about to a paragraph, you'll have achieved a level of clarity that will guide the rest of the process. The longer proposal should address these four aspects: what is the project; why is this important now; how will you accomplish the project, which includes making it clear that you're the right person to tell this story; what will result because of the project.

Jin Ding described it this way when she worked for the International Women's Media Foundation (IWMF): What's the project about; why you; why now; how are you going to do it?

Two choices of how to begin your proposal are to take people there by describing a setting in a way that engages people emotionally or by presenting informational aspects of the project straightforwardly. The latter is effective only if the information is surprising in some way.

Clearly explain why the work is important now, explain the consequences of inaction or how events of history are coalescing in significant ways or things are about to change.

How you'll make the work can give an overview of your plans, say what you've already done and, in the process, will demonstrate that you have become an expert on the topic and know exactly how best to represent it.

Granting organizations are increasingly more likely to support projects that have collaborations baked into them. Showing that you're working with organizations and others to produce the work and that the relationship will make things happen that make a difference can elevate your entry, or not, depending on the grant.

Follow advice in the editing sections of this book to determine which photos to submit and how to sequence them. The photos you submit will tell judges whether you're deserving of the grant. As with competitions, sequencing should be experiential more than informational. Take people on a journey. You don't have to submit the maximum number of photos. If you are choosing lesser-quality photos because they represent situations or informational aspects that you think are important, use text to present that information and submit a tighter, higher-quality set of pictures. Your entry is as good as the weakest photo.

Captions can be critical. Write them not to describe what's happening in the pictures, unless that's not clear and is important, but to give what's happening context. Tell a story with each caption and think of them collectively as if they were a narrative.

Avoiding Pitfalls

Here are some things to be aware of:

- Ensure that your project is best done now. If it could have been any time in the recent past or future, then judges will be less inspired. If you're touching an ongoing circumstance, then address it in a timely way.
- If your topic has been addressed many times, how does your approach differ from those?
- Scope is critical. If you're proposing a grand-scale project but the grant supports smaller efforts you're out. You can break a large project into component parts that are of a scale that a given grant does support. The opposite is true if what you're proposing is too narrow.
- Avoid presenting your opinion in the proposal. Don't be pedagogical or didactic. Instead, be engaging, convey your passion, knowledge and interest.
- Make it clear that there is enough left to photograph if the grant exists to support producing work.
- The title of your project is critical. It sets up judges for what to expect and gives them a starting point. Successful ones are usually a balance between peaking interest and being specific. Complete thoughts tend to be better; one- or two-word titles generally don't work in the grant world.
- Share your submission materials with people you respect to get their opinions. Ask them to read the proposal and then ask them to summarize what it's about. If what comes back is not what you intended then you can revise.

- Learn how the judging takes place. That can help with how you write your proposal, select and sequence the photos. If judges read the proposal and see the photos before they get together that's different from if they are sitting in a room together and hear the summary and see the photos at the same time. Whatever the format, try to create that setting with people you trust and present your submission to them, to refine your presentation.
- Most effort goes into applying for the grant. What if you get it? Extend your planning into what you'll do to execute the project along the expectations of the grant. Address the proverbial what's next before it becomes a last-minute effort.

Good luck.

Section 6.8 Work with a Business?

We are in a high tide moment for visual storytelling in another way. Brands, or companies, have increasingly been branching out from showing their products through traditional advertising to hiring visual storytellers who can convey the spirit of their products or services through compelling narratives of the lifestyles and settings where those products live.

A pinnacle example of this is when a company pays a visual storyteller to be their brand ambassador. I was walking by the North Face store Fifth Avenue in New York – the city not the state – a while back and was surprised to see a giant portrait of photographer/filmmaker Jimmy Chin in the window, so I went into the store and saw several large prints of photographs he'd made. Nice brand ambassadorship. Also in this realm, David Doubilet is connected to Rolex and Corey Rich has several active lifestyle business connections.

A variation is when brands pay photographers to post to social media, at the influencer level, where the number of followers the photographer has accrued is what attracts the brand that matches the photographer's ethos in some way. Feedspot is one space that connects brands with photographers through what it calls influencer marketing and blogger outreach. It's notable that seven of the top 20 photographers with *Feedspot*, as of this writing, photograph regularly for *National Geographic*. That's because a handful of *Natgeo* photographers were groundbreaking practitioners on *Instagram* under the auspices of *The Photo Society*, before NGS jumped on this bandwagon. Randy Olson has been the primary creator and driver of TPS, with George Steinmetz, Michael Yamashita, Gerd Ludwig and others – and Deb Pang Davis designed their original website. You must have been published in the print version of National Geographic to be considered for TPS membership.

I'm reading that as Instagram diminishes in popularity, influencers are also receding. But some other form will surely replace this.

What drives brand ambassadorships and influencer engagements is an expansion of photographers developing star power in the context of ever-expanding digital environments. Those who can sit atop their specializations become stars of sorts and can command or draw financial support for producing work because of their status. That dynamic has always existed but because there were fewer environments or markets where photography existed, there were fewer star photographers.

Yet another version of brand support is when businesses give money to visual storytellers or publications in support of specific efforts they're accomplishing. Among my favorites is *Camel Finds Water* a film about Trevor Gordon restoring a fishing boat and taking it on a re-maiden voyage. *Danner, Taylor Stitch, St. Archer Brewery* and *Feral* supported the film. These are called sponsorships.

Brands can initiate seemingly altruistic engagements, too, such as *Vueve Clicquot's Inspiration in Bloom* series, which engaged with six creatives to express their impressions of the year to come, as noted in AnOthermag.com Shini Parks is the creative director/photographer/brand ambassador in the mix of talents.

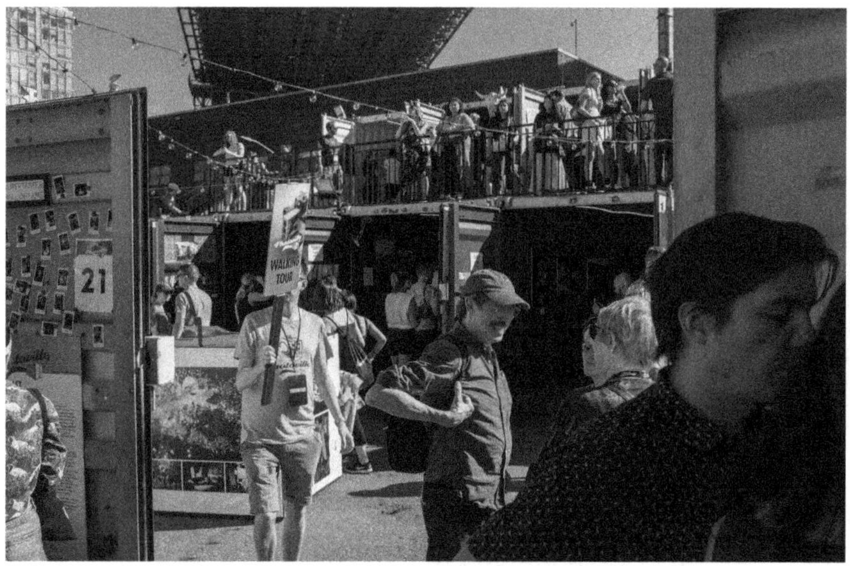

Photo 6.05 Attending photography events such as Photoville in New York City can elevate your career. You never know who you'll meet. That's Rick Smolan in the baseball cap during the 2019 Photoville. He's talking to Sarah Leen, who was then National Geographic director of photography. Rick has gotten corporate support for his projects for several decades.

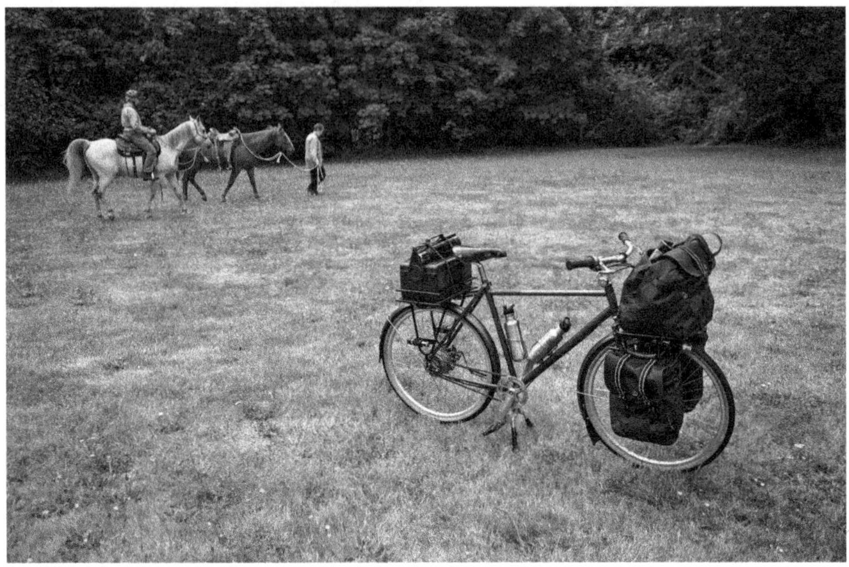

Photo 6.06 Long-term pdxcross team efforts and my resulting project about people who make bikes by hand lead to working with several brands and events, including *Oregon Manifest*, which created a competition for hand-built bike makers. The competition included a lengthy bike test ride. This is True Fabrication's bike near the start of the test as four-legged mounts passed by.

Patagonia is among outdoor brands that are really taking this model to its fullest potential.

These are all higher-end examples. They can happen at any level, including locally. Ben Wilson knew he wanted to work with businesses to tell their stories at some point in his career. So, while he was in one of my storytelling courses I encouraged him to connect with a local business. He ended up telling the stories of two Syracuse businesses, a brewery and a bike shop, using portraiture, documentary-style photography with introduced light, video and stop motion.

Eric Jackson and Mylz Blake applied their graduate course learning to create Black Cub Productions and were later joined by Ngozi Inyama as COO. Black Cub is a creative agency that focuses on cross-cultural stories that bring people together and work with organizations and businesses that support similar goals.

Another variation is contracting with a brand to produce an archive of images that they can use for a variety of communication needs, now and in the future. Updating that archive periodically would make this an ongoing relationship. You could become their go-to person as needs arise.

If you haven't connected with brands and are interested in telling entrepreneurial stories as part of your business plan, connecting with a business that you're interested in is the starting point. Producing a narrative with one gives you material to show the next, on the way to building out a potential specialty. The choices are whether you tell the brand's story directly, produce work where their brand appears or ask them to support work you create that is associative to their business' mission. An example of the associative would be if you photograph wild birds to approach companies that make or sell bird feeders or bird food. If you opt to tell a brand's story, you can contract with them to produce all their visual and social media content, even their website, if that's in your skillset.

Working directly with businesses through branded and influencer relationships are two ways that visual storytellers are creating more variations of income streams. Having a range of ways to generate income is critical or at least helpful. Here are some other ways people are generating income, just to make you aware of some possibilities that you might not have been.

- NFTs – Non-fungible tokens – are the buzz of the moment. As I write The Associated Press has, surprisingly to me, created its own space for NFTs, as are many other ventures. They are cryptographic assets on a blockchain with unique identification codes and metadata. What? As NFTs apply to photography, it's selling a unique digital rendering of a photograph or group of photographs. The advantage for photographers is that nearly all the profit from sales goes to them, as opposed to represented work sold through agencies or stock.
- Stock photography sales fell off a cliff a while back but seem to be reviving a bit now. That's a world unto itself that is worthy of a book-length exploration. If you aren't aware of it, stock means producing photographs that entities could apply as need to their uses. They tend to be photos that generically represent a topic, an object, a type of person or an idea. Compositionally and stylistically stock photos tend to be simple, so they're quick reads and can take on type for ads.

Earning money from stock, like grants, takes time except with stock the more time you put into it, the greater the return, in theory, because each purchase pays little, generally. Most of the work is on the front end and involves combing your archive for potential photos, prepping and keywording. A lot of people make photos specifically for stock sales, sometimes while they're on assignment or just going about their lives. Companies that represent stock include Getty which also owns, iStock, Shutterstock, Adobe Stock, Alamy and Dreamstime. Wirestock is a variation that connects your work to a range of stock venues and take a cut of sales. Each has different acceptance, submission and payment criteria and processes.

Stock could be worth your time if you can make photos that are more straightforward and can sustain the process and business aspects.

- More and more photographers are taking to YouTube and other online platforms to present how-to lessons and their observations about photography. Subscription-based platforms such as Patreon, Substack, Medium, Podia and Ko-fi offer varying services to present what you have to offer. In contrast to media platforms where how much you earn and use of your images are negatives. Becoming your own brand and the value of what you present becomes your primary income-generating stream.
- Creating in-person or online workshops is another option. Using apps such as Skillshare creates ongoing income without having to create presentations each time.
- I mentioned crowdfunding in the photo book section, but you can also crowd-fund to support other types of your endeavors.
- You can sell products through your website or partnerships with other entities that match your values and goals. Those can range from prints to digital files to zines to books to posters, films, anything that involves imagery and your creativity. These can be one-time or subscription-based purchases.
- Monetize your blog if you can commit to writing regularly.
- A lot of people do one kind of work to produce income to support another kind of passion-driven work. Photographing weddings or making portraits of people are common income producers. I think a largely untapped market is being paid to photograph people's daily lives. Jessica Ruíz is in that market in the L.A. area after graduating with a master's degree from Syracuse. What a gift it would be for a family to have a complete set of professionally made pictures or video of what their lives were like, to revisit for decades to come.
- Rethinking the business model has led to writing time-limited usage of work into contracts. The same work can re-generate income with the same client after the contracted time has lapsed.

Each of these takes more work to accomplish with the associated learning curves to become good at them. But that is the nature of being a visual storyteller today. We're able to say and create so much more diverse work but we must be able to do far more than was true not so many years ago. Those of us who have been doing this a while have to grow our skills and expand what we're capable of producing; those starting out have the advantage of learning from the outset what it takes to make a living.

Section 6.9 Get a Job?

If earlier in this section you answered that series of questions in a way that leads you to think that getting a full-time job is a better path for you then here's some advice on how to go about getting hired.

Whether you are a student, are just starting out post-education or are changing career paths later in life, my advice is that you make every aspect of what you're doing now contribute to getting the job you want. If you're a college student, your choice of minors or second majors can start to point to your specialization, which in turn projects you toward a path in the profession and a job. My undergrad major was in news editing and writing but I took art classes to develop my visual acumen, earned a second major in Spanish because I became interested in understanding more about the world, and took several geography courses for the same reason. Then in grad school, I took courses that expanded my photographic skills, picked up picture editing and design courses. So it was not surprising that 5 years after earning a master's I got a job as a picture editor at National Geographic. I had created the path through a series of choices but didn't know it until each subsequent stop enroute. And here I am now. Looking back, what I was really doing is determining what type of environment I find most engaging. The answer is situations where I'm dealing with the whole of the process, not just one medium and that involves making systems work better to accomplish more substantive results. It is the thrill of making things happen that wouldn't have by doing things more dimensionally or doing things that haven't been done. It was never about the job but what could be accomplished in each environment.

You probably don't know the exact job that you want. That's ok. Going through the process of getting hired will help you define and find specific jobs that help you figure out what really fulfills you. The job market is a world that you travel to uniquely based on your interests. Queries and searches lead to connections that lead to other connections and further queries, which lead to possibilities worth pursuing. This is a learning process that you teach yourself by doing. It can be frustrating not knowing what's next or exactly how to get there but trust me, you will learn of opportunities and you will find one that's a match if your effort is concerted.

Know from the outset that getting hired in the visual professions is more complex than a lot of others. You need to have more ducks in a row. That means that you'll have to have an active, responsive website with a range of work of the type that you want to be hired for. You will have defined and sustained a professional social media presence and all the ancillary materials – stationary, leave-behinds, promotional pieces – and the becoming known processes discussed in this book. Ideally, you will have identified a specialization to focus your energy on and be more appealing to potential employers because of that.

Do all you can to set things in motion, but serendipity is as likely to land you a job, more in the context of preparation meeting opportunity through chance. I got an internship in grad school because I happened to mention I was looking for one to another grad student. He knew of an opening and gave me a reference for that internship. I got it and then got hired into my first picture editing job because of that internship.

Make Connections

A lot of the hiring happens because of a connection between the person being hired and the one doing the hiring. It's up to you to create those connections – it's not as daunting as you might think. Here's how, as a student:

Go to workshops and meet people and hire people. Don't be afraid to introduce yourself, people in positions that involve hiring are there to meet people they might want to hire.

Sign up for reviews, which offer you a choice of who you want to connect with.

You can reach out to professionals and ask to shadow them to make a direct connection in settings that interest you. You might be told no by the first person you ask but keep asking, a lot of professionals enjoy helping people get started.

Join and be active in professional organizations.

Ask your professors to help connect you but be specific in what you're asking to narrow your request to something reasonable. Don't just ask who should apply for a job, describe what you're interested in and any details that can help your professor narrow in on suggestions of who to contact. Better yet, determine a range of settings that interest you and ask your professors if they know people in those settings.

Create Your Network

As you make connections with more and more people, you're creating your own network. You do have to stay connected with people for your network to remain active. If you think of them as one-time connections, you'll get minimal benefit from them. Write thank you notes after every engagement, ideally handwritten notes – that shows you care enough about them to spend the time, cost of paper and a stamp. It's reasonable to ask your network of professionals for advice and feedback but keep what you expect from them simple. If they see your request as a lot of work or you ask too often, you'll not stay on their good side.

Apply to internships starting as soon as you have enough work, as early as the summer between your second and third years. Don't put too much burden on that first internship. Any situation that is connected to the visual profession will have value, even if that's to realize you don't want to do it. Internships tend to build on each other. They provide real-world references and experience with which you can apply to better internships, many of which lead to full-time jobs.

I've been involved in the hiring process 30–40 times in a range of settings and types of jobs. Among those was Leo Hsu. The work that Leo submitted with his application for an internship at The Albuquerque Tribune is what made me consider hiring him. But it wasn't the most important variable, his personality was. One of his stories was titled *Aliens among Us*. Leo had seen the presence of "aliens" in everyday settings and made a fascinating essay. When I talked to Leo I learned that his mind was like a sponge, perpetually curious and driven to explore and understand. We hired him for who he is. Unfortunately, I left to start a job at National Geographic the day before Leo started his internship, so I didn't get to work with him, though we stayed in touch as he went on to earn a PhD in visual anthropology, and thereafter.

Know getting hired is as much about making it clear who you are as a person, what your values are, why you made the choices of what to engage with as it is the work you will show. You tell a potential employer who you are when talking about your work, when you write a cover letter and through how you respond to the people who are hiring you. Be curious and confident but humble when you engage. People hire the person not the work so help them understand how amazing you are.

If You Get an Interview

Most jobs require you to write a cover letter and send your strongest work. Keep your cover letter to one page unless they've asked for a longer one. Tell them something about you that gives them the sense that you'd be a good match for their environment. Speak directly about why you think you are a strong candidate, and worth their consideration. Offer why you want to work for them, both the entity and the people you'd be working for and with. How you convey these things can vary widely but should be unique to you and reflect your personality.

If you advance to the interview point, get to know the entity and who works there. Try to speak to someone who works there now to learn as much as possible. Arrive early, whether it's a virtual or in-person interview. Wear an outfit that is slightly better than what people wear in the day to day. I bought a nice suit to interview for my National Geographic interview and was dressed way too nicely compared to most of the people who interviewed me, so I felt a bit self-conscious – not a good thing. Who knows, maybe they just thought I REALLY wanted the job. I did get it.

A big part of interviewing is how you respond to their questions, some of which will seem direct, and others may not. Don't hesitate to ask a question in response to theirs, for clarification, if you're not certain of what they're asking or what to say. That gap can give your mind time to process a good response. My nature is to pause before answering a question, to let my response form before it comes out of my mouth. You can also rephrase the question to ensure you understand it. Or buy time by saying, "Let me make sure I understand, are you asking …"

Make your answer apply to how you'd work in the job you've applied for. Questions you might be asked:

- What inspires you? I'd say it's better to speak to what you do to become inspired and how that applies to this job than trying to answer generally.
- Whose work do you follow or whose work do you admire? Start by describing the type of creators that you respond to. Then have a few people in mind, some of whom work for this organization, others outside of it. Don't list friends or super obvious people. The direct connections you can make to the setting you're applying to the better.
- What would you bring to the job? This is a variation of wanting to know how you act in the workplace. You can tell them a story of a situation where something you did is a reflection of what you'd bring to this job or you can describe yourself in terms that will matter in this workplace.
- Tell us something about you that we wouldn't know from reading your resumé and seeing your work. Here too you want to answer this in a way that puts you into the job you're applying for and explains how your personality is a match to the job. Speak about how you would work in their environment, how your personality would mesh with the demands of the job and how you'd interact with people you work for and with.
- What do you see yourself going 5 and 10 years from now? This is one that you might think is looking for specifics but answering generally is advisable. Speak in larger terms about what you value in your professional pursuit and how those will carry you forward.
- And the killer: What are your weak points? This one is a trap. What you likely hear is them asking why you're a failure, what you're lousy at. What they really want to know is how you respond to challenging situations. It's better to respond in a way that shows them how you respond to situations when you're at first not sure of what to do.

Always have about three questions in mind to ask them. And you can follow up some of their questions with questions to show that you're really interested in that topic as it applies to their workplace. Your questions and how you phrase them help you understand the setting, but they equally tell them what you care about.

Follow Up

Thank them on the spot for considering you, tell them your impressions of the interview and why you're even more excited by the prospect of working there. Then follow up with a hand-written note to the key people.

If you do get the job, wonderful. If not, ask yourself what you can do for the next interview that would increase the chances of getting that job. Refine your site, your presentation, your answers, your questions.

And move ever forward.

Being a Staff Photographer

A friend who has worked for a medium-sized newspaper for a few years wrote the other day and among other things was describing how frustrating work is, how much has changed for the worse. I thought it might be helpful to offer some thoughts on how to make your staff photographer's work life better. (I'm using the title staff photographer to include working for any entity that produces and "publishes" content for a community, such as news organizations, hospitals, universities, government, businesses, outdoor and environmental organizations, etc.)

The best staff photographers have always been those who directed much of their work life by always having and being able to execute better ideas for stories than what the assignment system would produce. They were respected in their organizations and were deeply connected to the communities they served. These traits are now essential, not just so you can work on things that you want to, but because to stay working in this world and be content you have to be perceived as having value beyond taking pictures and producing videos. If you become known as someone who feeds the beast with great content, who connects your employer more strongly with the community and you are great to work with you'll be of greater value to the organization and your day-to-day will be less fraught, more rewarding.

How to Create the Best Work

Having a variety of ways to set work in motion is the trick. Here are some:

- Set a goal of setting at least two ideas a week in motion.
- Know which people who initiate content – writers and word editors if in a newsroom – are the most visually literate. Check in with them regularly, know what they're working on at the idea stage, express interest in and join efforts that have the greatest potential. And sell your ideas to them.
- Always have work in progress or waiting to be done that requires a range of time to produce. Have ideas that you could turn quickly to

fill a need, ones that would take a day or so to accomplish and ones that would take a few days, weeks or longer but that you'd work on piecemeal. Create one effort that is yours personally, that you care about and periodically connect with indefinitely.
- Develop specialties within your community – journalists call them beats. You might care about criminal justice, religion, education, the outdoors, sports or if you're in a topical setting develop a specialty within that setting. Get to know the people and what's happening within your specialties, ideally getting people to call you when notable things transpire. Change specialties over time to build a dimensional network in your community.
- Manage your schedule before it's managed. Tell the people you answer to what you have in the works, when you need to do what you need to do, to be sure that works for them.
- Always be aware of what your boss's needs are, or will be, and offer to help meet them. Telling your boss "I can take care of that for you" reveals commitment beyond yourself and will likely be an effort that pays forward.

Creating Added Value

The more you create value through what you do, beyond the standard expectations of your job, the more you'll be valued. For instance, you can become known as the person who solves specific problems before they become problems or people come to you because of your specific point of view, anything that is valued and attributable only to you.

At the White House, we realized that the more the president valued what we did, the better work the photographers would be able to do. Among the things we did to be valued was to select the best photos every week and print those in a booklet. Eric Draper gave a new book to the president every week. It was extra work, but the added value produced better work which then reinforced our value.

- Sharing a photo with people you photograph, even asking them what photo they'd like for you to make, for them, will give you standing in the community that grows. I gave a print to a restaurateur I photographed in Portland, Oregon, who told me it was the best photo he'd ever had made, that he framed it and put it on his fireplace mantle.
- Photograph your co-workers doing what they do and share those photos with them.
- Ask your boss what you can do to help, every day, or better yet know what's needed and present a solution.

- Connect with high school, community college or university journalism and art programs to teach photography, as a guest or a full course.
- Host online experiences for your community. These can be to talk about specific projects you've done, the staff's best work from the year, anything. Formats can vary from podcasts, live conversations, pdfs that readers download, q&a sessions and more.

Developing Credibility

The more dimensionally you approach your work life, the better off you're likely to be.

- Regularly tell your coworkers how much and why you appreciate something they've done.
- Bring together coworkers to do reviews of work. Encourage everyone to bring at least one example of work others have done that they think is successful, then talk about why those efforts work well and what it took to make that happen. You can make this visually centric but make it open to writers, editors and others. This will become infectious.
- Educate your coworkers about what visually strong content is. When working with writers and editors on efforts, tell them why it's working well, or not well, for imagery and offer an approach that would lead to strong visuals. Post strong work in the newsroom, bring in guests to talk to newsroom gatherings, ask outsiders for critiques that you then share.
- Avoid being demanding. The worst thing is to be perceived as someone who has to have it their way. I'd have regular verbal combat with one newspaper section editor. She'd rebuff most of my input. When I realized that she perceived that I was telling her what to do and she didn't like that, I backed up and offered that when I suggest something, it was just an idea that comes from wanting to offer the best visual content possible for the section. "It's your section, your decision," I said. Thereafter we had the best working relationship and most of my offerings happened.

Planning for Change of Job

There's a sizeable Facebook group called *What's Your Plan B*, comprised mostly of visual journalists who lost their jobs. If your job ended tomorrow, by choice or not, what would you do? I'd advise that you be able to answer this question long before you must. You can start working now to make that possibility less cataclysmic.

First, define what you'd like to do. If you want to keep doing what you're doing but at a different place, start reaching out to potential future employers to establish a relationship, let them get to know you and your work. Identify several, not just one.

If you want to do something completely different, start doing that now, in your spare time, or if you can, build it into your current work life. For example, if you want to become an independent visual producer with a specialization, start producing work like that now. As you're working and you meet people who might hire you in the future, create an ongoing connection with those people so that when you go independent you've already established a client base.

This happened to me. My last newspaper position was going to eliminate so I took a buyout. I saw this coming a couple years out and with my wife's encouragement and support started to form my own business of working directly with photographers. It took an immense effort and thankfully within a few weeks of my job ending, I was earning a living as an independent. That income just kept growing.

I've known a lot of photographers who changed careers completely, by switching to a new passion, from roasting coffee to making beer and wood-fired pizza. There is a lot of stress involved regardless of the transition. But to a person, they say they are in a better place than they were.

Take Care of Yourself

Regardless of your path, it's easy and too common to devote most of your waking hours to making a living. As a profession this has sadly been a standard expectation. The notion of work-life balance is too simplistic, as if Lady Justice were the model. There is lasting value for your health and well-being if you can determine your own balance on this spectrum of work/not work.

Try This

- Create or refine your website based on ideas presented here.
- Research, devise and execute a social media plan for your professional path.
- Create a set of promotional materials specific to your type of photography.
- At some point initiate a narrative of book depth and create the book. "Book depth" can be of any length if what is presented is complete and dimensional.
- Determine which competitions are a match for the type of work you create and enter three of them. Then watch the judging if you can. Evaluate what was awarded.

- Identify and apply for a grant if that's appropriate for the type of work you do.
- Consider what kinds of businesses might be a market for your work and then devise a plan to connect with them and pitch your idea.
- If getting a job is your goal, start setting that in motion long before you need it. Create and keep fresh your resume and website; go to workshops; meet people; get to know the market you want to enter; ask people for help; produce work that appeals to that market. Make your educational or current experience as productive as possible to the goal of getting a job.

Conclusion

The Inability To Not

A quality that all of the many hundreds of photographers I've worked with share is this: The Inability To Not Tell Stories With Photographs. Removing the double negative: They are all compelled, they must bring a camera to their mind's eye. Everyone has a unique why that drives their compulsion. For some, it is the need to connect with people and the camera allows that to happen. Others are driven by being able to express themselves through the photographic form. Others feel like they have to say things about life on the planet and the camera is their choice as the mechanism of expression. Yet others get a kick out of the photographic process alone no matter what's in front of them.

Knowing what truly drives you is a critical step in the process of more completely being able to achieve your fully realized why. And once you have this clarity decisions in all aspects thereafter will be clearer, or at least you'll have the checks in place to know if you're staying along your path.

This is not an easy or automatic profession. So, if you aren't compelled and willing to do what it takes to make it, step aside now because there are plenty of people who are. As Gregory Heisler warns, you may be in love with the idea of being a photographer but aren't willing to put in the work to become more of one than you are now.

The only way to achieve and sustain a professional life is to put yourself out there, get out of your comfort zone, test yourself beyond your current limits, constantly. Challenge yourself to make photographs as you never have and create evermore dimensional narratives. Ask what was rich and rewarding, what was meh or unacceptable and do more of the good, less of the not-so-good. Not everything will be easy, even when you are perfectly aligned on your path. There will be a sense of accomplishment, a self-fulfillment that is unique, each time you achieve a heightened effort.

I've seen this growth brighten the lives of most of those I've worked with. Seeing their sense of accomplishment is what satisfies mine. If this book has helped you advance and elevate your why, then that makes me happy.

Randall Roberts was my boss in Albuquerque. He'd say as we were leaving after typically long days, "Thanks for stopping by." I've carried that sentiment forward every place I've worked.

Thank you for stopping by.

DOI: 10.4324/9781003287544-7

Acknowledgments

How to even begin? Every experience with every person I've encountered on the path to this writing is embodied on these pages. Everyone was like a magnetic field, either attracting or repulsing. Thinking of them collectively now is like watching a Marvel movie intro. Those that linger with warm embraces are the people who were most giving, patient, thoughtful, challenging and inspirational. This book would double in length if I were to name names with the intention of mentioning everyone who has been an influence. I am an editor so let me attempt a shorter naming.

Sergeant Joseph Cotton and his wife showed me as an 18-year-old, U.S. Air Force Airman, how rich a marriage can be, and they were the first Black couple I'd ever been around. A first, professional influence was Sam Kimura, from whom I took my first university-level photography class, at the University of Alaska at Anchorage. I learned from Sam how to make and print pictures, but more importantly, he and his family invited me into their home. That connection, as a 20-year-old still in the Air Force, taught me that we are what we do. While I was an undergrad, Professors David Gitlitz and Linda Davidson opened my eyes to the world, as we walked across Spain, speaking only Spanish while exploring art, history and architecture, on the medieval pilgrimage route, El Camino de Santiago de Compostela.

This book is stronger because of the feedback I got from Zun Lee and Nathaniel Brunt.

A handful of people have been there in ways that mattered in many phases of my life. I've been in awe of what high school classmates Phil and June Simpson have accomplished. They created Silver Hills Winery outside of our hometown of 1,800 in Nebraska and hosted delicious meals most weekends while running the family farm. Loup Langton, Melissa Farlow and Randy Olson became lifelong compatriots starting with grad school. I am a visual editor because of Bill Kuykendall and Mike Zerby, two of my grad school professors. Vince Musi and Callie Shell have been heartmates since the mid-80s – and Vince officiated Deb and my marriage with their son Hunter as ring bearer while Callie made photographs. David Griffin, Kathy Moran, Sarah Leen and Bill Marr have been ever present, whether in person or not. Editors Tim Gallagher and Sue Schmitt taught me that leaders don't dictate, they inspire. Julia Dolan, Steven Josefsberg and Lisa

Hostetler expanded my understanding of art. Gregory Heisler taught me to see anew, again. Jim Shahin enlivened my brain, every time we talked. Lexine Alpert is the embodiment of compassion, as Elizabeth Krist is of caring, Zun Lee is of what matters, Janet Jarman is of dedication, Dennis Dimick is of knowledge, Rick Smolan is of creating community, Andrea Wise is of doing right.

From Albuquerque Tribune cohorts I learned how to be a David in a world of Goliaths. National Geographic colleagues taught me that place can be the essence. The whole Copley Chicago crew taught me that it's not what but why and how that matters. From Eric Draper and the White House crew I learned to fully engage with history in the present tense. pdxcross mates showed me what's possible when we share a labor of love. Oregonian days taught me the value of supporting each other and the cost of not doing that. From Syracuse University days, I learned mostly from students by continually being challenged to create environments in which they could fully realize their potential and to listen. I'll be forever indebted to Peter and Aphrodite Tsairis for The Alexia experiences. And from the hundreds of photographers I've worked with directly, I've learned how to create and talk about visual storytelling more completely with each of you. I hope I've become a better person as a result.

And to the memories of time editing books with Michele McNally.

Who matters in your life? How can you make that connection richer?

Dean Lorraine Branham hired me at Syracuse University. Her death from cancer left a void and made me realize anew that it is the people in our lives who matter most.

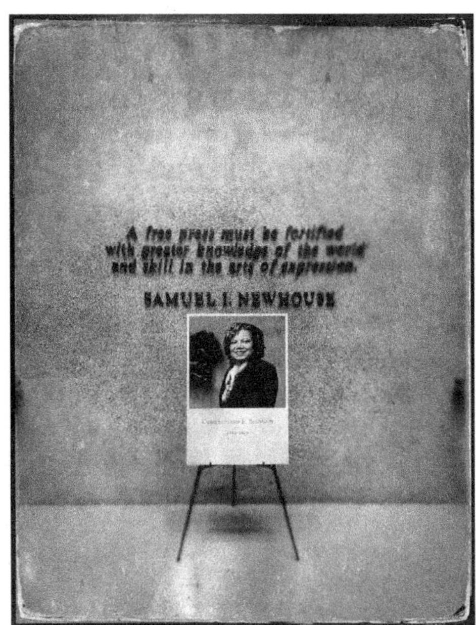

Appendix A

Self-Assignments

Among the many things I learned from creating and evolving courses at the university level for nine years is that assignments were really the most important aspect of teaching and that they could be created at either end of the spectrum. They could be crafted to ensure that students learned what you were teaching them, a giving back of what you had presented, essentially. Or they could be crafted as opportunities for students to apply what they learn during the course in real-world ways.

The first approach is how I was taught so I started there. It became clear fairly soon that the former approach has limited value. Students tended to produce less dynamic photographs than I had hoped and the spread of grades, as a reflection of the strength of their work, followed the usual, a few As, mostly Bs and some Cs. The few students who were able to match what I thought was important for them to know did well, the rest not so much.

Several goals became clear after a few semesters and I continually revised assignments to achieve those goals, which included:

- To have each assignment produce a professional-level set of photographs.
- Every assignment was to create multiple images and would build narrative robustness progressively.
- To have each student produce a level of work.
- To have each student's work be different from all the others for every assignment, as a reflection of helping them define their unique path into the profession. That meant that each assignment had to be crafted in a way that students could bring themselves to them, as opposed to everyone doing the same thing and then measuring everyone by and against that sameness.
- To have most assignments result in multiple outcomes, which meant that students had to produce more than photos and have a sense of how the work they created would best be expressed on different platforms – from short films, to web presentations, gallery exhibits, books, zines, slide shows with or without audio and more. Expectations increased as students progressed from basic to advanced courses.

- To think of assignments as choices that each student makes as to what they are going to engage with. Each choice brings clarity to the next choice and the cumulative choices define their specialization and their path into the profession.
- To have every student step out of their comfort zone in a variety of ways.

Once I had greater clarity of why in what can be accomplished through assignments, the assignments helped students produce stronger work.

What follows is a collection of those assignments that you can try, whether you're a student, professor, amateur or professional. Each assignment lays the foundation for the next. Each one is intended to advance your way of seeing, uniquely to you and collectively help you define your specialization.

My advice for people who struggle with a starting point for any of these assignments is to answer these questions:

- If you could choose the ideal thing to have in front of your camera, what would that be?
- If you could choose to spend a month doing anything, what would that be, what would give you the greatest joy? Put yourself in that situation with a camera.
- Who would you like to get to know better, whether or not you know them now? Get to know them through your camera.
- What are you really good at now, photographically, and what could you be doing better? Focus at least some effort on getting better at your weakness.

What have you never achieved that you'd like to achieve through your photography?

Here they are:

Light on a Person

Being able to see varying qualities of light in a setting and then translating from how it looks to your eye to how the camera renders light is a skill that you can develop. This approach is the opposite of the default approach of choosing to photograph someone from an angle to primarily show what they are doing. And remember that we see light as it falls on objects and reflects to us.

Learning to see light as an independent variable is the primary learning objective of this assignment. Other objectives are how to relate to people while photographing them, how to place people within settings and making photos from various distances to say different things about people in settings.

What to do: Go with someone you can photograph into a setting that has multiple light sources coming from different angles – I used the chapel on campus at Syracuse University for this assignment because it had as many as 14 different light sources in some spots.

First, map the light in the space. Just look at the light, independent of all other aspects of the scene. Determine how many light sources there are and what the hierarchy of those sources is – that means which is brightest, second brightest and so on. Light sources can be windows, doorways, reflections off the floors or walls, lamps, exit signs. See how the light falls on and reflects off surfaces at varying angles and distances from the source.

Then choose three different settings within the larger space, each of which has a different quality of light. One spot could be vibrant, another somber, a third somewhere in between. There could be little contrast between the brightest light source and the dimmest in one spot; one source could be super bright compared to others in another spot. You can make test photos to see how your camera sees the light.

Then once you've chosen three spots where the quality of light is distinctive, place the person you're photographing in one of the spots. Walk around the person to see how the light changes from different angles and in combination with what makes for the most effective background, determine the best angle from which to photograph the person.

One thing to consider is whether there is a catchlight in the person's eyes, meaning is there light reflected in their eyes, which can be a spot, or a wider source being reflected. If there isn't a catch light their eyes will look dead and that's usually not good.

Photograph the person by exploring the light as fully as you can from three distances, close to them, middle distance and farther away. You'll see that you must reinterpret the light and recompose and probably reposition the person from each of the distances.

Color is next.

Respond to Color

Advancing your seeing of color in a setting and using it interpretively to convey qualities of the setting is the objective of this assignment. Bring forward what you learned from the light assignment to this one and you'll see that composition is equally important.

Think of color in three ways: including the color of objects; excluding the color of objects; factoring color temperature of light sources in a setting. Here are the challenges that address each consideration.

Color of objects: Choose an active or dimensional setting in which you can engage with different aspects of the setting for a good bit of time, at least a few hours. Pick a color from the setting that in some way personifies a unique quality of what's going on. Lara Solt chose to train her eye on pink at a county fair to reflect the energy and brightness of the fair.

If the setting is somber, choose a less vibrant color. Challenge yourself to not just see the color but use it in a way that is expressive. Also be aware of colors in the setting that detract from what you're striving to say with your focused color, or those that pull your eye away from what is most important – that's the excluding facet of seeing color. You'll find that some colors in a setting help convey what you're saying, others take away from it, depending on where the colors sit on the color wheel and within the setting.

If the color temperature of the light is the same throughout this setting you've chosen, then find another where there are at least two, for instance, a warm light source and a cool one. Make photographs that use color temperature as a critical component, qualitatively – a warm indoor light juxtaposed against a chill outside light temperature, for instance. If you don't have a meter that reads the color temperature, turn off auto white balance, choose one of the presets – sun, shade, incandescent, fluorescent – and take an overall photo of a setting. You'll be able to see the different color temperatures as a starting point for deciding where and how to make photographs.

Three Distances with Technical Variables

In the light on a person assignment, I suggested making photographs of the person from three distances because from each distance you can say different things, as explained in Section 2.5. Let's take that a step further. As you relearn how to make photos, I'd suggest that you photograph every setting you're in from three distances.

The objective of this assignment is to create a set of photographs that convey a range of qualities where the varying distance from what is being photographed is the prime variable of expression.

Choose a setting to photograph that you can enmesh yourself with, where activities take a while to come to fruition, are tactile and interactive and ideally repeat themselves. All the better if there are various qualities of light within the settings. For example, settings where someone is making something or caring for someone or attending to an animal.

Go through the process of engagement with the person or people you'll be photographing, getting to know them, their surroundings and what is likely to happen. Read the light and color, then choose a distance. You can start with any of the three distances.

Each view will require you to speak to different aspects/qualities of the person and what's happening. You'll have to see the light and color and compose and wait for moment value to come to fruition anew from each distance. You'll have to pay attention to and respond to each distance differently in the pursuit of saying something new as you move closer or further.

Think of each distance as a range, not a set distance, that you explore. For instance, from nearby you can engage with the smallest aspects of what's in front of you, from how their hands are working to how light is falling on their eyes to photographing objects within the scene, each from a different distance.

Some people don't like for you to get super close to them as you're making pictures, at least at first. They must get used to it. Make a few frames close to them and then step back to a middle distance or further, like a slow dance. Get close again as things evolve. Do this several times and most people get used to you being close to them. You can also move your camera in at arm's length from you to get close by using the screen to compose instead of the viewfinder.

Then photograph from middle and further distances.

Respond to the setting fully from each distance and you'll create a set of notes from which you can create a visual score. The intention isn't just to make pictures from different distances, it's to create photos that speak to the greatest range possible of what transpired in front of your camera. And that produces a more diverse set of pictures from which you can build a narrative, a song.

Bring forward what you learned from light, color and distance assignments and apply them to these compositional exercises.

Compose Fully

It's worth confirming that composition is the intentional placement of elements within the frame, three dimensionally. The objective of this assignment is to create a diversity of full-frame photographs that have different starting points within the photograph.

Choose an active setting that you can fully engage with for at least an hour. Frame your compositions without putting the starting point of the photograph in the middle of the frame – that's where the eye lands first. Place the point anywhere but the middle, at different edges of the frame and at different depths within the frame. Adjust the rest of the composition as the starting point moves. This is probably going to be difficult and that's the point.

Ensure that you are creating foreground, middle ground and background regardless of where the eye starts. Break the frame in some of the compositions.

For a further challenge, combine this assignment with the distance assignment and compose it differently three times at each of the three distance ranges. Chances are you had to recompose in the distance exercise. Doing it again will reinforce the learning.

Change Your Route and Timing

The objective of this assignment is to enliven your sense of where photographs might happen.

Regardless of where you are on the learning spectrum, there are things you can do to open your seeing eyes wider. Most of us travel regular routes in our day-to-day lives and can become null to the experience. We might pass by without noticing potentially rich photographic possibilities. This is true in reality and metaphorically.

If you are attuned to as many possibilities to make strong photographs as possible then you'll be making more of them. Who knows what might happen by connecting with some aspect of the daily flow of your life more completely?

An exercise to tap unrealized potential is to stop somewhere along your regular route and engage with that setting. This could be a business you've had a passing interest in, a group of people who gather, a bus stop, a farmer working their field, a construction site, a landscape, an interesting person, really anything or anyone. Engage with the setting, and the people in a way that leads to making pictures. Maybe you stop and see that then is not the right time to be making pictures so figure out when is and return.

Or, just stop somewhere, sit and observe; hit pause on your life and *really* see the familiar anew.

The opposite is to change your regular route, and open your eyes to things you're not accustomed to seeing. Then engage and make pictures of what intrigues you or simply piques your curiosity.

A third approach is to change the time that you travel from place to place. Leave for work early, or go in late, which changes when you make the return trip, too.

Engagement is the critical component, regardless of which of these approaches you take. You must connect with the setting and its people to make telling photographs.

The Quotidian

The objective of this assignment is to activate your awareness of daily happenings and attune your seeing to make compelling photographs of them.

I learned the word quotidian in Spanish (cotidiana) before English, while walking the pilgrimage route from southwestern France to Santiago de Compostela, Spain, as an undergrad. David Gitlitz and Linda Davidson, the professors leading seven of us on this medieval experience, encouraged us to pay attention to the cotidiana as we walked day after day along a route that as often as possible included Roman roads, bridges and paths – David carried a map that Franco had drawn in 1936 that included these landmarks. They'd heightened our senses as to how history played into the present with every step of the 600 miles.

One of three final exams was to go into a church and describe the architectural revisions to the structure in 50-year increments through the 700-year life of the church, connecting each revision to the style of its time, en Español. Talk about having to pay attention to details big and small.

Walking and really seeing was a mind and eye-awakening lesson in understanding that we can understand a lot by engaging with the daily flow of life. I can still conjure multi-sensory scenes from that walk as if it were yesterday.

This assignment is simple: Slow down your mind's eye and pay attention to things that repeat, that happen every day and make photographs that convey the qualities of those things. This can be as simple as what the stove top looks like when you're cooking at a time when a swath of light strokes the surface or how people are standing in line at the coffee shop and there's a most bizarre combination of color combined with body language or light falling on your aging pet makes her look like a puppy or how a sliver of light sneaks into the bathroom and falls on the roll of toilet paper that your roommate left dangling to the floor.

Within the daily flow, photograph things that repeat multiple times while challenging yourself to engage differently with each new engagement.

Do this within a given setting over time and you'll make a cohesive set of photographs that speak to something that would have been lost to time. Vivian Maier did this. So did Gabby Jones in photographing the bathroom she shared with five roommates for an assignment in one of my courses. Gabby is now an independent photographer based out of New York.

Manifest the extraordinary in the ordinary.

Photo a Day

The objective of this assignment is to actuate your mind's eye in new ways.

I recently met a photographer who challenged himself to make intentional photos every day, in his case of wildlife. The first of those days was seven years ago and he's done it every day since. That's impressive.

Making at least one photo every day might seem unachievable before you do it but once done, you'll thank yourself. I tried it for six months before assigning a class to do it and was amazed by the resulting photographs and the awareness that grew from the experience. This is the quotidian idea extended, in that it can include the little or big things in life but you have to make at least one picture every day.

Don't fret too much about what you put in front of your camera. Part of the benefit of the effort is to realize that you can make compelled photographs of most anything once you've fine-tuned your intention. It can be as simple as responding to the light or the colors in each setting or recognizing the beauty you find in your partner or your pet or a flower.

Once awakened, this ability to make photographs of the "nothing" will translate to when you put yourself in a more purposeful and potentially chaotic situation. It's a way to train your eye and your mind to fully respond to settings. And you'll make a set of photographs that wouldn't have existed.

As I write this, I'm gathering photographs of my two kids, Holly and Ben, that I've made of their everyday lives from day one, photos made using the same premise as the photo a day assignment. These happenings would have passed to history and patchy memory but made photos as life happened. Now they and their kids will be able to see, and remember, so many of their lives big and little happenings. It's a gift.

Day in the Life of Someone

The objective of this assignment is to develop the interpersonal skills that it takes to fully engage with someone while photographing them.

This expands on the *light on a person* assignment by photographing the daily flow of life of someone you know and making an intentional set of portraits of that person. Starting with someone you know alleviates you from the burden of meeting someone and getting to know them well enough to photograph them intimately. I have students pair off and photograph each other's life for this assignment. That teaches them what it's like to enter someone's life to make pictures and what it's like to be photographed as you go about your life.

Being able to make pictures within people's lives requires a range of skills, from establishing trust, deciding how much to talk to the person, how to stay in someone's space for several hours without becoming annoying, so they might allow you to come back. Oh, and then there's all the dynamics involved in making pictures – determining why you're making pictures (what are you striving to say about the person) and then how best to make those pictures.

Schedule to be there during a busy day and be there from the moment they awaken to when they call it a day. That doesn't mean you have to be in their face with your camera every second. You shouldn't. Step into the next room for a while or take a walk and give the person a break from you.

Some photographers share photos as they make them, on the back of the camera, and some don't. But definitely share a set of them with the person you've photographed.

A critical thing is to go beyond simply documenting the happenings of the day. Say something about the person, and build an overarching narrative or several small ones. One of those should be a set of portraits that together express who they are. Photograph the spaces in which they exist, without the person in the photos, to say something about them independent of their actions and physical attributes.

As with all assignments, strive to make this one connect to your larger specialization, to get as much value from the experience as possible.

Photograph Five Strangers

The objective of this assignment is to develop your ability to make revealing photographs of people you don't know.

Meet five people who you don't know and gain their trust enough to be able to photograph them as they go about their lives, for an hour or two.

And make their portrait. Use the same approach to making pictures and building small narratives as the last assignment.

Based on what you've come to know about the five people, decide which of the five would lead to the most compelling narrative if you were to continue photographing them over a period of time.

That requires getting to know each person, talking to them about their lives and what matters to them and about their lives going forward. Generally, the more compelling narratives will come not from people who have an interesting past – you can't photograph their past – but from those who have an engaging and dynamic present.

This too is an assignment I developed for the first course I teach. Shweta Ghulati met five people and of them one was active in the anti-racial movement, lived in a one-room apartment and was about to give birth. The student was able to photograph her activism, her life at home, socializing with friends, the birth of her child and the first few weeks of the baby's life. That's dynamic. Shweta is now a visual editor at National Geographic.

Photograph One Block

The objective of this assignment is to develop your ability to craft narratives with place as the starting point.

Choose a block that interests you in a locale of your choosing. The block can be urban, residential, industrial, big or small. Get to know the block by meeting people and hearing their stories, by doing research at the library and city offices about its history, by spending time there throughout the day and night, during the week and on weekends. Take pictures during this process but think of those photos more as taking visual notes than building a narrative, though you may end up using some of them. Being there with a camera will also get people used to knowing you as a photographer.

Then determine the why, what story could you tell about this block, what kind of a narrative do you want to build and what's the best approach to making pictures to achieve it. In some cases, a set of portraits of people on the block, paired with architectural photos will be the best. Another might be telling a narrative of one business or person or family or setting on the block that is representative of the whole. You can use a non-fiction or illustrative approach, depending on the specialization that you're developing. Add other mediums that would further expand the expression.

You could give back to the block by hosting a projection night to present them with your visual narrative. Or make a short-run publication to give to people that can also serve as a promotional piece for you.

The takeaways are to get to know a setting, develop your research skills, become comfortable introducing yourself and becoming known, defining a narrative, approaching the image making uniquely to achieve the narrative, editing the work into outcomes and sharing what you've done.

Photograph an Event, Three Times

The objective of this assignment is to develop your storytelling ability with an event as the starting point.

For those of you who want to or currently do make a living photographing events, here's one for you. That includes those of you who want to elevate your image making and storytelling when photograph family events big and small to those who photograph big events such as state fairs, protests or political conventions.

If you are new to photographing events, I'd suggest starting with smaller local events that happen repeatedly or over a period of days, such as international festivals, or county fairs. Think beyond one-off, less dimensional events, like music performances because they don't offer as much potential.

Start by learning who's in charge of the event and who is participating in them. Connect with the people involved before the event happens, as early as possible. Sometimes the most interesting narratives happen before the event. For example, in advance of the Multnomah County, Oregon, Fair one year, Faith Cathcart learned that one person had won the pie baking contest for several years and photographed her life as she prepared for the upcoming fair's entry, which included getting her grandchildren involved in the whole process and making many pies before achieving one that she thought was good enough. It was a rich narrative, more interesting than just photographing at the fair. The Why will determine if the before of an event produces a better narrative.

Learn the back stories of events and a clear why will point you to a stronger narrative than if you just show up and start making pictures of whatever the activities are. This process also puts you there at the right time so can be more efficient and productive, which can be a good argument for using this approach if you work for a publication. Readers will be rewarded with a deeper connection to the event through your narrative even if they were there.

Use this approach intentionally three times, either by returning to the same event to make a more complete narrative or going to three different events to build on your ability to define the narrative.

You'll know when you've landed on an engaging narrative when you feel compelled to connect with someone or something specific.

Place and Person Engagements

The objective of this assignment is to further define your specialization and expand your storytelling ability to its fullest form with person and place as starting points.

This assignment has two parts that can be separate or linked to each other. I use these as the primary assignments in the second course I teach because they give students time to develop an idea, connect and reconnect with what or who they're photographing multiple times and as a result work through most of what it takes to produce a successful group of narrative-based photographs. The two parts are: photograph a place and photograph a person.

Coming up with an idea and then accomplishing everything it takes to begin making pictures is challenging and time-consuming. Giving the option of letting the person part of the assignment grow out of the place assignment is a more efficient approach that produces deeper and more comprehensive narratives.

With this two-part assignment, you would be able to make a set of photographs of pretty much anything, or anyone you determine through your specialization.

Photographing Place

Bringing yourself to this assignment means that you can choose to build a narrative about a single place or if you want to lean more toward the conceptual, you can approach place as a theme, such as a home. Places can be settings that share certain qualities or where similar things are done or they can be a personal expression of spaces that matter to you. Define what type of place would be the richest experience for you to explore and craft an approach that will expand your visual vocabulary.

Photographing Person

Similarly, you can choose to photograph a single person or a group of people who are similar or different but have a thread that holds a narrative together.

In both cases, your why will determine how best to define your approach. If you want to be known as a portrait photographer of a particular ilk then making a set of portraits that hold together as a group would be a good approach for you. That approach could incorporate both place and person in one set of photographs.

An example: Say your general area of interest is aviation and you love to meet people who fly planes. That's your why. Realizing the why would be to develop a body of work that presents subsets of people who fly types of planes, each of which is connected to a different type of experience and/or period of time. A starting idea then is to develop a project around crop dusters. That would include portraits of them, photos of them prepping the planes and flying, working with farmers and ag industry folks and overviews/landscapes as they fly through them. (I worked for a crop duster when I was in high school in northeast Nebraska, loading 50-pound bags of fertilizer into the plane.)

A second subset to further your specialization could be to photograph the world of pilots who fly World War II aircraft. A third could be about learning to fly and so on. The critical component of this specialization is that there is a diverse market for the work you'd produce, from businesses to organizations to journalistic outlets.

Essay based on Idea, Theme, Word

The objective of this assignment is to create a cohesive set of photographs based on a concept, quality or idea that holds them together.

This assignment flips the paradigm and uses the approach as a starting point. Creating a set of pictures that hold together because they come from an idea or issue or concept or share a theme. This type of project's success depends on the clarity and depth of your perception and how you realize that expression in a set of pictures.

This approach to narrative is called an essay, where each picture presents a different idea or concept or aspect of your core idea and the sum of the photos creates a complete iteration, as opposed to a narrative in which photographs are connected by the flow of occurrences.

This form can take many shapes. The crop duster example above is an essay in an overall concept that utilizes individual narrative threads.

A pure essay example is Cornell Watson's "Behind the Mask" series, which expresses the weight of racism. Each photograph in the series speaks to and touches Cornell's interpretation and speaks to how the people in the photographs have experienced racism in America. Only Cornell could produce this body of work because he brings deep personal experience to every aspect of the making of the photographs. There is clarity at the project level and in each setting.

Another is Naomi Harris' photographic essay about Trump supporters, a collection of portraits.

Other concepts and ideas speak to how cell phones have taken over daily life, what riding a subway is like in different countries, revisiting your high school classmates, making portraits of people who share a physical trait such as red hair, portraits of people before and after they compete in physically challenging events, photos of your kids every year on the same date for 21 years … You get the idea.

Wide Open: Self-Initiated Projects

The objective of this assignment is to produce a career-defining body of work.

An essential ability for photographers of all types is to generate and realize ideas and to initiate the creation of focused, dimensional work on your own. You will create a self-fulfilling path forward by creating the type of work that you want to get paid to do.

Most photographers I know use self-initiated projects as a way to drive their work lives, others to create work that challenges themselves in fresh ways and others to point their careers in new directions. They can be a way to evolve.

The crop duster idea above is this type of project. The realization of the idea can exist in a range of settings – editorial, advertising, commercial and non-profit or as a film from short to long form – and in various media, from print to digital, still to short films, single to multiple images on responsive web sites, social media and fertilizer trucks.

People are increasingly creating teams of creators who can expand on the lead person's capabilities, to be able to offer completely realized concepts to potential clients.

Self-initiated projects are gifts that you give yourself.

Appendix B

Visual Vocabulary

We work in a visual medium but many of the people we work with are not visual. We must use words to convey our visual pursuits, ourselves and the profession in a way that non-visual people will understand. And in a way that presents what we do in its best light to all audiences. This is our responsibility.

Our choice of words conveys our level of experience and understanding, they are a verbal form of our visual vocabulary. Here's a selection of words that present a lesser choice and a better choice for your vocabulary:

NO: Shoot; shooter; shots. As in "I'm going to shoot an assignment; you're a good shooter; you got some nice shots."

YES: Make or create or craft; photographer, visual storyteller, visual journalist or genre-specific designation such as nature photographer, artist; photographs, images

Naomi Rosenblum tracks the origins of the terms shoot or shooter to the early days of photography because people saw it as a parallel to hunting and the achievement of making a successful photograph as equal to getting the shot, or killing an animal. Centered compositions in films are even called crosshair framing. Time has shifted the context for the term shoot. I dare you to say that you're going to shoot the president if you're anywhere near the White House. Nearly daily mass shootings that result in thousands of deaths taint the photographic connection to shooting. Using any form of the word shoot connected to photography is at best insensitive, uninformed and suggests you're stuck in the past.

NO: Get access

YES: Earn entry; gain trust

This is in the context of connecting with people to make their photos. The deeper the connection, the more important earning the privilege of making photographs comes into play. Saying you get access is fine if it's a high-security environment that requires a process for access but not when you earn an entry by relating to and showing respect for people.

NO: Subjects

YES: People

Calling the people you're making pictures of "my subjects" is derogatory. It diminishes them to objects and makes the experience more about you when it should be about the people you're photographing. I guess you can say subjects when you're an artist and you're using people in front of your camera to say something that's coming from you, or a portraitist doing studies.

NO: Give voice to

YES: Amplify people's voices

People you're photographing have voices, they have lives that are meaningful, they have opinions and values. They are people. When you say you are giving voice you are making the interaction about you; the expression comes from a white privileged perspective. At best, your work will amplify people's voices, which shifts the power to them, recognizes their voice above yours.

NO: Collaborate

YES: Just describe the interaction

Collaborating with people you're photographing is another in a long string of terms that becomes a short-form way of saying what you mean. Collaborate comes from the good intention of not treating people as subjects but rather letting them be involved in the process of deciding how your interaction with them happens and with full knowledge of what will result from the exchange. So just say what you're doing, how you're interacting and what will result because of the unique way you're connecting.

NO: Unbiased

YES: There is no such thing as unbiased

This notion of being unbiased is a myth that largely comes from white privilege antecedents. No one is unbiased. We all carry our life experiences to the choices of what we put in front of our cameras and how we choose to interact with those settings and people and then what kinds of photographs we make of them. Just be honest and say where you and your photos are coming from, your perspective, impressions and experience related to the whole of their making.

NO: Truth, truthful

YES: Aspire to present a reality of those you're photographing, not yours. Be honest, representative, respectful, accurate, fair, unaltered

Truth as a concept dates back to the early days of photography when photos were perceived to be more truthful than paintings. That definition of truth was accuracy. Photographs could be more accurate renderings than paintings. But the truth soon after the turn of the 20th century started to really mean that what was pictured is the truth, the whole truth and nothing but the truth. Photographs can't be truthful in the simplistic principle of truth's meaning, which is that something happened and my photo of that is exactly and wholly how it happened. What might be true for you won't be for others. Just look at the various truths of the January 6, 2021, attack on the U.S. Capitol is presented in the media.

Again, be more specific, explain further, don't use the shorthand term.

Visual Journalist vs Activist vs Advocacy

Know where your work falls on this spectrum. The more it is one, the less it can be the others. The journalist strives to accurately represent what happens, without altering what happens in any way; advocacy is active support, it argues for an idea, a cause, a policy. Activism sits somewhere in the middle of the other two.

NO: I like that photo

YES: Say why you find the photograph successful, engaging, compelling or the opposite

We can like butterscotch ice cream more than chocolate chip. That's our taste. Just saying you like a photo has no meaning beyond your preference and if you're arguing for one photo over another you have to say with greater depth and complexity what it is about that photograph that succeeds more than others under consideration.

NO: My story.

YES: The story I'm telling

Like *give voice to*, saying *my story* makes it about you, it's the possessive form. Instead, form the expression in a way that makes it about the people or places you're photographing. It is their story that you're striving to do justice to.

NO: My vision

Better: My visual language, my interpretation, my way of seeing

My vision is a grossly overused expression, as in, "My vision for this story is …" FDR had a vision for what it would take to bring the USA out of the depression. Vision is a big deal as it applies to endeavors, using it to describe small things is self-inflating. Be more specific. Say instead: my idea, my approach, my thoughts on this, my visual vocabulary for this effort will be.

NO: My style

YES: Visual language, approach, way of seeing

Style is usually a technical or aesthetic layer that you apply to your image making either in camera or in post processing.

If you are really speaking to what distinguishes your imagery from everyone else, your visual language, then calling that your style is a shallow rendering. A parallel is in clothing fashion, which offers new styles with every season. Style changes over time and is generally a superficial modification. Your approach to creating work should evolve intentionally and grow from a series of choices and experiences and successes and failures. Styles applied to work one year won't carry over to the next whereas your visual language builds on itself.

The words vision and style are similar in nature.

NO: Multimedia

YES: Multiple discipline

Multimedia is a redundant term. Media is plural, so connecting multi to a plural word makes no sense and is grammatically incorrect. But somehow it stuck and grew to mean a specific genre that uses interview-based audio as the primary narrative with supportive video or still photos sitting under the spoken text.

Saying you're producing a multiple-discipline project and then describing the approach and how each discipline advances and elevates the project is a much more informed and intelligent way to talk about your work.

NO: Cover; capture

YES: Make photographs of or in a larger sense produce a body of work on; make moving pictures or video of

I'm going to cover x event is a common expression. Be more specific. I'm focusing on photographing this aspect of this event that is happening.

Capture is a word that most often means making moving pictures of something. It's offensive for reasons that are like the word shoot. People were captured in Africa and enslaved. Animals are captured because they misbehaved or are ill. Here too, be more specific about what you're doing. If you made a video of something, say that.

Words to know:

Graphicacy: This word is the equivalent of literacy and numeracy except instead of applying to words and numbers it speaks to the visual realm. The term dates to 1965 and historically has referenced maps and diagrams more than photographs but as visual media have become more diverse and widely used, the term's usage and throw has expanded.

Computational photography: Photos that result from digital computation instead of optical processes. It's a term that is more comprehensive than digital photos. It will include new forms of creation as they're developed, such as epsilon or light field photography, which creates multiple image iterations simultaneously that can be refocused after they're made, or AI photos of people created completely digitally.

Documentary: This is a genre that meant something specific when it was first used in the second half of the 19th century. It came from the word document and meant that a photograph was an accurate visual representation of an object, a place or a person. It was a document.

The word has meant different approaches through the decades. Around and after 1900, the documentary approach meant that the photographer was producing work with a social value or commentary, often with the intent of bringing about change. Different sub-genres grew in different countries where political climates affected the intention of the genre.

Societal commentary has remained a core attribute of the genre but two ends of a spectrum have come to being. One is based on photojournalism's principles of not altering, only capturing things as they happen and the photographer being a neutral voice; the other says that if the intention is pure and valid, any approach to the making of images is valid. You can create or recreate scenes, alter images and post process to your heart's content as long as those choices are in the service of meaningful results. John Grierson, a founder of the documentary film approach, called this the creative treatment of actuality.

If you don't know that different ways of thinking about documentary exist, and you object to any form that is not like the one you practice, you'll sound at best uninformed. That doesn't preclude you from adapting either approach, knowingly.

It's also important to know that regardless of the approach there will always be a point of view.

Photojournalism: Know that the origin of this word is two words: Photography and journalism and the intent was that they were and would be inseparable – words and pictures together as they address news events that are then presented in journalistic environments, mostly newspapers, news magazines and news sites. Historically and largely currently people in charge of publishing environments value words over pictures, which is reflected in relative staffing and budgets for the two mediums.

Incumbent in the photojournalistic genre is producing truthful representations of whatever is photographed by following a strict set of ethical practices that largely involve not altering images, not controlling situations and are dependent on first amendment rights in public settings. Fewer and fewer people refer to themselves as photojournalists as the ability to make a living from that genre alone diminishes with each year's passing. Visual journalism has grown as a moniker because it can incorporate other media, especially the moving image. Visual storytellers is another term that allows for more interpretative and impressionistic approaches to telling visual stories. If you call yourself a photojournalist, you're excluding yourself from about 80 percent of the market that hires people who can tell stories visually.

Global South: This is a far better term to use than third world or developing nations. It's a geographic distinction as opposed to lumping swaths of the planet together based on their as the primary consideration. Third world imposes a value, is judgmental, global south is descriptive. The term has been around since the 1950s.

Othering: This is the practice of framing people based on how they are different from the dominant "norms" of a society. It's a bad thing to do yet much of documentary practice has historically involved the photographer taking on a "subject" that is different from themselves, and often of those who are in compromised situations. The assumption has been that the photographer is helping those who are in "lesser" circumstances and while the intention might have been good, the production of images alone rarely helped those pictured. Some think that simply making the "public" aware of those who are afflicted is value enough. That is changing with greater discussion of the negative effects of "parachute journalism," the increased creation of organizations that advance the work of those who have traditionally been underrepresented in the profession and a recognition that awareness from personal experience can create a richer and more nuanced set of photographs. Among the effects of this trend is to redefine what is considered good photography, as those who were previously excluded, either intentionally or unknowingly, are being hired.

The oppressed, victim photography, poverty porn: This is the tendency to depict those who are marginalized in a society only as the sufferers, the inflicted, afflicted and generally non-contributors. It's a variation or extension of othering. Most often such photography is a gross simplification of circumstances and generally serves a purpose independent of those being depicted. Avoid doing this by striving to be complete, dynamic and complex in settings that are outside of your experience and fully engage with and understand the people you're photographing and involve them more in the making. The idea of collaborating with people you're photographing grew in part out of this tendency.

The Gaze: This is the notion that the person behind the camera is superior to those in front of the camera in some way. There are many different types, the male and female gaze, the imperial and post-colonial gazes. The most prevalent is the male gaze, which typically objectifies women in front of the camera. Look at the many camera equipment ads with scantily clad women for examples of how the profession is guilty of this. Please learn more about this on your own.

Scopic drive: This is the force that drives the gaze, generically. It is human nature to see, to look at others or be seen by others. This concept also incorporates our mental, aesthetic and emotional responses to the visual.

(Gaze and scopic drive are worthy of extensive conversation and deeper understanding.)

FWIH *(filler words I hate)*: Pet peeve of mine is excessive words that add nothing: Sorta, kinda and like. Add ummm to the mix and that's the complete set of auto-fill words. Like, umm, you know what I kinda, like, mean, sorta? Listen to yourself and if you hear these words coming from your mouth, ask if they added to what you were saying. If not, challenge yourself to eliminate them. Precision and clarity of expression is the goal.

Appendix C
Resource Guide

Here is a collection of resources that I started to build a few years ago to help expand my awareness of what's out there and to share with others. I wouldn't call it a complete list, if that's even possible to achieve. I apologize for the U.S.-centric nature, that is where I live. I hope you find it helpful nonetheless.

Photographic Agencies/Collectives

Magnum
VII
Redux Pictures
Contrasto (Italy)
Panos Pictures (UK)
Agence Vu (France)
Contact Press
Focus (Germany)
Visum (Germany)
Noor
Luceo
Prime
Grain
Razón
Agencia zur (Argentina)
Eyemade (London and Paris)
Moment (Scandinavia)
Oculi (Australia)
Fractures Photo Collective (Spain)
Webistan (Afghanistan)
The Cause Collective
The Photo Society (NGM photographers)
Farm Security Administration (Historical)
Facing Change/Documenting America
Authority Collective

Natives Photograph
https://nativesphotograph.com
Thuma, Myanmar
Her Pixel Story, Kashmir
The Packet Collective, Sri Lanka
The Confluence Collective, Darjeeling-Sikim Himalayan
Kaali Collective, Bangladesh
Photo Circle, Nepal
See in Black
Assembly
The Photographic Collective, Africa
Juntos Photo Coop

Photo Festivals (Gatherings)

Visa Pour L'Image, Perpignan, France
Contact Photography Festival (Toronto)
Le Recontres d'Arles, France
Pingyao, China
Photoville, Brooklyn

Photo Reviews (to have work reviewed)

NY Times Reviews (must apply, for students and early career photographers)
Photolucida (Portland, Oregon)
Houston Photofest
Center (Santa Fe)
NYC Photo Festival
Chico Hot Springs Portfolio Review
Festival La Gacilly-Baden Photo, Austria

Photography Competitions and Grants

World Press
Pictures of the Year (POY)
American Photography
Communication Arts
BOP (NPPA)
CPOY College Photographer of the Year
Critical Mass (run by Photolucida)
The Alexia Grants – Student and Professional
FotoVisura Grant
Critical Mass/PhotoLucida
Magenta Flash Forward

Communication Arts Photography Competition
Lensculture
Independent Book Publishers Award
London Street Photography
Soros Open Society
BD Photo Competition
Ian Parry Scholarship
The Tierney Fellowship
Photocrati Grant
The Center grants – Project Launch, others
Documentary Project Fund
Aaron Siskind Foundation Grant
Carmignac Gestion Photojournalism Award
Getty Image Grants/Editorial Photography
Anja Niedringhaus Courage in Photojournalism Awards
Inge Morath Award
W. Eugene Smith Grant – Student and Professional
The Aftermath Project
Magnum Foundation
National Geographic Society Grants
Tim Hetherington Trust
Mack Annual Research Fellowship
Howard Chapnick Grant
International Automotive Photography
Wildlife Photographer of the Year
British Journal of Photography Awards
Lucie Foundation Scholarships

Organizations

NABJ – National Association of Black Journalists
https://www.nabj.org/?
NAHJ – National Association of Hispanic Journalists
https://nahj.org
AAJA – Asian American Journalists Association
https://www.aaja.org
ASMP – American Society of Media Photographers
https://www.asmp.org
NPPA – National Press Photographers Association
https://nppa.org
Society for Photographic Education – Students
https://www.spenational.org/join/register
Color Positive

https://www.color-positive.com
Authority Collective
https://authoritycollective.org
Diversify Photo
https://diversify.photo
Black Women Photographers – and Grants
https://www.blackwomenphotographers.com
Natives Photograph
https://nativesphotograph.com
The Photo Society
http://thephotosociety.org
WPOW (Women Photojournalists of Washington)
https://www.womenphotojournalists.org/index
Kamoinge (African American collective)
https://kamoingeworkshop.squarespace.com
Open Society Foundations (Also give grants)
https://www.opensocietyfoundations.org
Market Photo Workshops – South Africa
https://marketphotoworkshop.co.za
Photoville
https://photoville.com
Photowings (Has many interviews with photographers)
http://photowings.org
Social Documentary Network
https://socialdocumentary.net/cms/MemberBenefits
Photoevidence
http://fotoevidence.com
Bronx Documentary Center
https://www.bronxdoc.org
New Orleans Photo Alliance
https://neworleansphotoalliance.org/calendar/

Women-Specific Organizations

Women Photograph
https://www.womenphotograph.com
Firecracker in the UK
https://www.fire-cracker.org
MFON
http://mfonfoto.org
IWMF – International Womens Media Foundation
https://www.iwmf.org
Girl Gaze

https://girlgaze.com
Women in Motion
https://www.kering.com/en/group/kering-for-women/women-in-motion/
Female Photographers
https://femalephotographers.org
Women Focus
https://www.womenfocus.org
We Women
https://www.wewomenphoto.com
Visual Thinking Collective
https://www.visualthinkingcollective.com
Black Women Photographers
https://blackwomenphotographers.com

Photo Book Publishers

(These are mostly small operations)
Ceiba Press
Sturm & Drang
Mack books
Aperture (larger)
Dashwood books
Gost books
zno
pierre von kleist
TBW Books
Gnomic Book
Kris Graves Projects
Edition Patrick Frey
Phaidon (larger)
Twin Palms
Princeton University Press
Kehrer Verlag
Chronicle Books
Minor Matters
Red Hook Editions (Jason Eskenazi)
Powerhouse
rockynook
Daylight
Dewi Lewis
Nazraeli Press (High Quality)
Steidl (High Quality)
Loose Joints, Marseille
Session Press

PSG
Capricious

On-Demand Printing

Aristan State
Blurb
Readymag
Newspaper Club (newsprint)
Star Press (Minneapolis)
Edition One
Artifact Uprising
Mixam
Artisan Craftsman

Web Site Creation

Visura*
Photoshelter*
Squarespace
Format*
https://www.format.com
Behance
Wix
Virb
aphotofolio
dunked
Viewbook
semplice (word press)
Adobe portfolio
Cargo collective
**More than site creation*

Reading List: Books on Photography

Understanding Image Making

Anything written by Teju Cole
Understanding A Photograph
John Berger, 2013
La Furia de las imágenes, notas sobre la postfotografía (the fury of images, notes on photography)
Joan Fontcuberta, 2018
Camera Lucida, Reflections On Photography
Roland Barthes, 1980

New Ways of Seeing
Grant Scott, 2020
Photography, The Key Concepts
David Bate, 2016

About Photo Books

Publish Your Photography Book
Darius Homes and Mary Virginia Swanson, 2011
Self Publish, Be Happy, A DIY Photobook Manual and Manifesto
Bruno Ceschel, 2015
The Photobook, A History, Volumes 1–3
Martin Parr, Gerry Badger, 2004
The Chinese Photobook, from the 1900s to the present
Martin Parr, Wassink Lundgren, 2016
Photographers Sketchbook
Stephen McLaren, 2014
The PhotoBook Review – published by Aperture
PhotoBook Journal – including a lengthy list of book publishers

About Seeing

The Mind's Eye
Henri Cartier Bresson, 1999
on Composition and Improvisation
Larry Fink, 2014
on Photographing People and Communities
Dawoud Bey, 2019
The Nature of Photographs
Stephen Shore, 2007
Color Rush, American Color Photography from Stieglitz to Sherman
Katherine A. Bussard and Lisa Hostetler, 2013

About History

Picturing Us, African America Identity in Photography
Edited by Deborah Willis, 1994
A World History of Photography
Naomi Rosenblum, fifth edition
Photography Until Now
John Szarkowski, 1989
The Oxford Companion to the Photograph
Photography, The Whole Story
Juliet Hacking, Prestel, 2012

Documentary Photography and Photojournalism

Documentary Photography Reconsidered, History, Theory and Practice
Michelle Bogre, 2019
The Documentary Impulse
Stuart Franklin, 2016
Understanding Photojournalism
Jennifer Good and Paul Lowe, 2017
Bending the Frame
Fred Ritchin, 2013
Truth Needs No Ally, Inside Photojournalism
Howard Chapnick, 1994

Producing Work

Photo Work: Forty Photographers on Process & Practice
Edited by Sasha Wolf, 2019
The NEW Black Vanguard
Antwaun SARGENT, 2019
Telling Tales: Contemporary Narrative Photography
Various, 2016
Imaginarium
Claire Rosen, 2017
Conversations on Conflict Photography
Lauren Walsh, 2019
Timeless
Photographs by Kamoinge, 2015

Visual Editing

Picture Editing & Layout, A Guide To Better Visual Communication
Angus McDougall and Veita Jo Hampton, 1990
A Photographer and Picture Editor Demonstrate How to Choose: The Right Picture
Ken Heyman and John Durniak, Amphoto, 1986
Get the Picture – A Personal History of Photojournalism
John G. Morris, Random House, 1998
Words and Pictures
Wilson Hicks, 1952
This Equals That
Jason Fulford and Tamara Shopsin, 2014
Visual Impact In Print
Gerald Hurley, Angus McDougall, 1971

Making a Living

The Freelance Photographer's Guide To Success, Business Essentials

Todd Bigelow, 2021
Legal Guide for the Visual Artist Tadd Crawford and M.J. Bogatin

On Teaching

The Missing Course, Everything They Never Taught You About College Teaching
David Gooblar, 2019

On Audio Storytelling

Out On The Wire, the storytelling Secrets of the New Masters of Radio
Jessica Abel, 2015

Index

Note: *Italic* page numbers refer to figures.